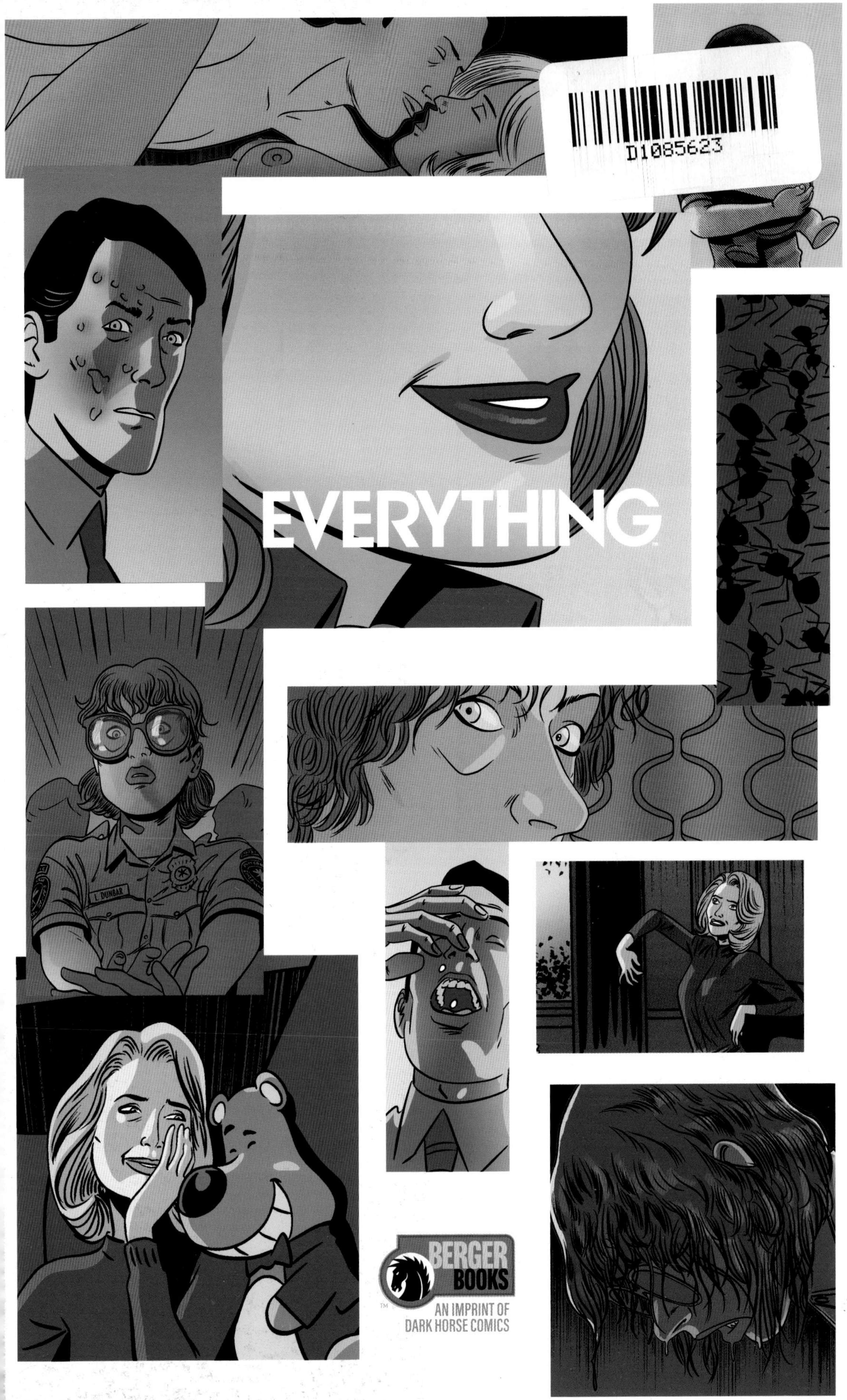
EVERYTHING
L. DUNBAR

BERGER BOOKS
AN IMPRINT OF DARK HORSE COMICS

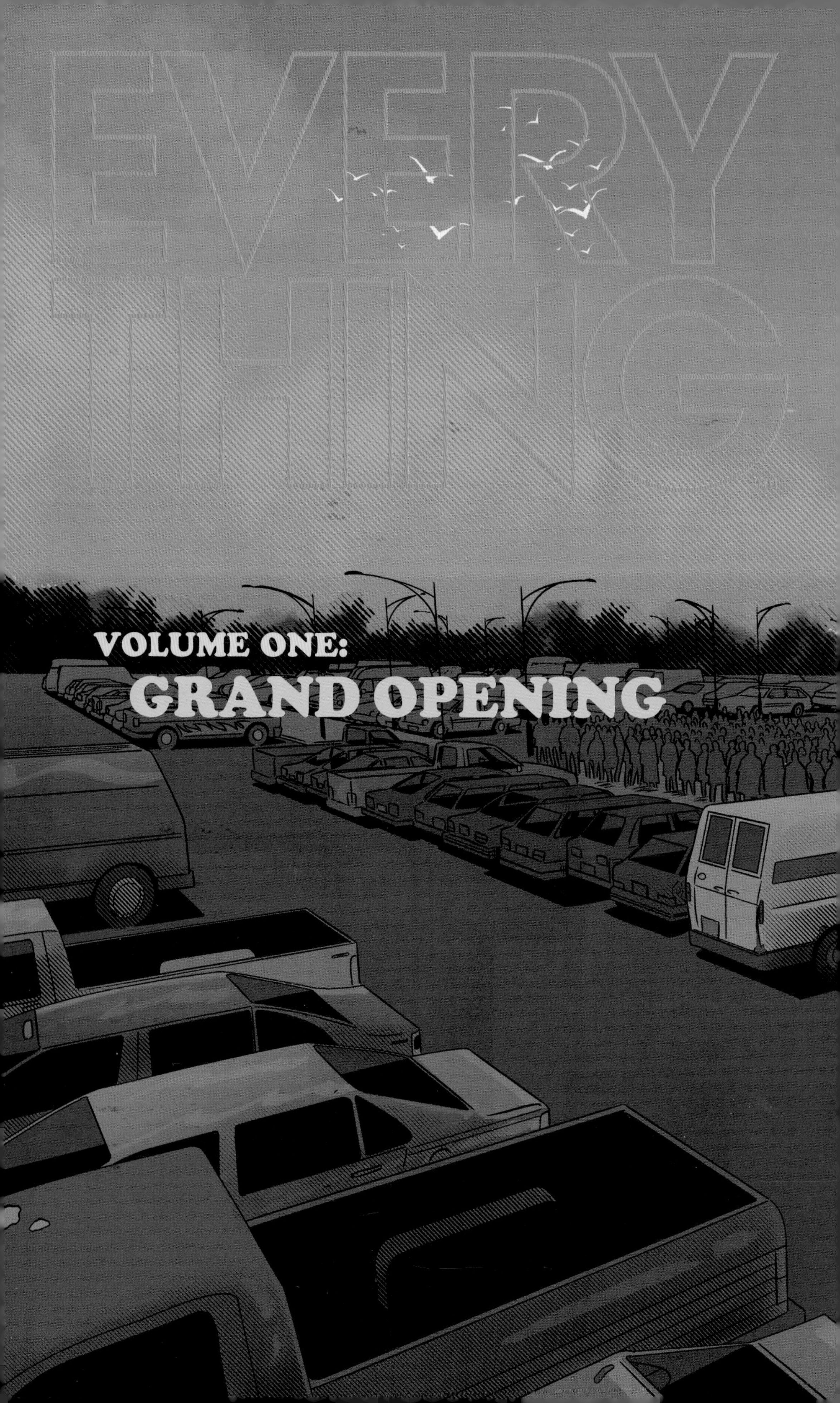
EVERYTHING
VOLUME ONE:
GRAND OPENING

Christopher Cantwell
writer

I.N.J. Culbard
artist

Steve Wands
letterer

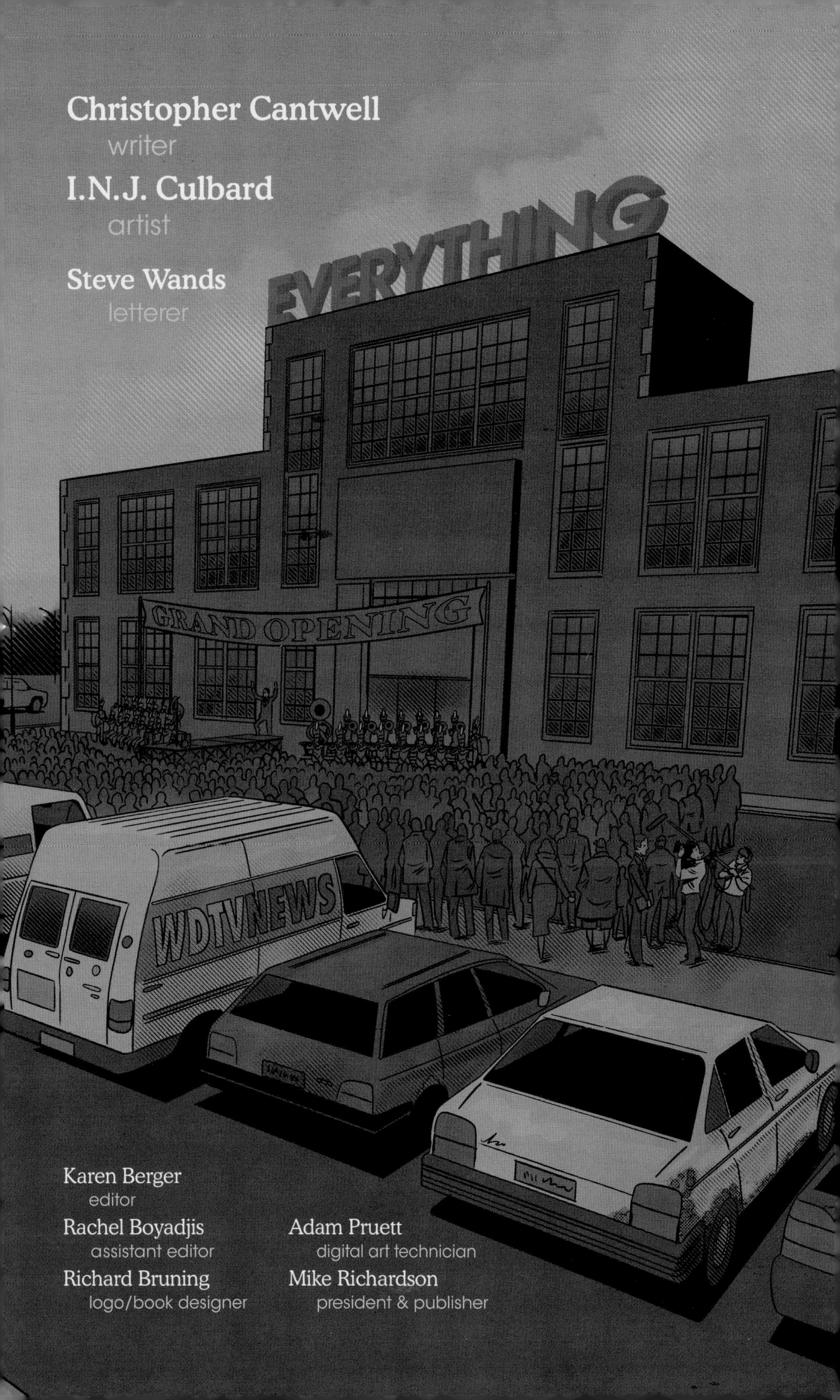

EVERYTHING
GRAND OPENING
WDTV NEWS

Karen Berger
editor

Rachel Boyadjis
assistant editor

Richard Bruning
logo/book designer

Adam Pruett
digital art technician

Mike Richardson
president & publisher

Everything and Nothing.

I love this idea that both go together. In our story, you can get everything at Everything, which ultimately amounts to... nothing. No amount of stuff can make you happy or complete, just like the Grinch learned in his battles back in the day with Whoville. I feel this same way when it comes to our ability, seemingly, to now have everything. In 2020, I can watch any TV show from any era (theoretically), enjoy any movie, listen to any song ever made, and buy anything I can conceive of with a few clicks of a button. Despite infinite options, it kind of leaves me wanting... nothing. I instead feel the need to push away from the table, and maybe go for a walk.

To enjoy Nothing for a while.

I think that INJ and I are trying to accomplish a similar feeling in the way we're telling this story. We're trying to give you everything by kind of giving you nothing. We're trying to show that anything and everything can happen by showing very little, and by telling a tale that many would call "a slow burn." For me, it comes from love of stories like *Twin Peaks*, one of my all-time favorites. For much of that show—especially in the beginning—you're asking yourself "what the hell is going on?" but not in a bad way. We're trying pull off something similar here. In terms of the really weird stuff, there are only glimpses. We had the idea to entice you in, just like the Everything store would do if it came to your hometown. Whether it's Holland, Michigan or the township of Twin Peaks, things seem perfectly safe and fine... but that's when circumstances can mutate into their strangest and most frightening.

Speaking of David Lynch, *Blue Velvet* does this so well! What's the scariest thing Lynch could think of? A suburb. It's these mirages of the American Dream, these paltry manifestations of a perfect life—in the form of cookie-cutter houses and friendly corporate chains—that are the most insidious threats that might exist in our reality.

I'm not saying anything new.
I'm just talking about something that really bothers me.

But as importantly, this book is fun for us. INJ's crisp art and classic "friendly" faces allow us to really start some shit and get under people's skin. I also love retro sci-fi imagery, so it's so fun for me to play around with what exists under the store—in the form of Mind Helmets and shock troopers and hints of other dimensions. I'm also a massive fan of the film *Fat City*, a story that I believe more than any other illustrates that sadness and being at the bottom of the barrel can have a kind of beauty and romance, that the opposite of happy is as important to the human tapestry as typical joy and satisfaction. Lori's favorite movie, *The Call of San Berdoo*, is modeled on *Fat City*. Lori knows every line by heart, because in her own words Lori is trying to figure out how to be "happy with being sad."

That kind of feeling seems more real to me than the promise of any department store sale or cheap platitude. If anything, I always find myself more wary of those promises and the people who believe in and defend them. They always strike me as militant, and kind of fascist in their optimism. Fuck that. Sometimes you just gotta say "I don't feel good today," and be okay with it. That's a big part of life.

Mine, anyway. Everything can't exist without Nothing.
It just remains to be seen if Everything will ever be able to accept that.

• Christopher Cantwell •

Chapter 1:
"Grand Opening!"

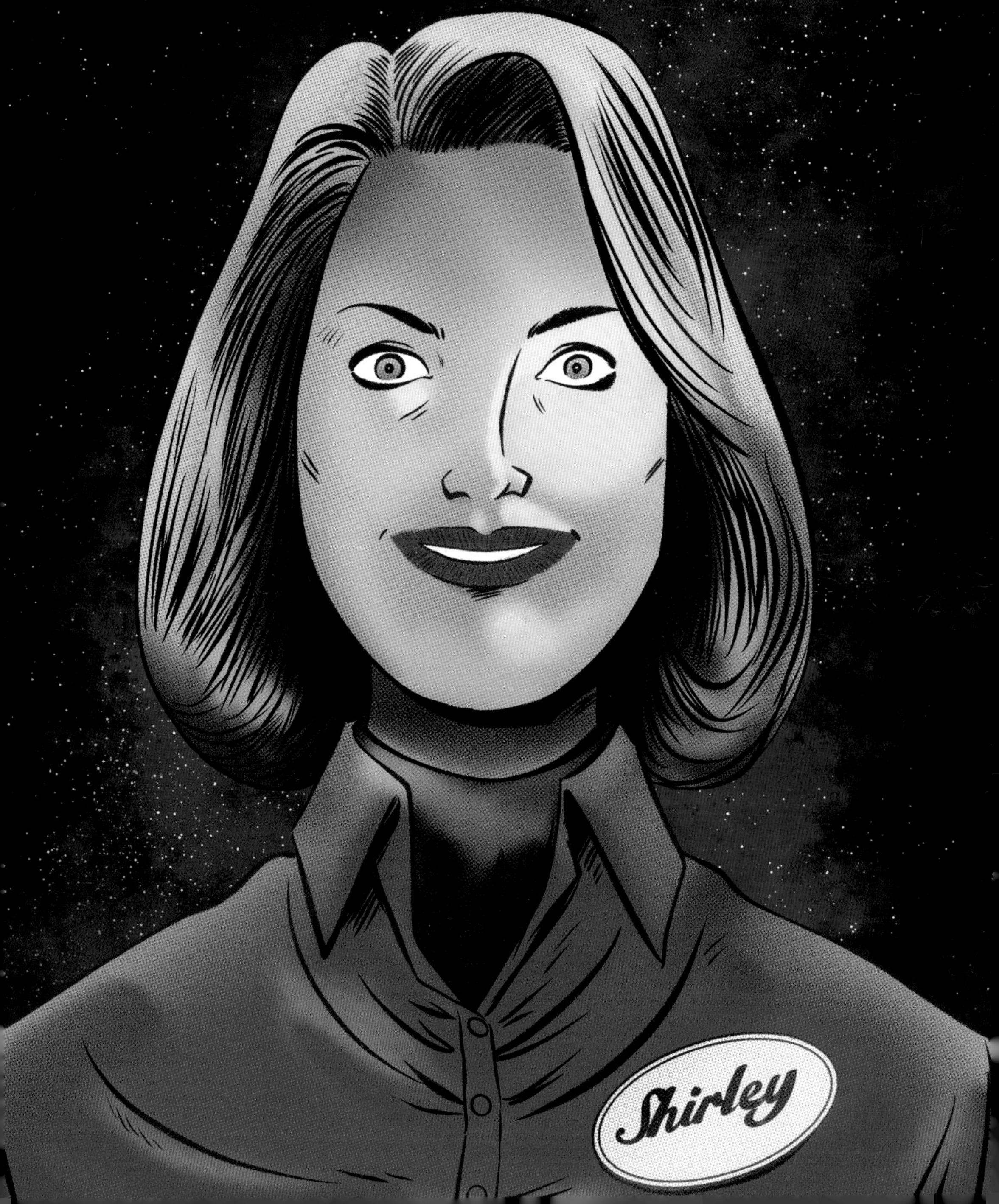
Shirley

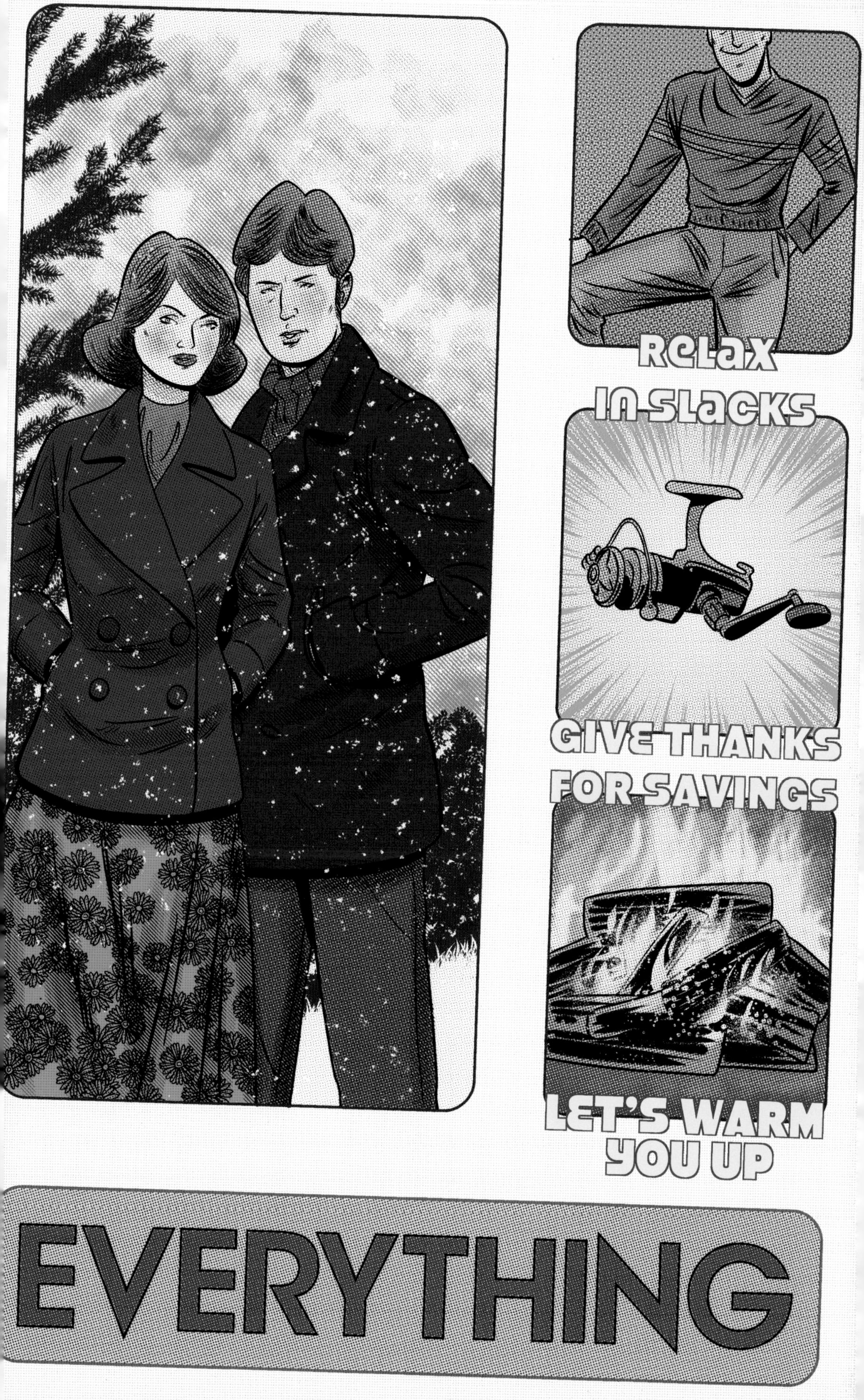
RELAX
IN SLACKS
GIVE THANKS
FOR SAVINGS
LET'S WARM
YOU UP
EVERYTHING

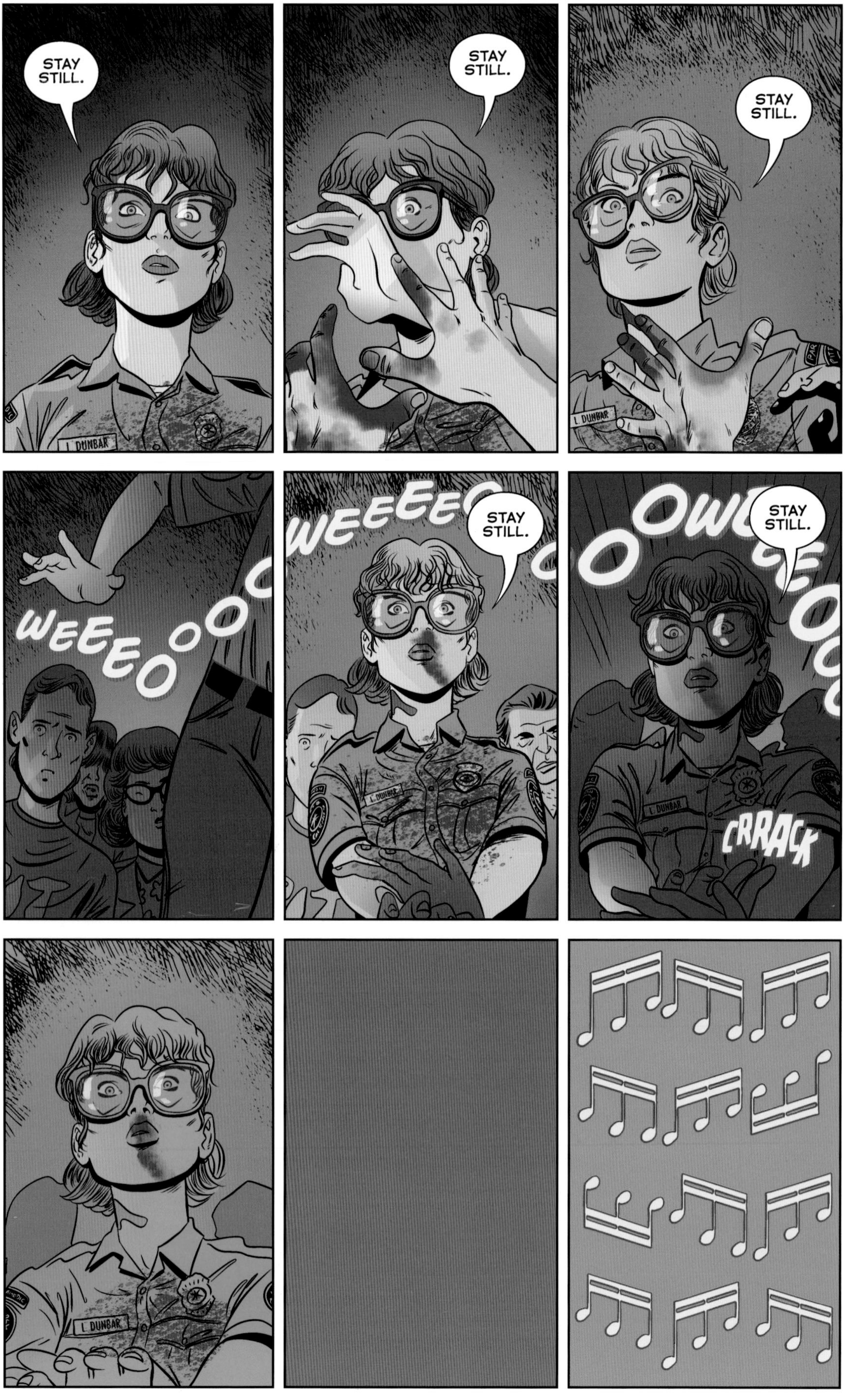
STAY STILL.
STAY STILL.
STAY STILL.
WEEEOOOO
STAY STILL.
STAY STILL.
CRRACK

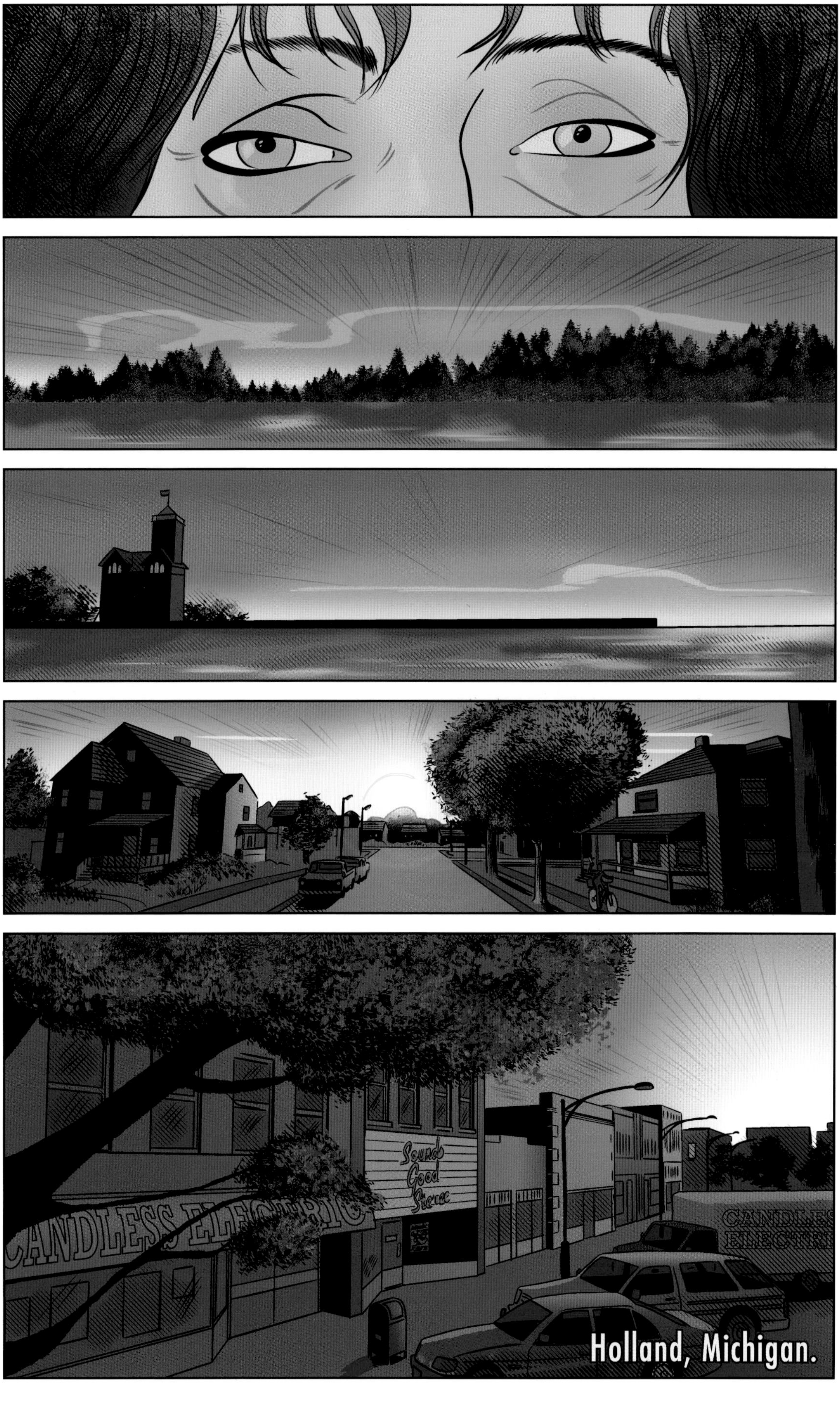
CANDLESS ELECTRIC
Sounds Good Stereo
Holland, Michigan.

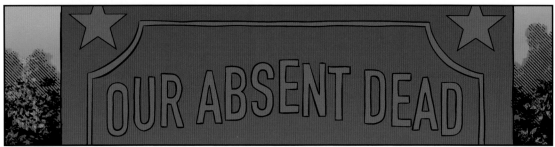

OUR ABSENT DEAD

$350

October 10th, 1980.

EVERYTHING.
ON SALE.
FOREVER

'S COFF

OK HO

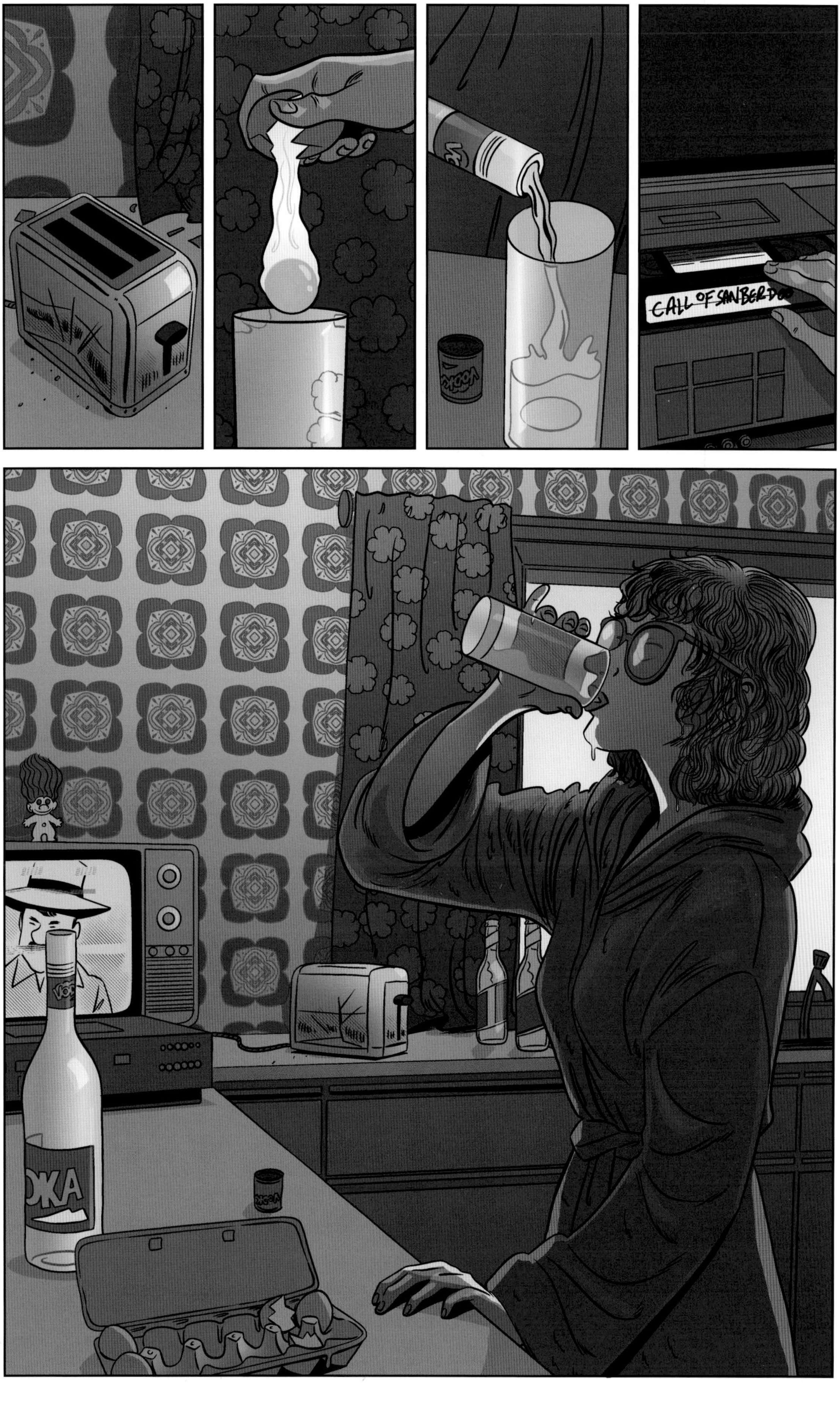

CALL OF SANBERDOO

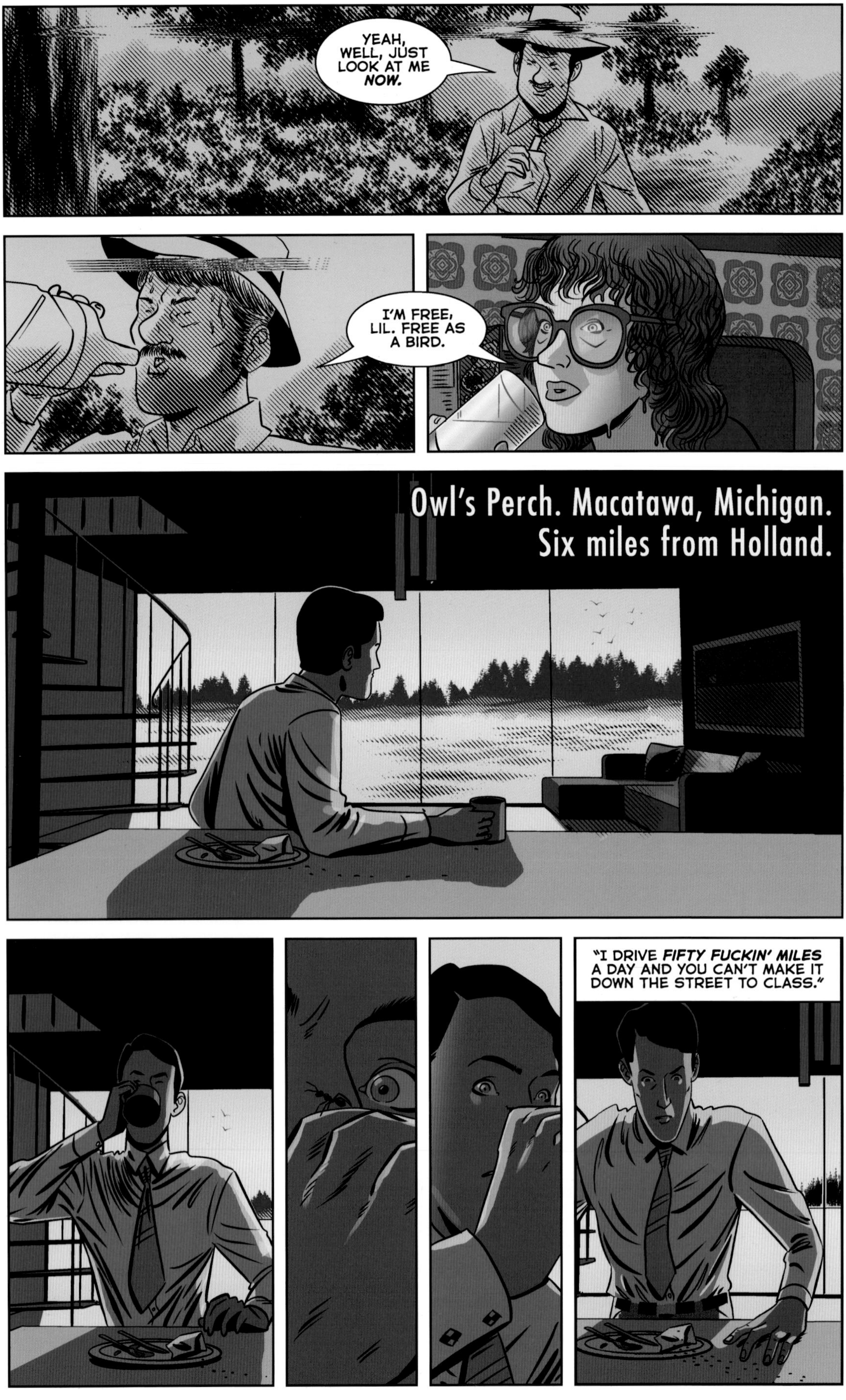
YEAH, WELL, JUST LOOK AT ME NOW.
I'M FREE, LIL. FREE AS A BIRD.
Owl's Perch. Macatawa, Michigan. Six miles from Holland.
"I DRIVE FIFTY FUCKIN' MILES A DAY AND YOU CAN'T MAKE IT DOWN THE STREET TO CLASS."

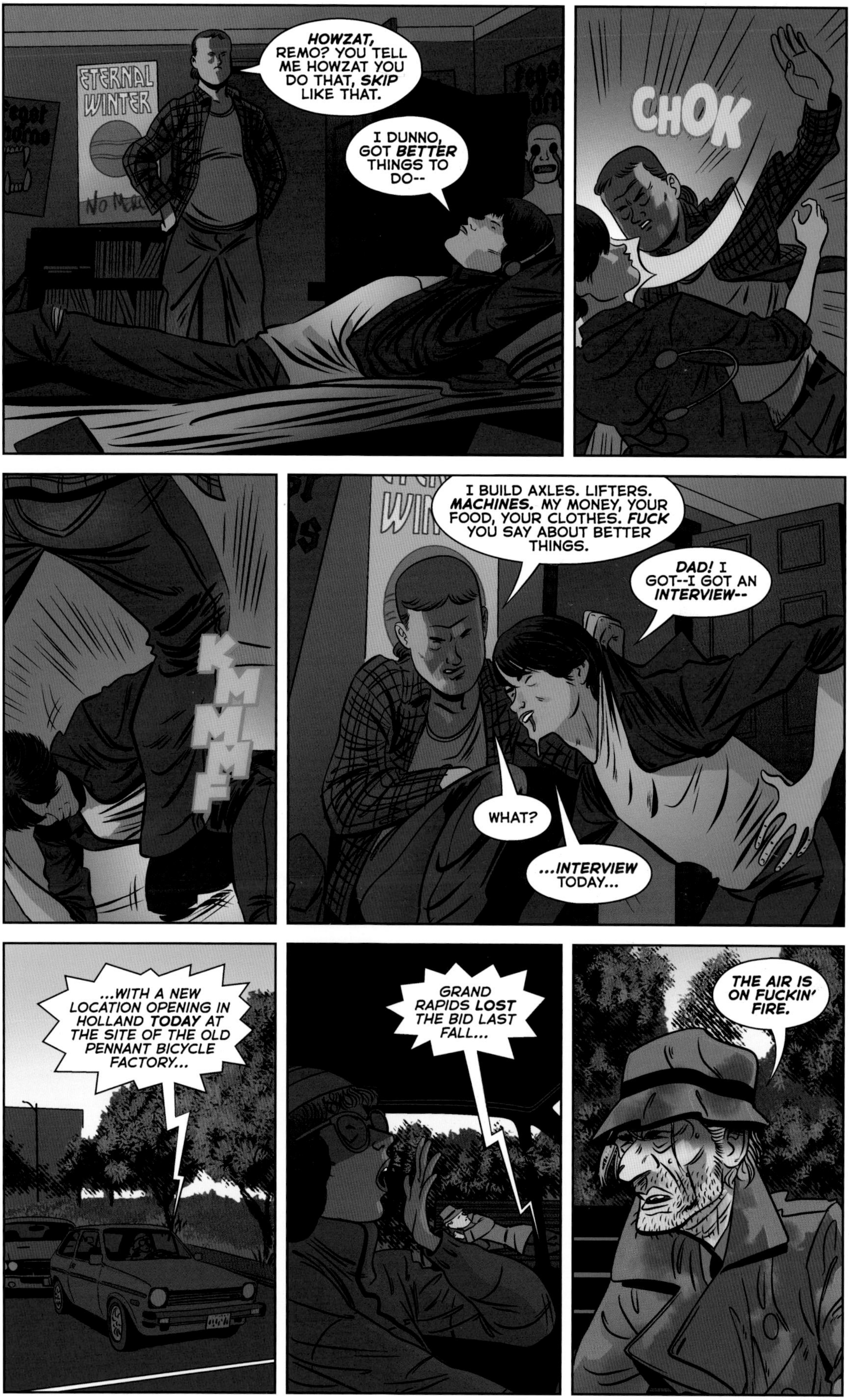

ETERNAL WINTER
NO MERCY
HOWZAT, REMO? YOU TELL ME HOWZAT YOU DO THAT, SKIP LIKE THAT.
I DUNNO, GOT BETTER THINGS TO DO--
CHOK
KMMMF
I BUILD AXLES. LIFTERS. MACHINES. MY MONEY, YOUR FOOD, YOUR CLOTHES. FUCK YOU SAY ABOUT BETTER THINGS.
DAD! I GOT--I GOT AN INTERVIEW--
WHAT?
...INTERVIEW TODAY...
...WITH A NEW LOCATION OPENING IN HOLLAND TODAY AT THE SITE OF THE OLD PENNANT BICYCLE FACTORY...
GRAND RAPIDS LOST THE BID LAST FALL...
THE AIR IS ON FUCKIN' FIRE.

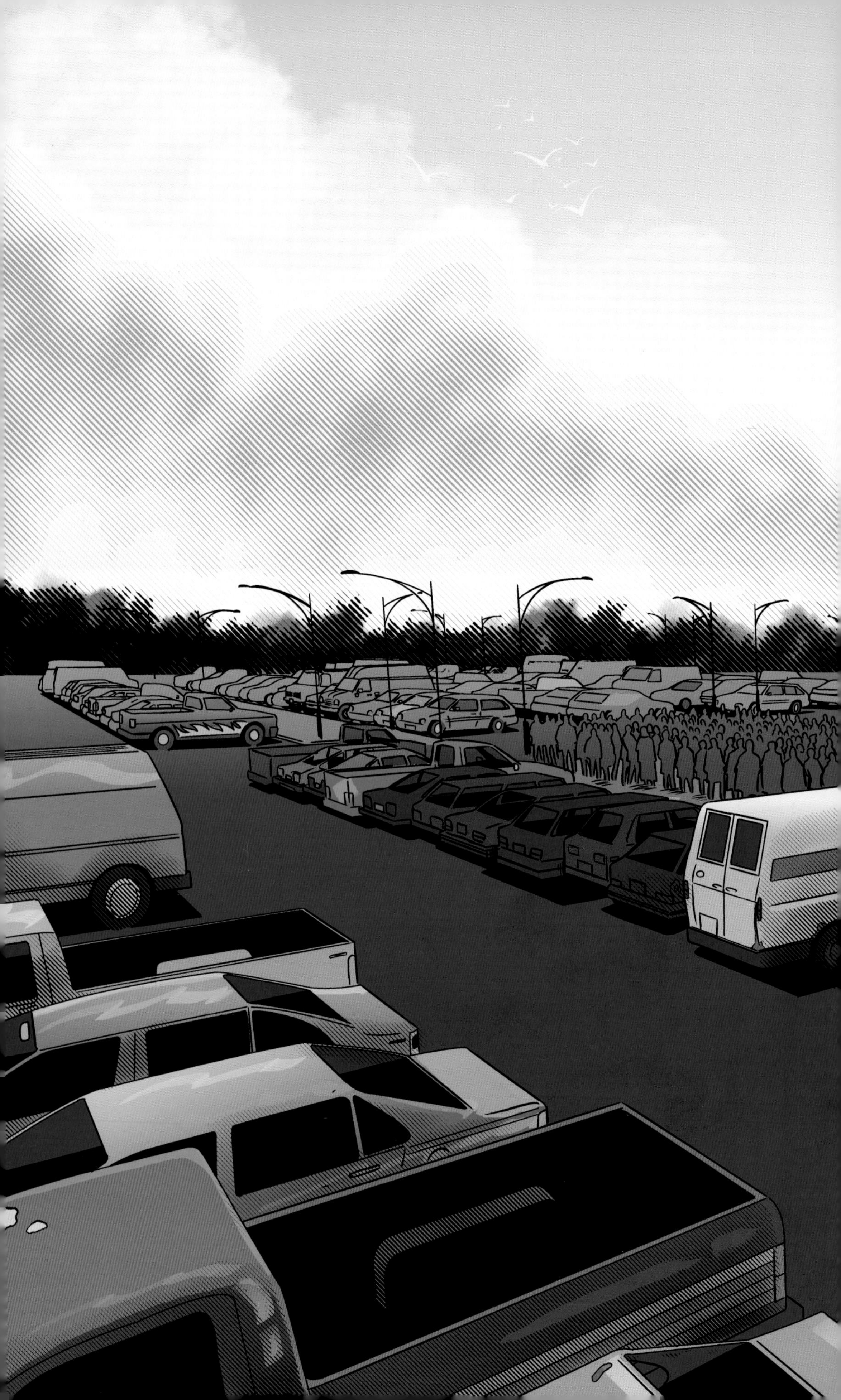

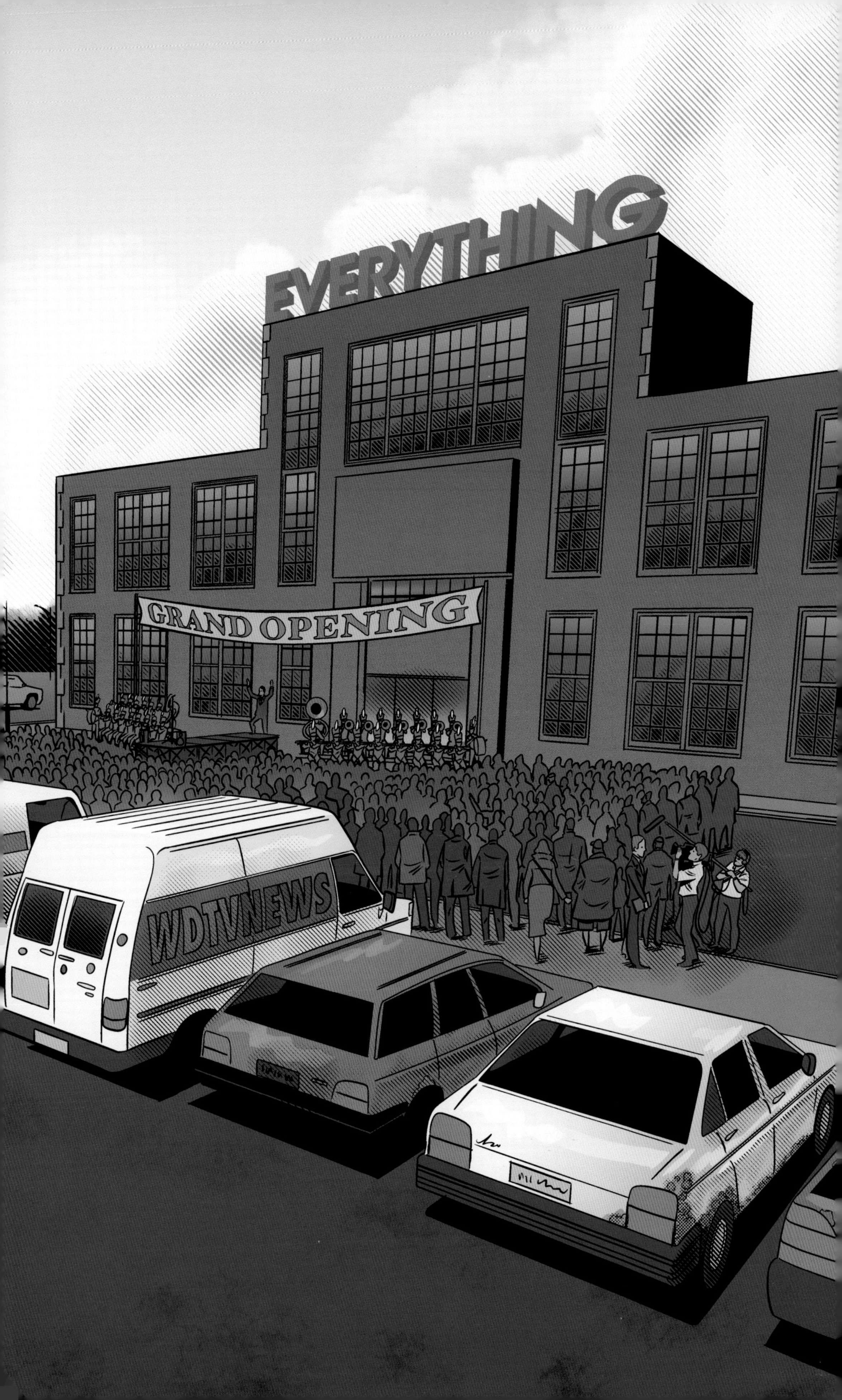
EVERYTHING
GRAND OPENING
WDTV NEWS

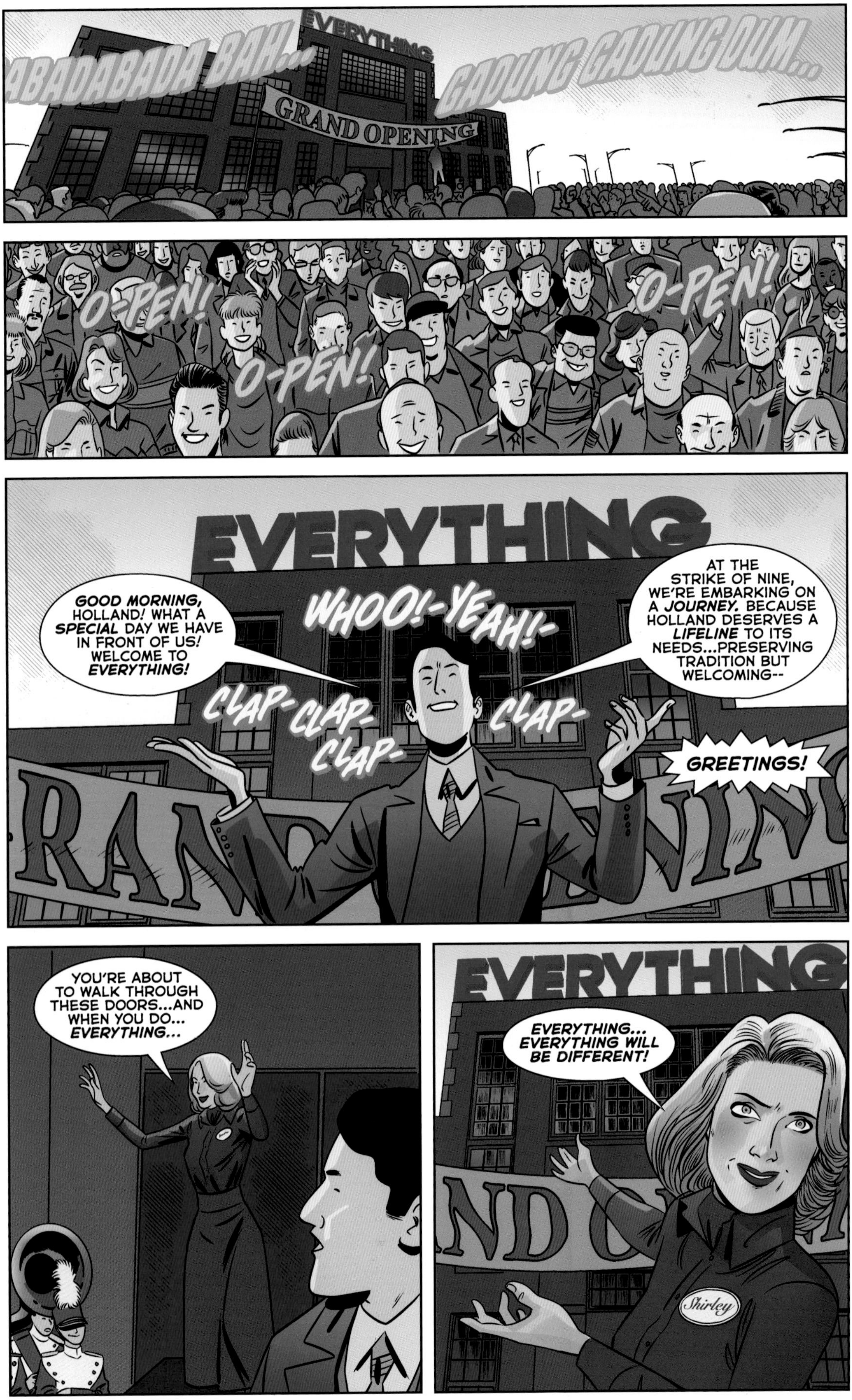
EVERYTHING
GRAND OPENING
...BABADABADA BAH...
GADUNG GADUNG DUM...
O-PEN!
O-PEN!
O-PEN!
EVERYTHING
GOOD MORNING, HOLLAND! WHAT A SPECIAL DAY WE HAVE IN FRONT OF US! WELCOME TO EVERYTHING!
WHOO!-YEAH!-
CLAP-CLAP-CLAP-
CLAP-
AT THE STRIKE OF NINE, WE'RE EMBARKING ON A JOURNEY. BECAUSE HOLLAND DESERVES A LIFELINE TO ITS NEEDS...PRESERVING TRADITION BUT WELCOMING--
GREETINGS!
YOU'RE ABOUT TO WALK THROUGH THESE DOORS...AND WHEN YOU DO... EVERYTHING...
EVERYTHING
EVERYTHING... EVERYTHING WILL BE DIFFERENT!
Shirley

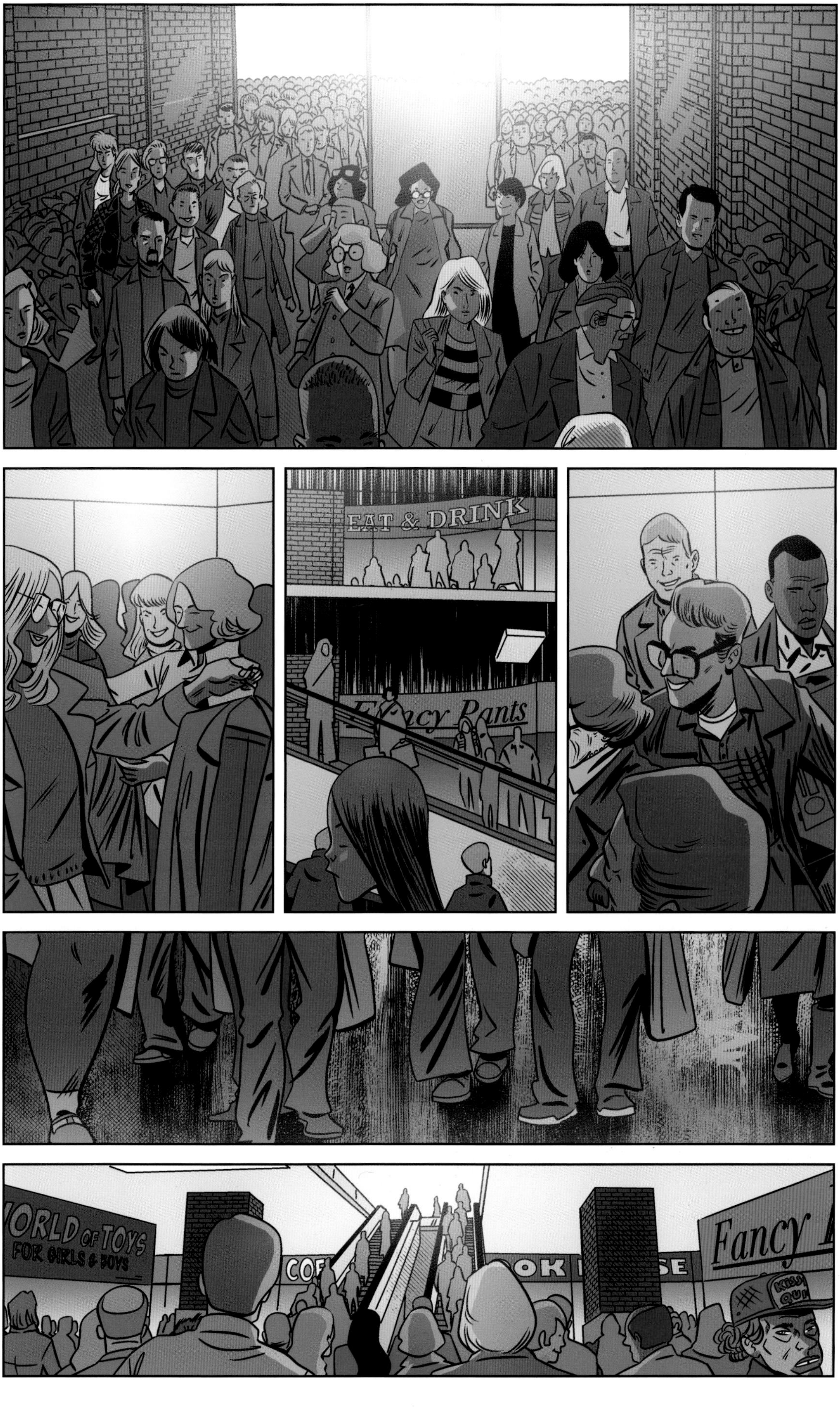
EAT & DRINK
ncy Pants
ORLD OF TOYS
FOR GIRLS & BOYS
COF
Fancy

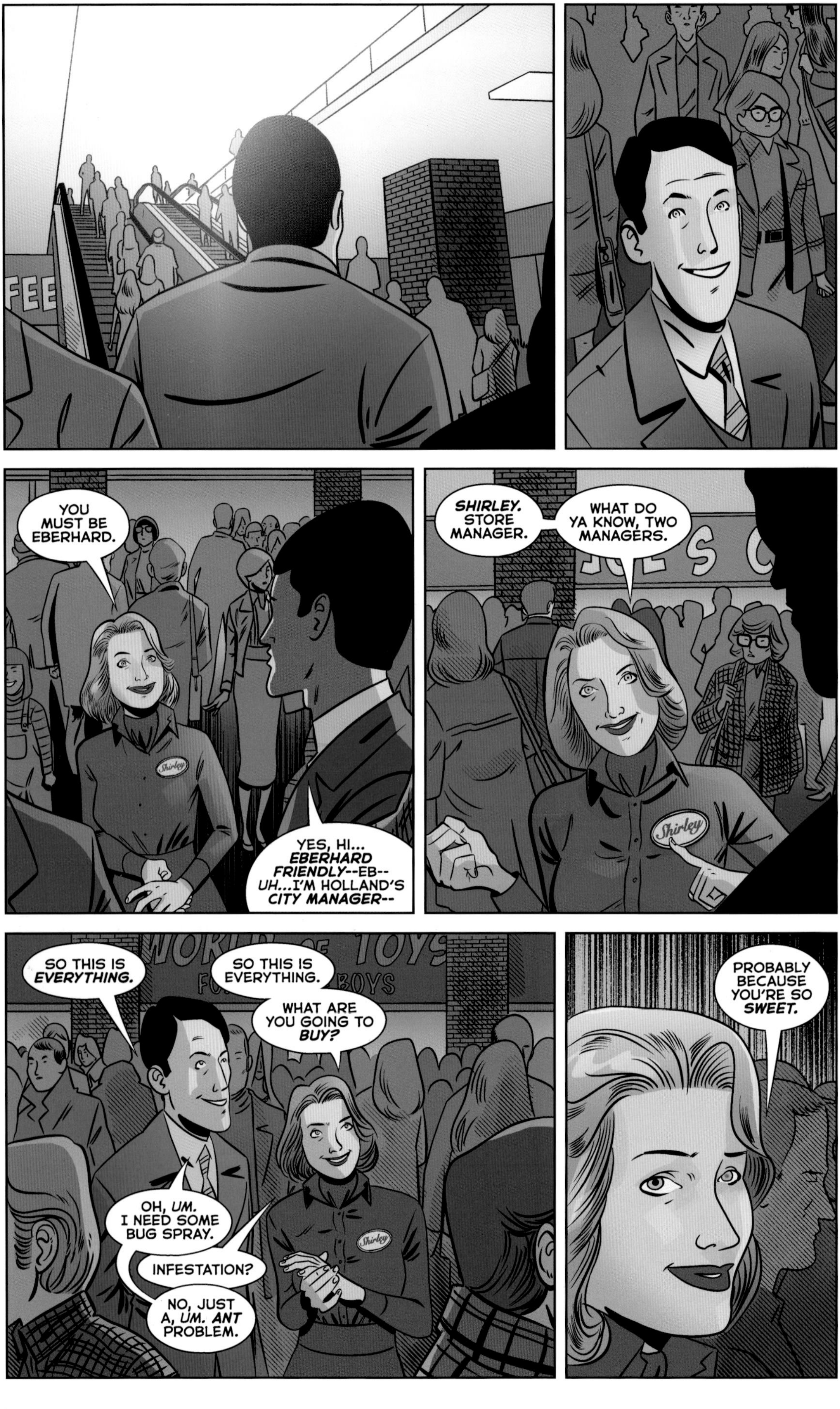
YOU MUST BE EBERHARD.
YES, HI... EBERHARD FRIENDLY--EB-- UH...I'M HOLLAND'S CITY MANAGER--
SHIRLEY. STORE MANAGER.
WHAT DO YA KNOW, TWO MANAGERS.
SO THIS IS EVERYTHING.
SO THIS IS EVERYTHING.
WHAT ARE YOU GOING TO BUY?
OH, UM. I NEED SOME BUG SPRAY.
INFESTATION?
NO, JUST A, UM. ANT PROBLEM.
PROBABLY BECAUSE YOU'RE SO SWEET.

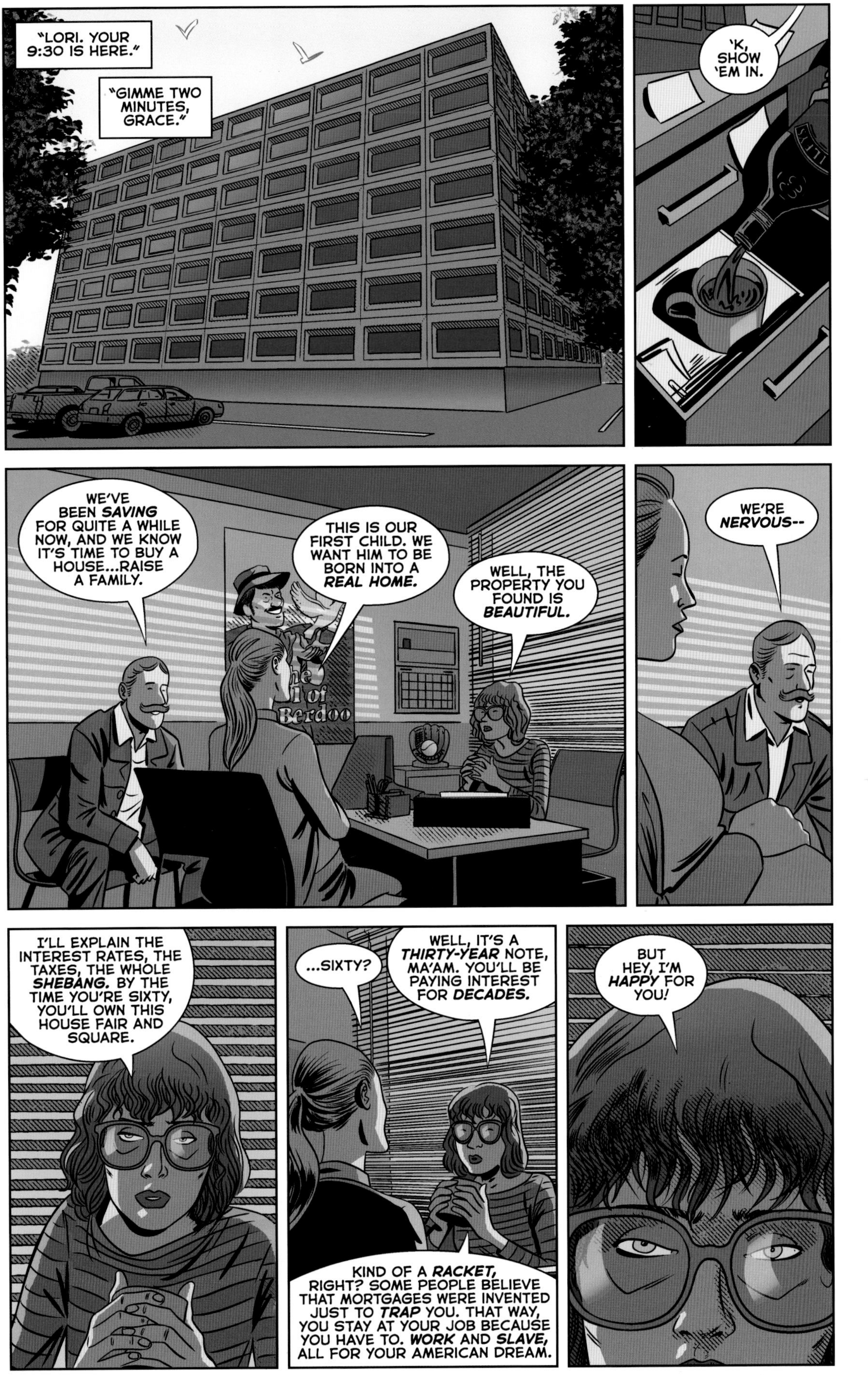
"LORI. YOUR 9:30 IS HERE."
"GIMME TWO MINUTES, GRACE."
'K, SHOW 'EM IN.
WE'VE BEEN SAVING FOR QUITE A WHILE NOW, AND WE KNOW IT'S TIME TO BUY A HOUSE...RAISE A FAMILY.
THIS IS OUR FIRST CHILD. WE WANT HIM TO BE BORN INTO A REAL HOME.
WELL, THE PROPERTY YOU FOUND IS BEAUTIFUL.
WE'RE NERVOUS--
I'LL EXPLAIN THE INTEREST RATES, THE TAXES, THE WHOLE SHEBANG. BY THE TIME YOU'RE SIXTY, YOU'LL OWN THIS HOUSE FAIR AND SQUARE.
...SIXTY?
WELL, IT'S A THIRTY-YEAR NOTE, MA'AM. YOU'LL BE PAYING INTEREST FOR DECADES.
KIND OF A RACKET, RIGHT? SOME PEOPLE BELIEVE THAT MORTGAGES WERE INVENTED JUST TO TRAP YOU. THAT WAY, YOU STAY AT YOUR JOB BECAUSE YOU HAVE TO. WORK AND SLAVE, ALL FOR YOUR AMERICAN DREAM.
BUT HEY, I'M HAPPY FOR YOU!

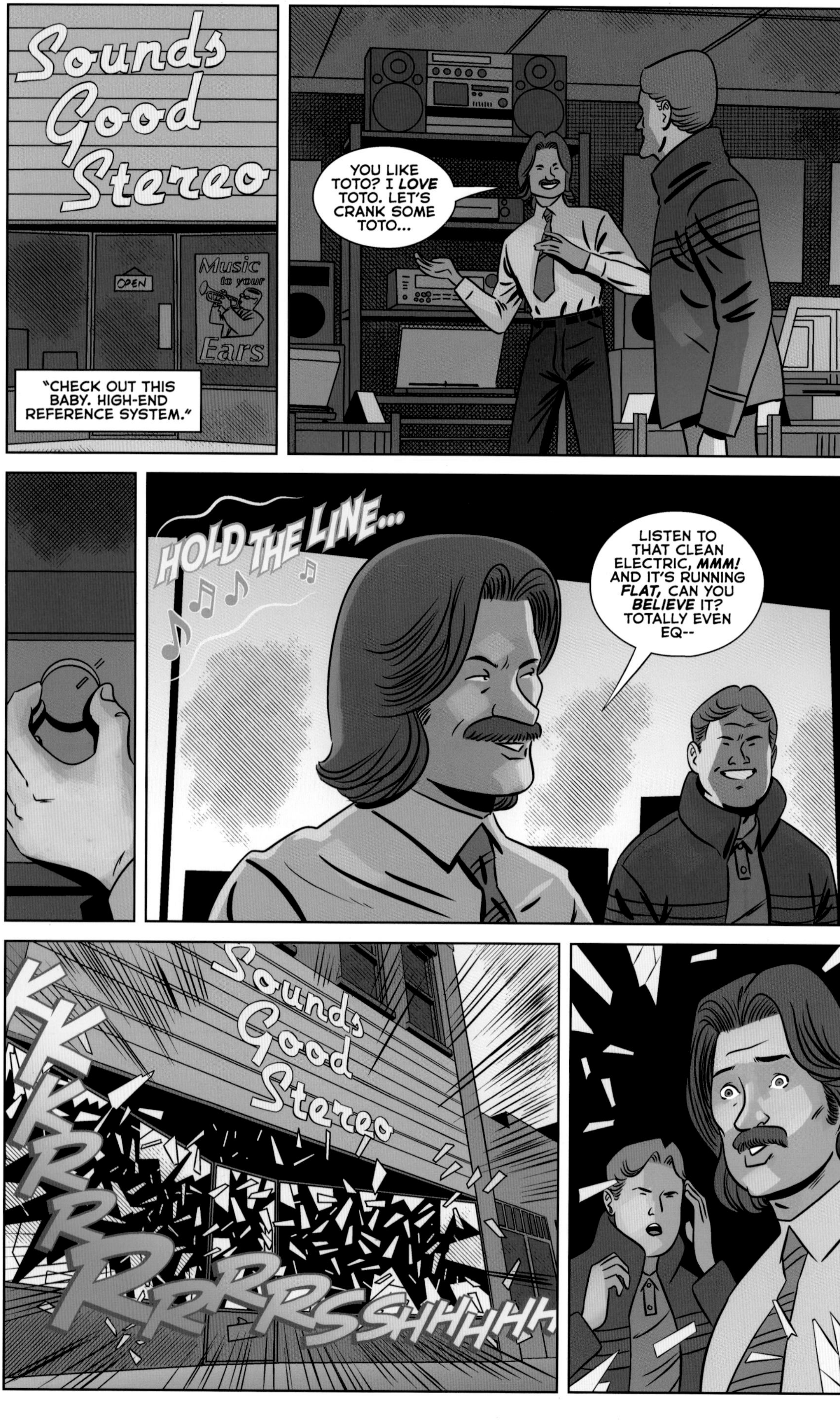
Sounds Good Stereo
OPEN
Music to your Ears
"CHECK OUT THIS BABY. HIGH-END REFERENCE SYSTEM."
YOU LIKE TOTO? I *LOVE* TOTO. LET'S CRANK SOME TOTO...
HOLD THE LINE...
LISTEN TO THAT CLEAN ELECTRIC, ***MMM!*** AND IT'S RUNNING ***FLAT,*** CAN YOU ***BELIEVE*** IT? TOTALLY EVEN EQ--
Sounds Good Stereo
KKRRRRRRRSSHHHHK

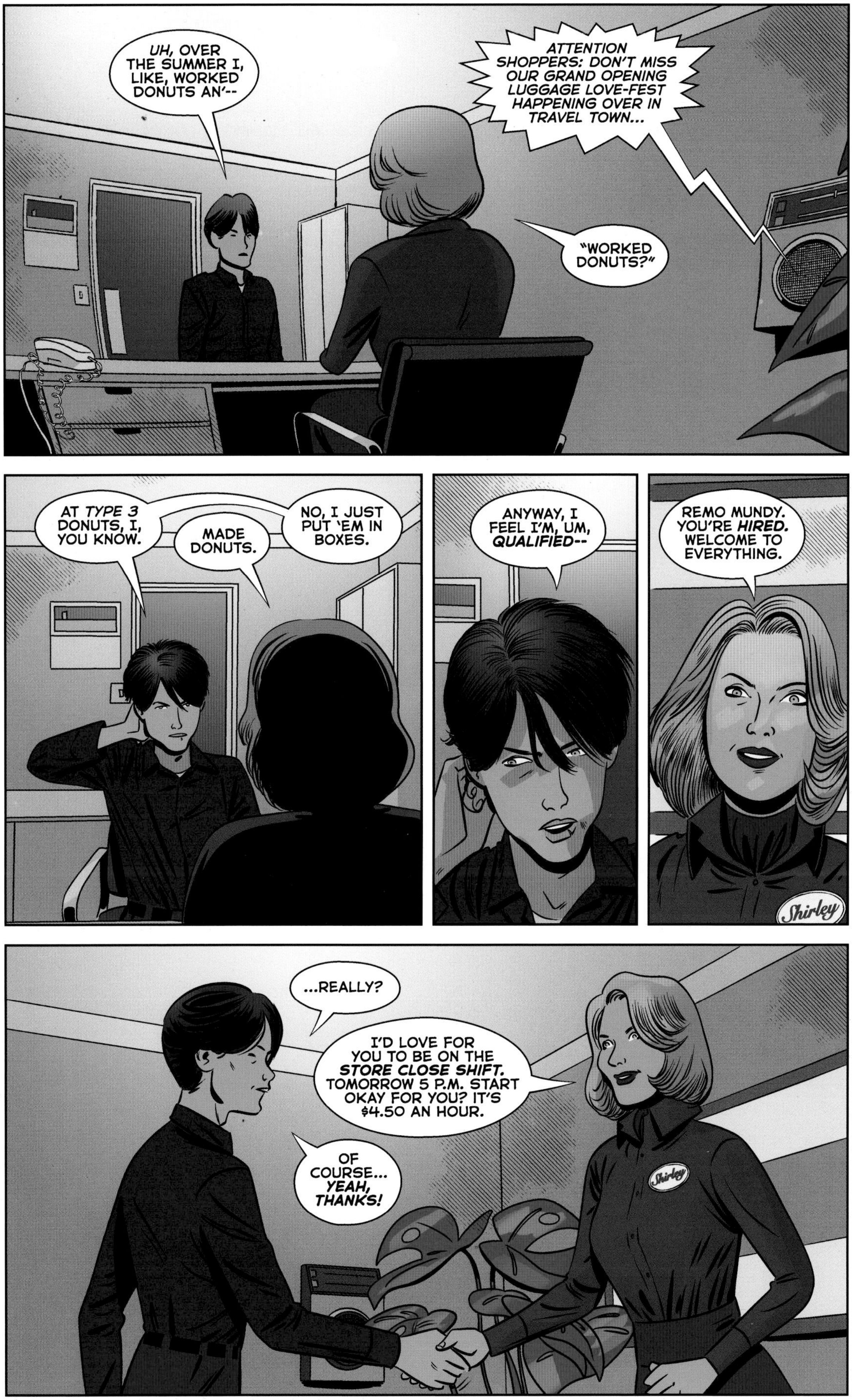
UH, OVER THE SUMMER I, LIKE, WORKED DONUTS AN'--
ATTENTION SHOPPERS: DON'T MISS OUR GRAND OPENING LUGGAGE LOVE-FEST HAPPENING OVER IN TRAVEL TOWN...
"WORKED DONUTS?"
AT TYPE 3 DONUTS, I, YOU KNOW.
MADE DONUTS.
NO, I JUST PUT 'EM IN BOXES.
ANYWAY, I FEEL I'M, UM, QUALIFIED--
REMO MUNDY. YOU'RE HIRED. WELCOME TO EVERYTHING.
Shirley
...REALLY?
I'D LOVE FOR YOU TO BE ON THE STORE CLOSE SHIFT. TOMORROW 5 P.M. START OKAY FOR YOU? IT'S $4.50 AN HOUR.
OF COURSE... YEAH, THANKS!
Shirley

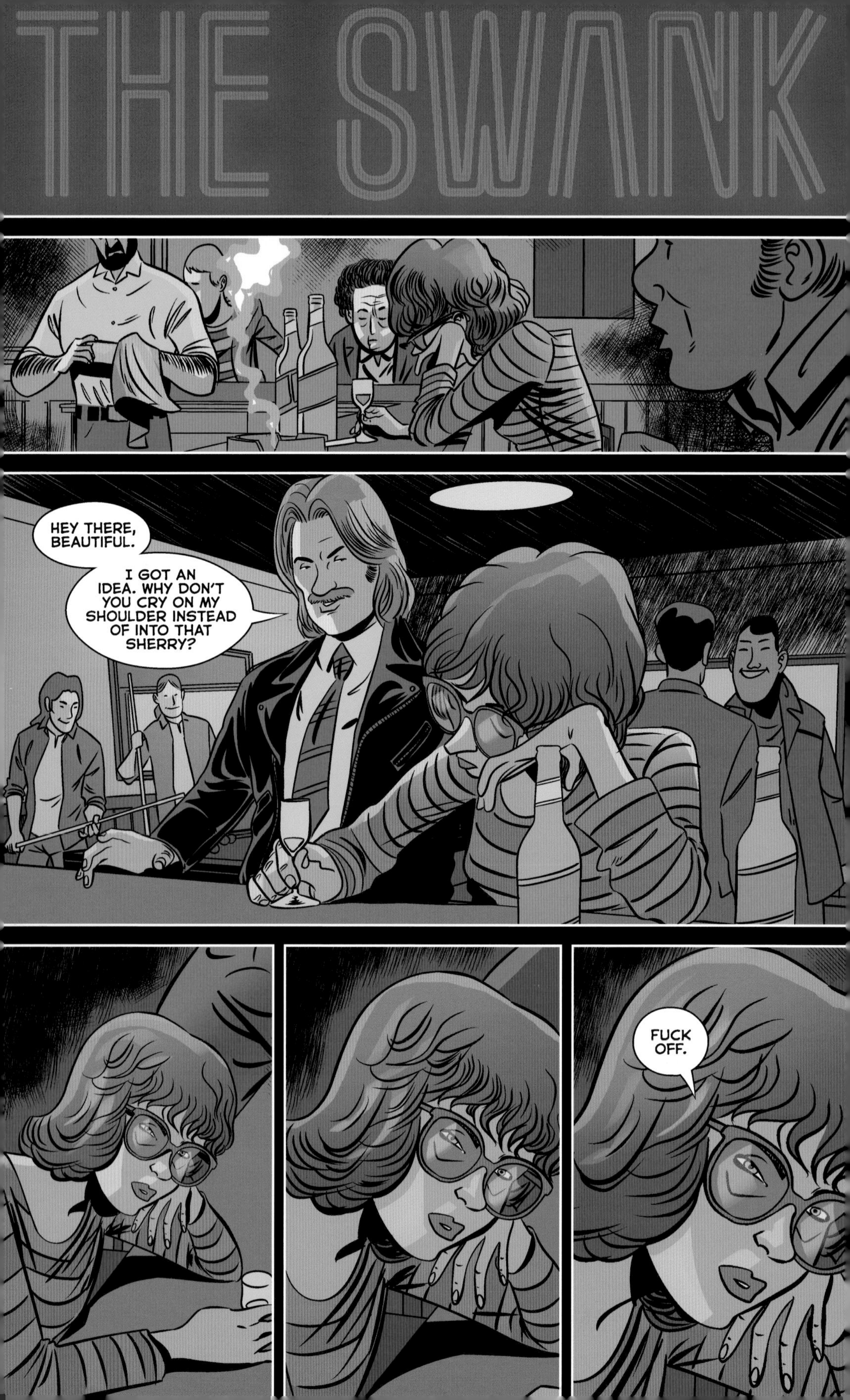
THE SWANK
HEY THERE, BEAUTIFUL.
I GOT AN IDEA. WHY DON'T YOU CRY ON MY SHOULDER INSTEAD OF INTO THAT SHERRY?
FUCK OFF.

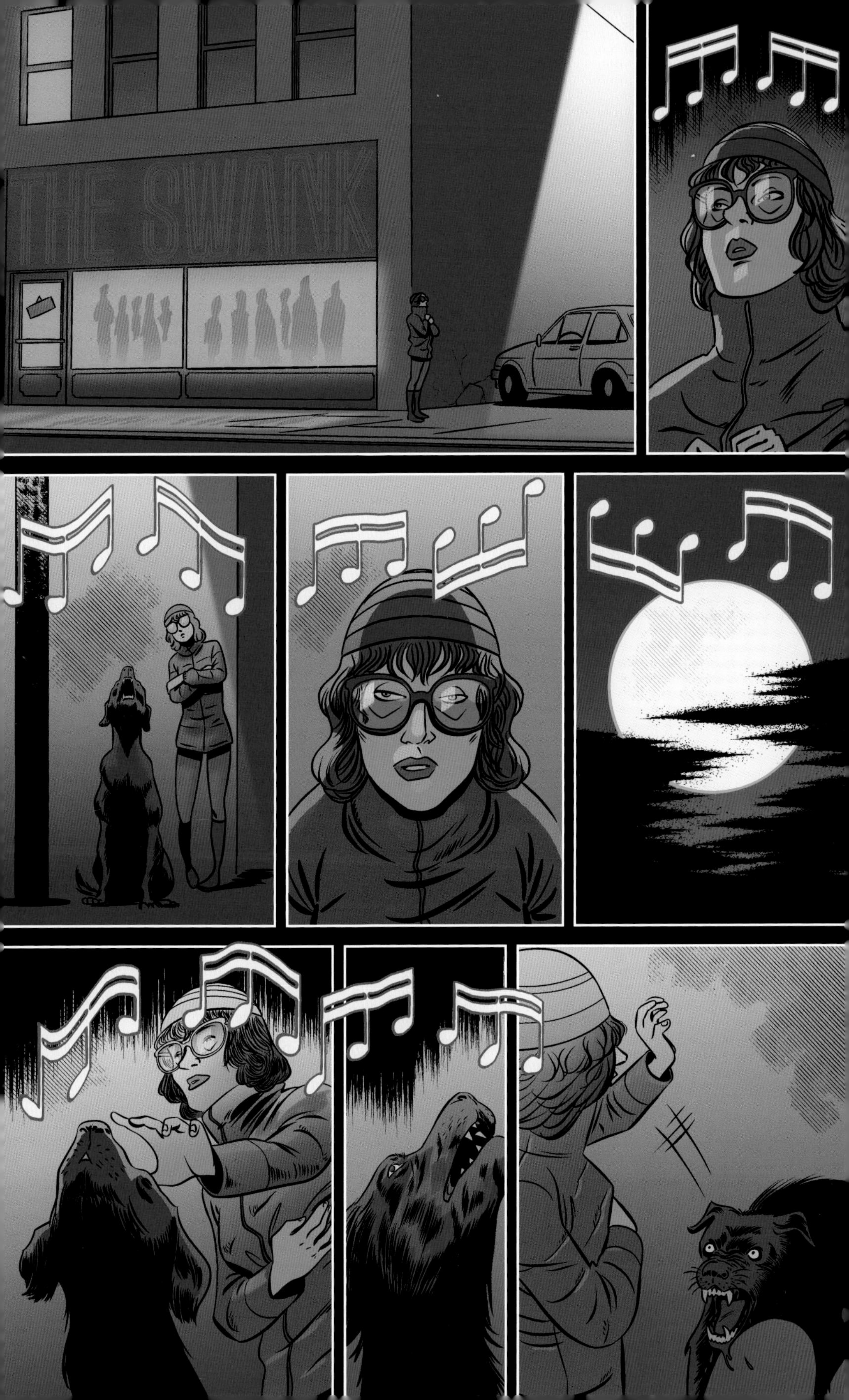
THE SWANK

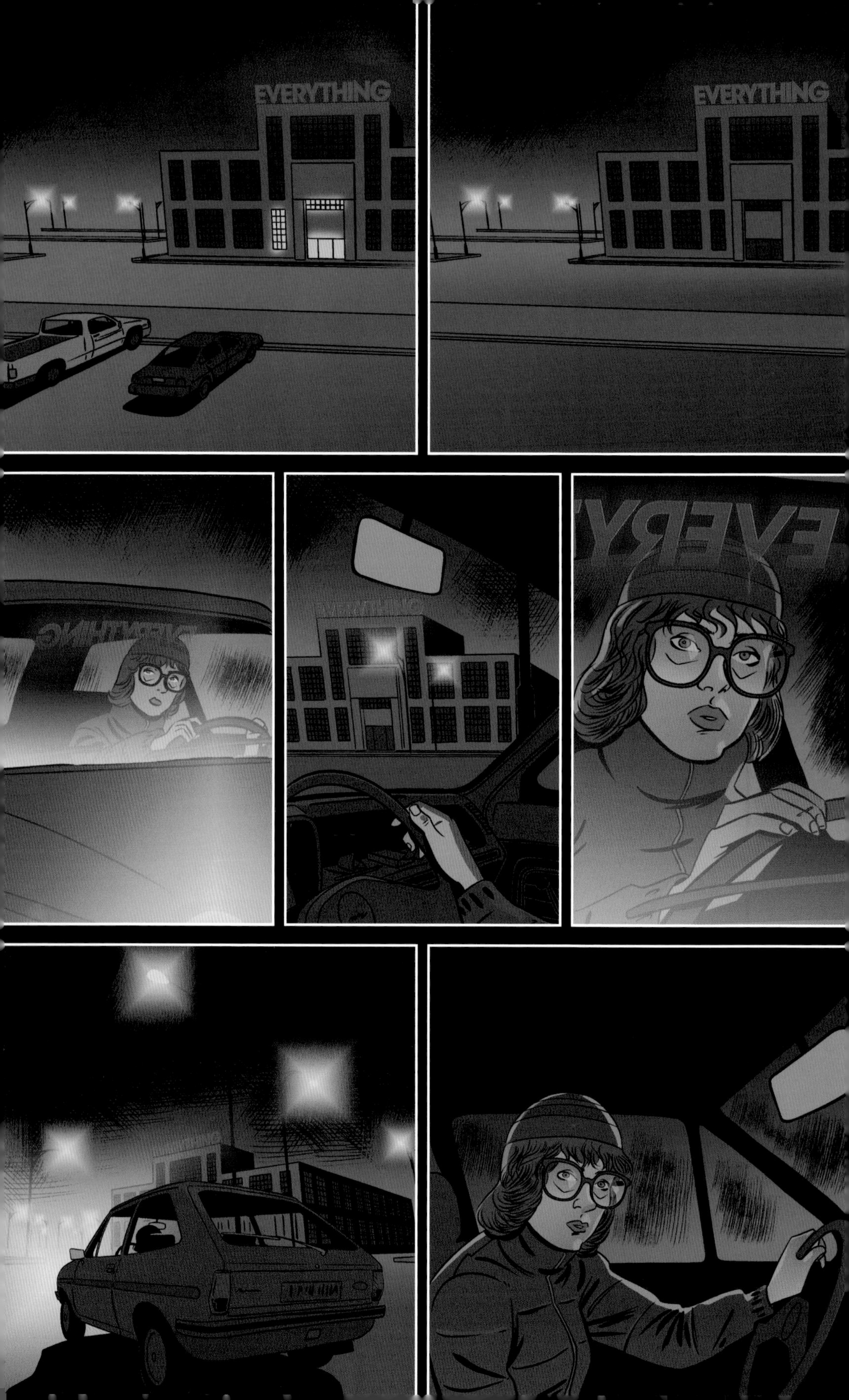
EVERYTHING
EVERYTHING

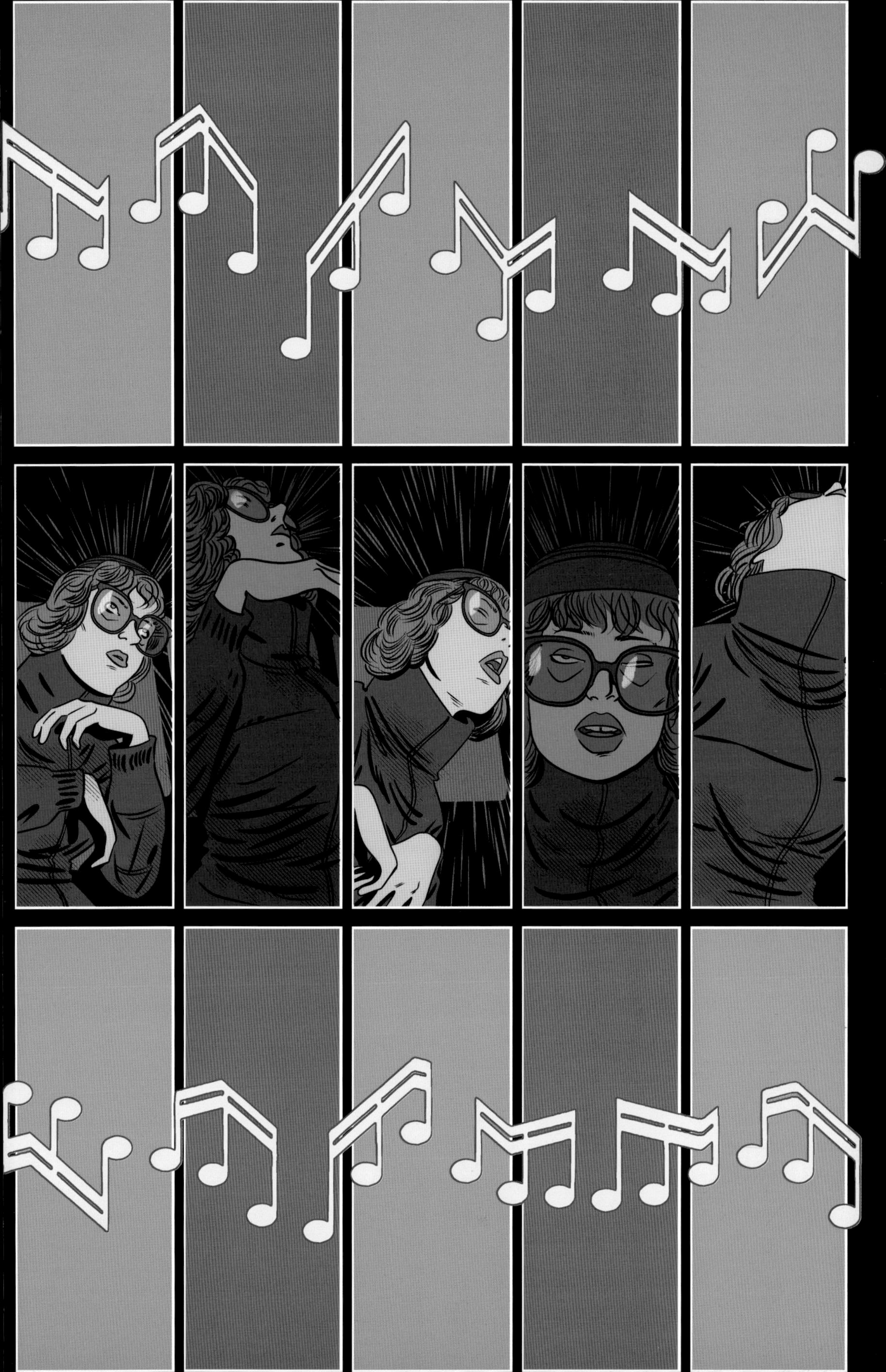

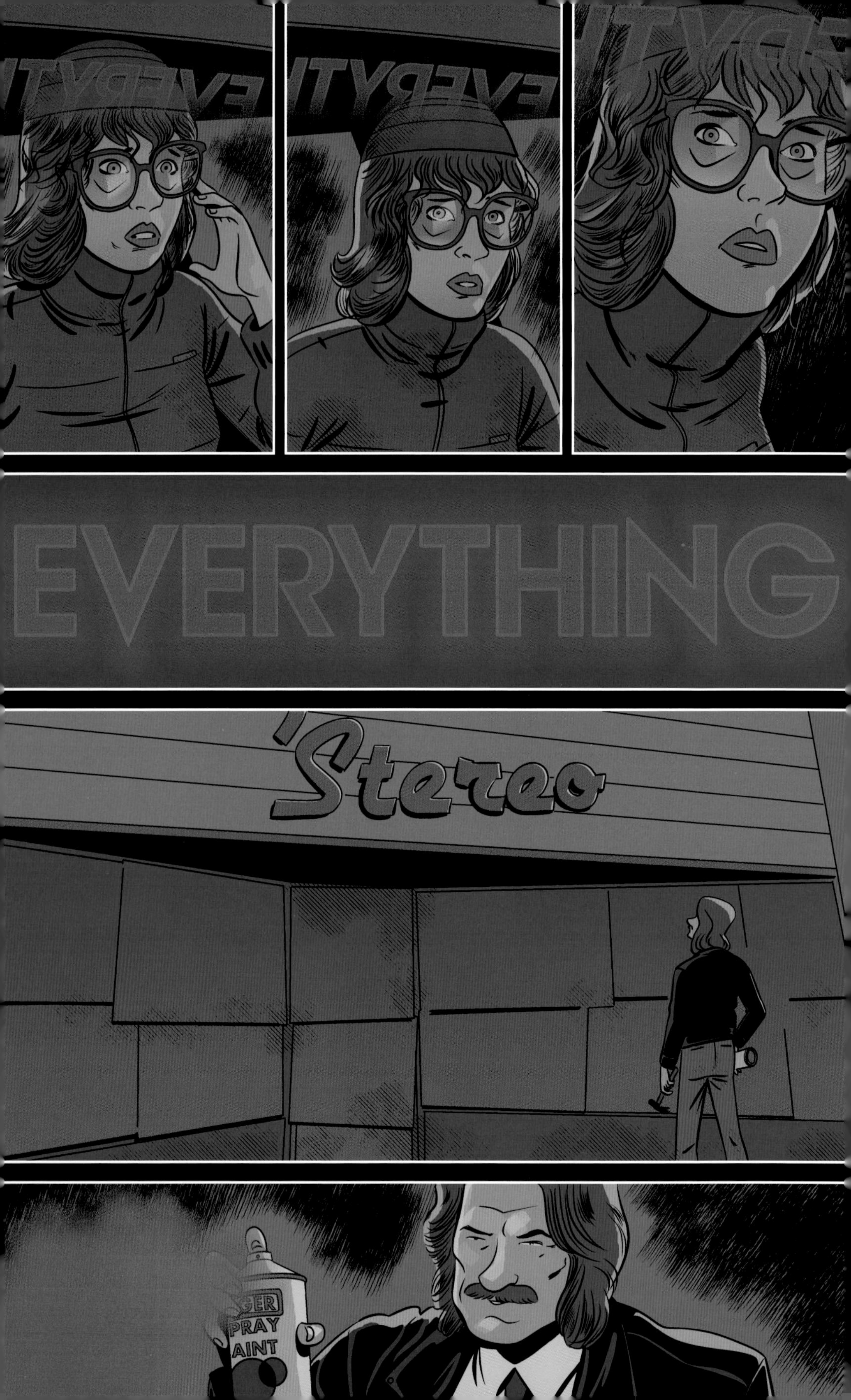
EVERYTHING
'Stereo

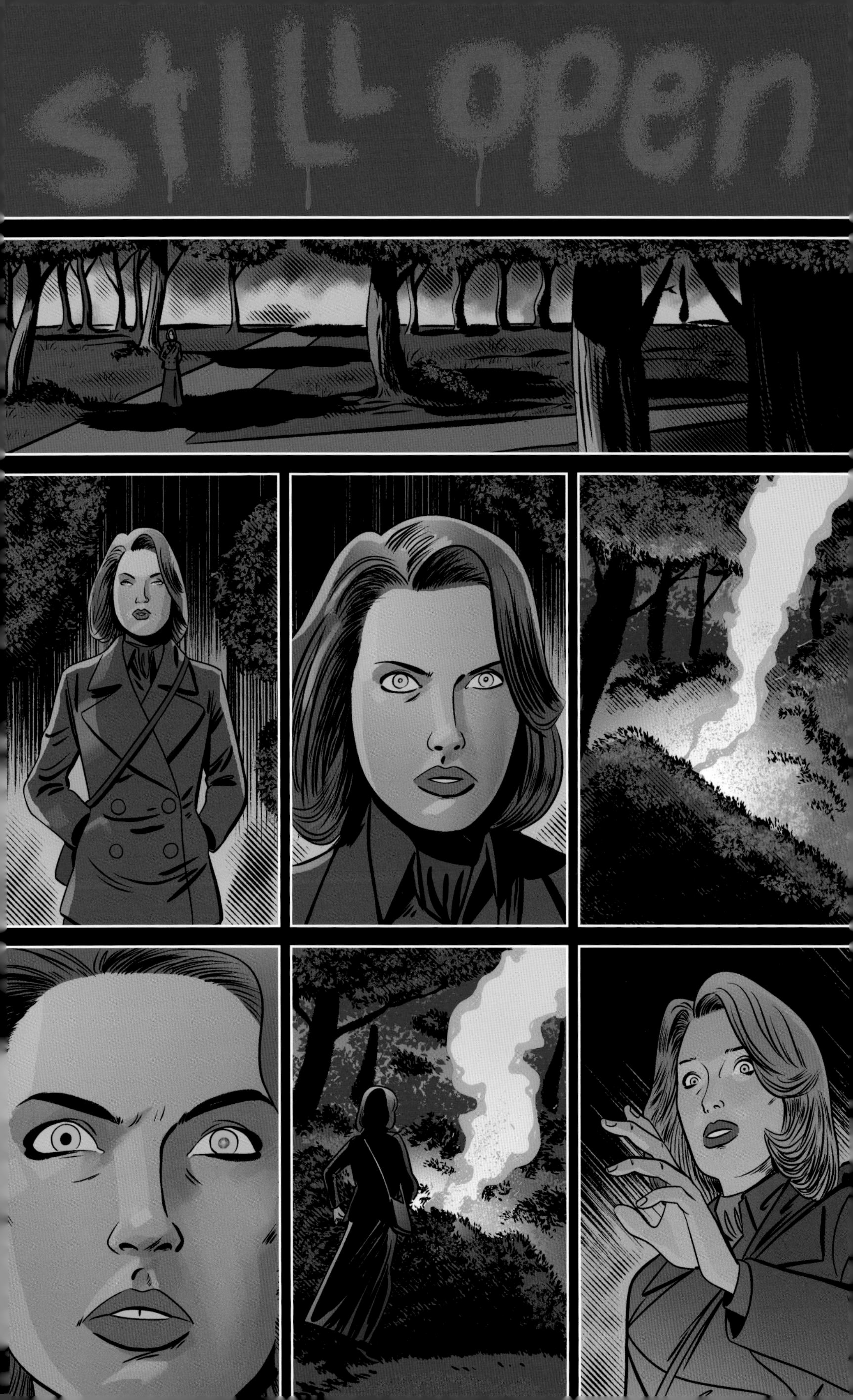
still open

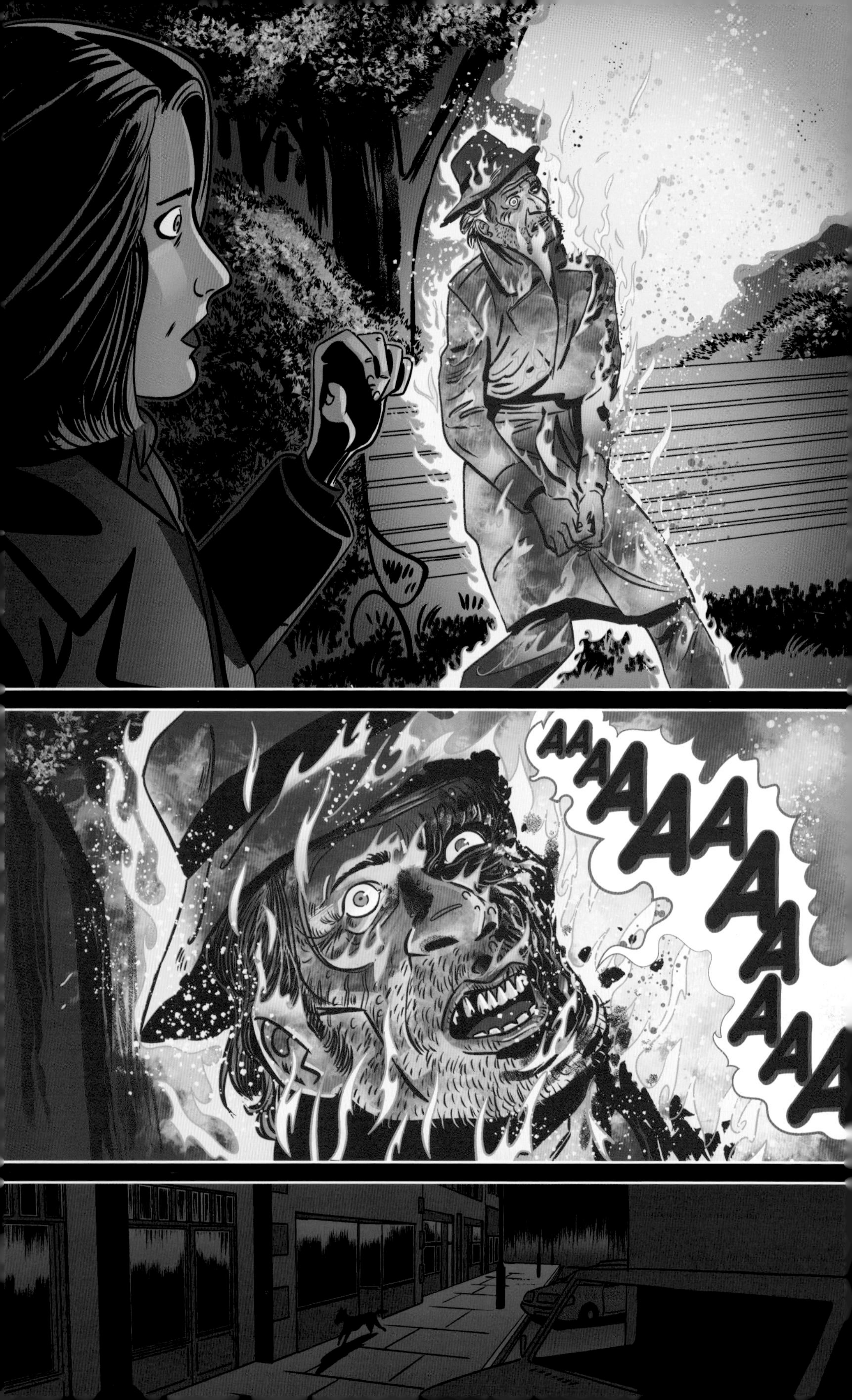
AAAAAAAAAAA

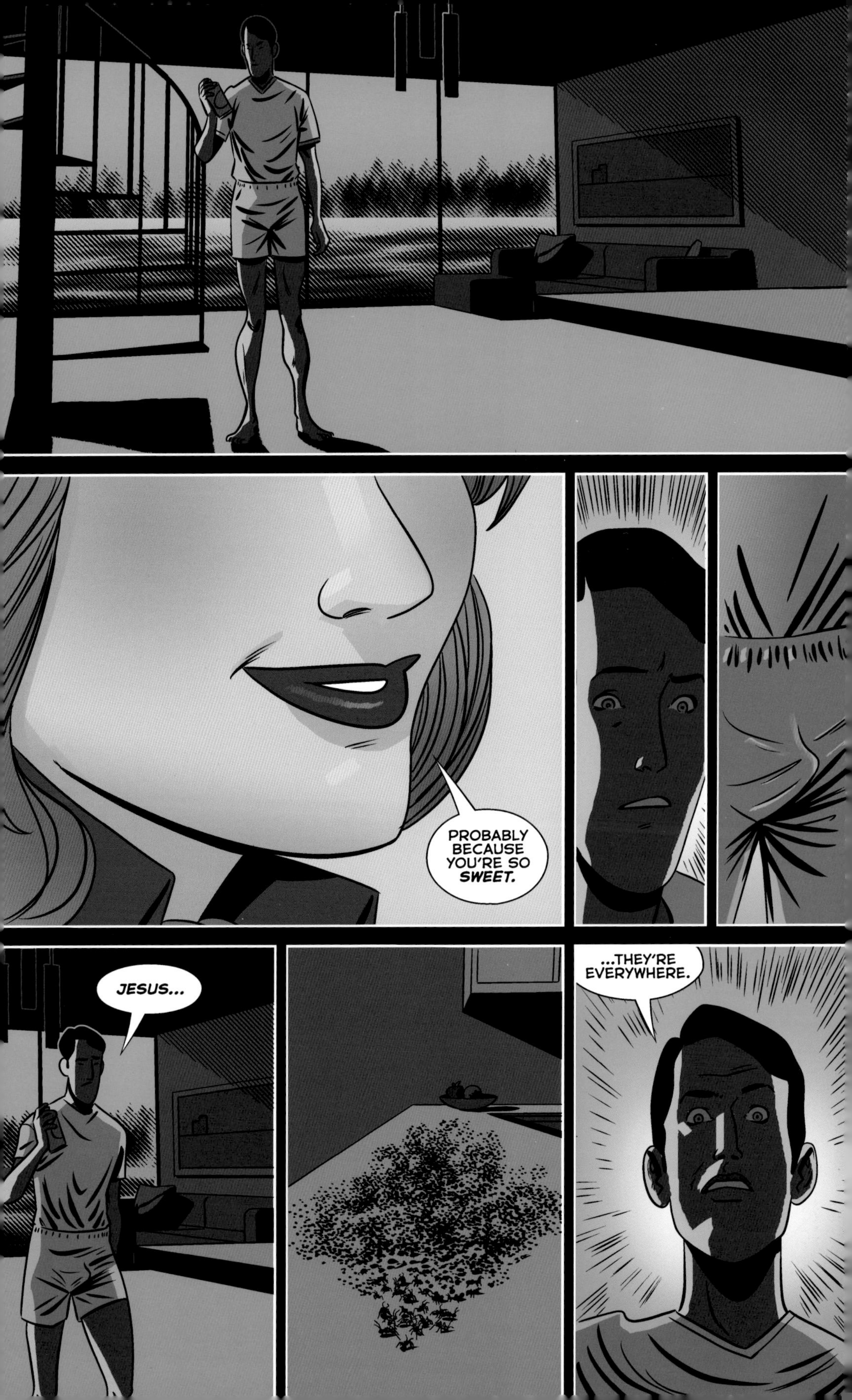
PROBABLY BECAUSE YOU'RE SO SWEET.
JESUS...
...THEY'RE EVERYWHERE.

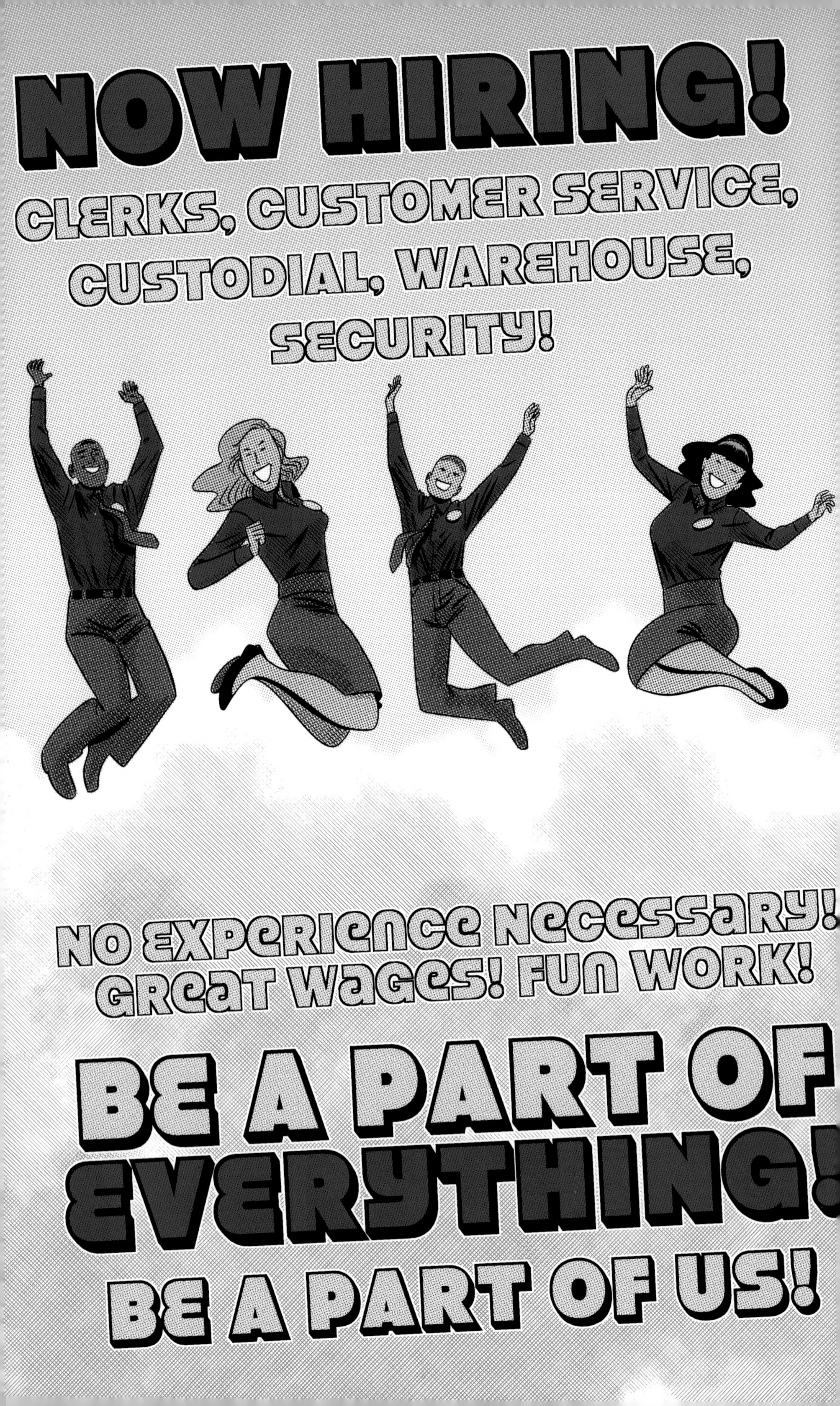
NOW HIRING!
CLERKS, CUSTOMER SERVICE, CUSTODIAL, WAREHOUSE, SECURITY!
NO EXPERIENCE NECESSARY! GREAT WAGES! FUN WORK!
BE A PART OF EVERYTHING!
BE A PART OF US!

Chapter 2:
"The Evil That Never Arrived"

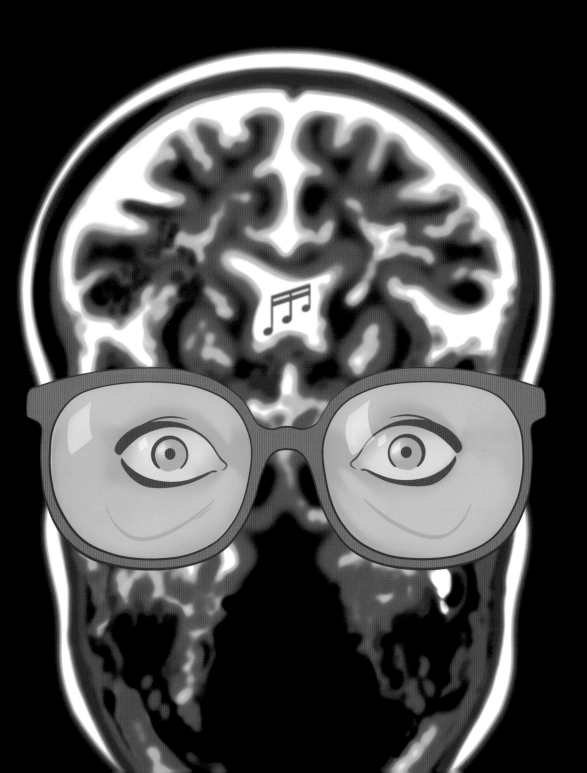

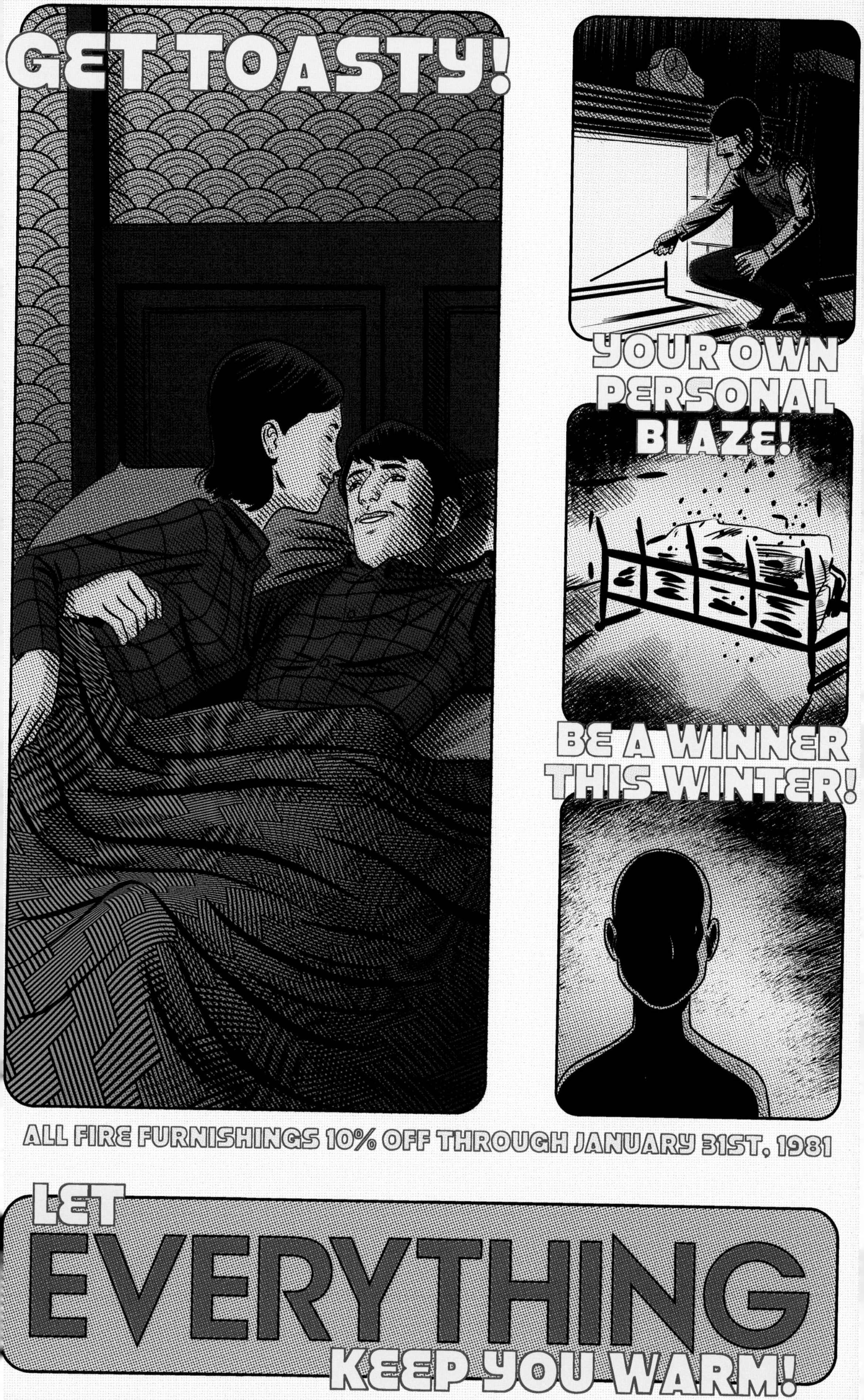
GET TOASTY!
YOUR OWN PERSONAL BLAZE!
BE A WINNER THIS WINTER!
ALL FIRE FURNISHINGS 10% OFF THROUGH JANUARY 31ST, 1981
LET EVERYTHING KEEP YOU WARM!

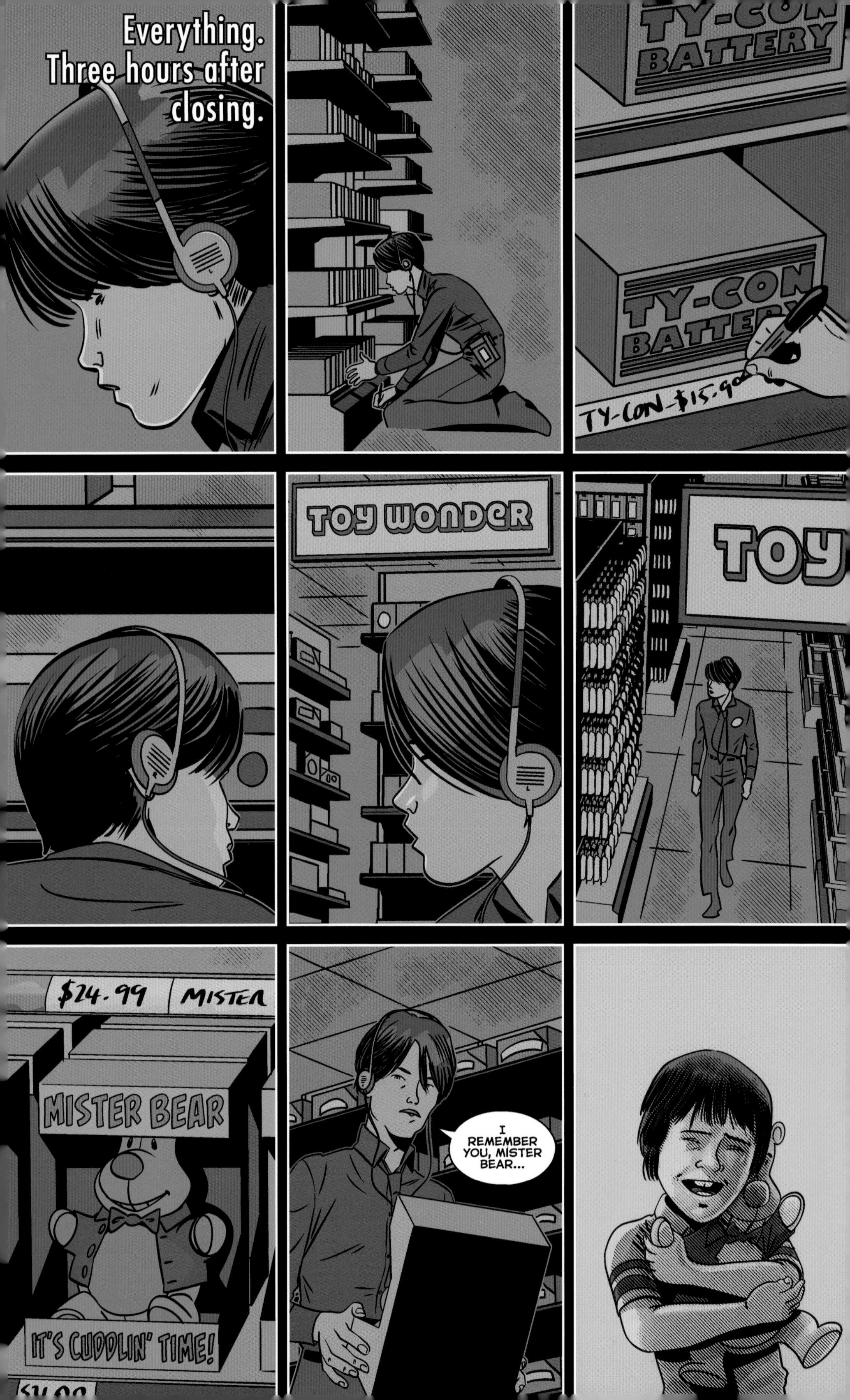
Everything. Three hours after closing.
TY-CON BATTERY
TY-CON BATTERY
TY-CON-$15.99
TOY WONDER
TOY
$24.99
MISTER
MISTER BEAR
IT'S CUDDLIN' TIME!
I REMEMBER YOU, MISTER BEAR...

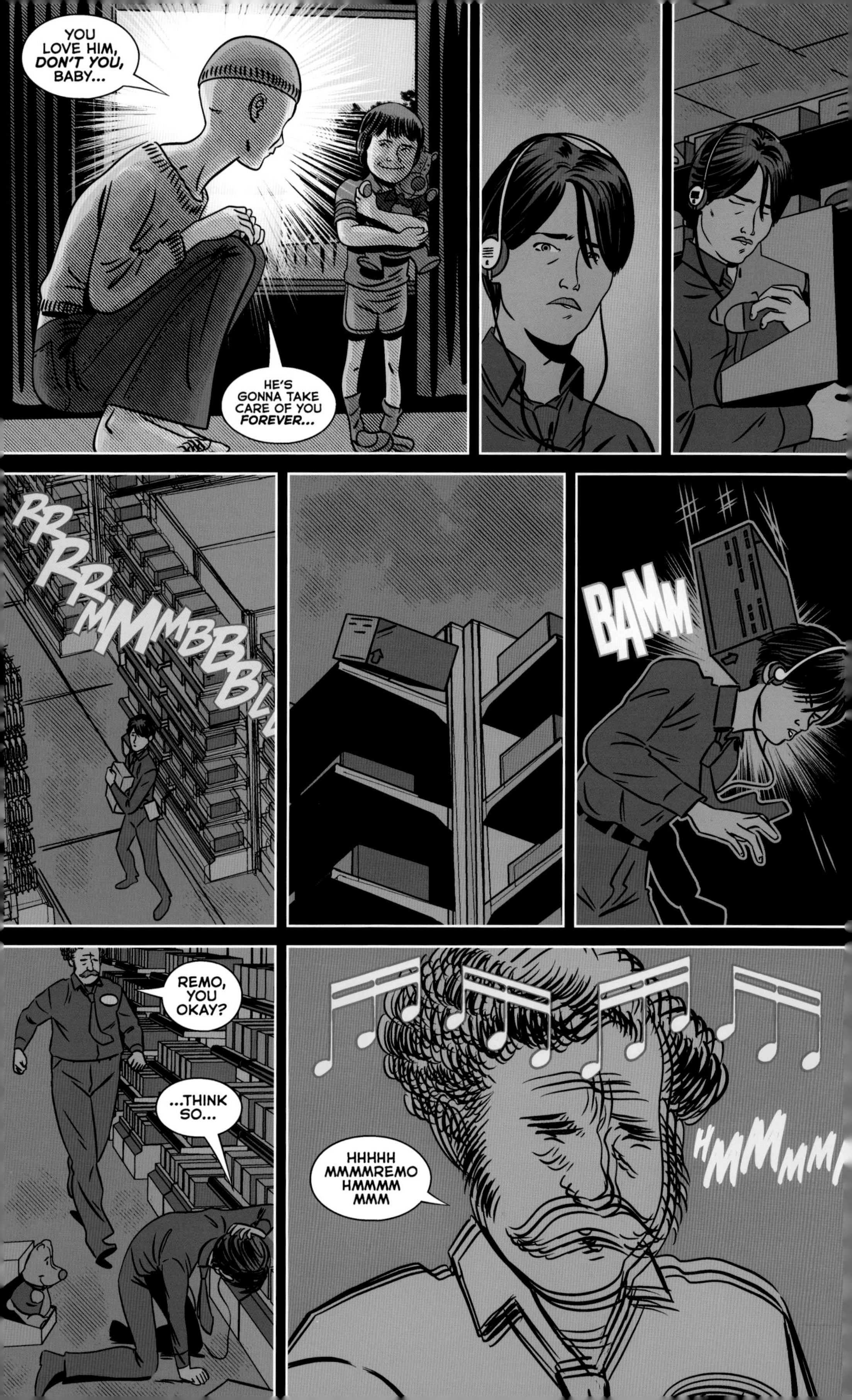
YOU LOVE HIM, *DON'T YOU,* BABY...
HE'S GONNA TAKE CARE OF YOU *FOREVER...*
RRRRMMMMBBBLL
BAMM
REMO, YOU OKAY?
...THINK SO...
HHHHH MMMMREMO HMMMM MMM
HMMMMI

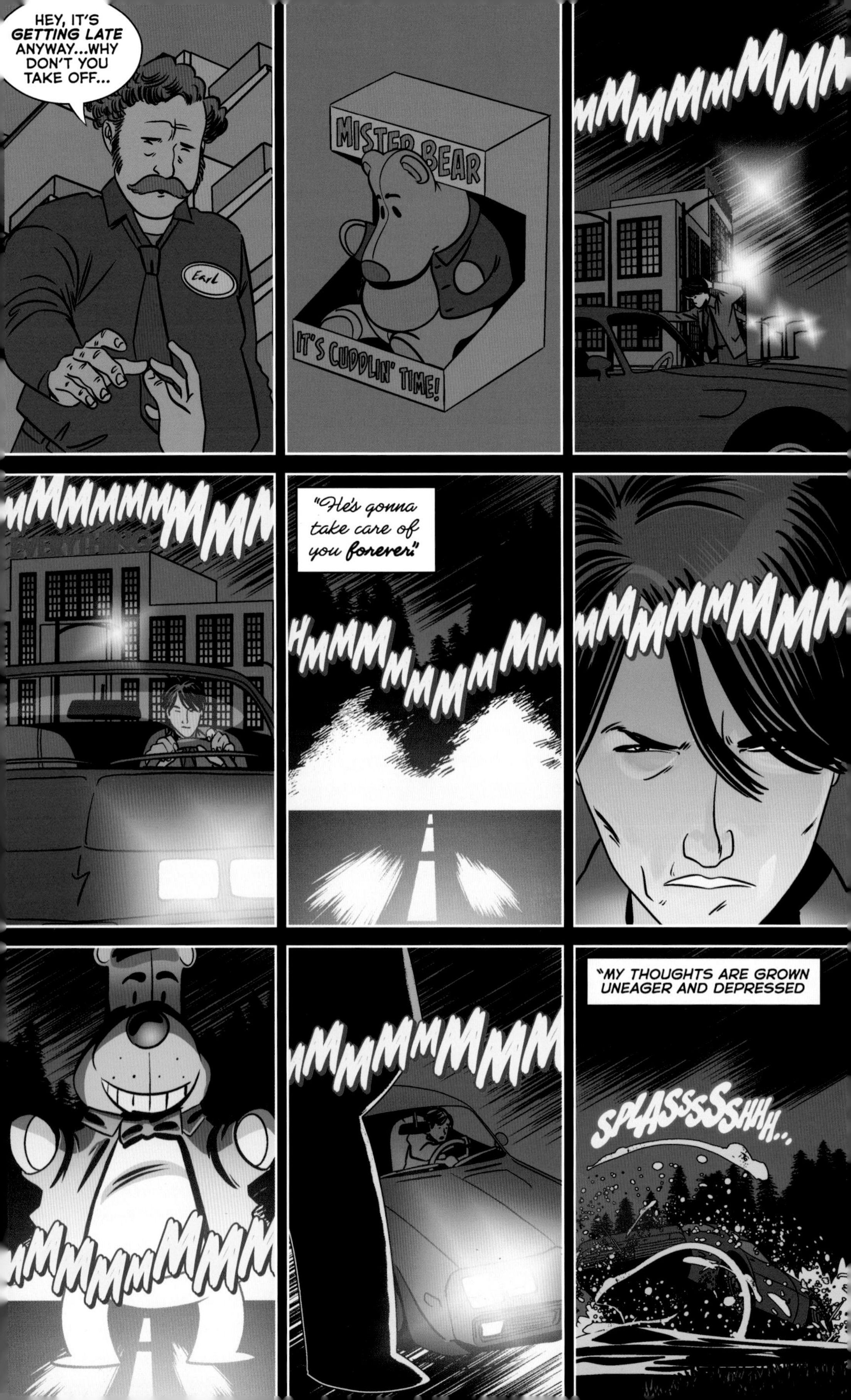
HEY, IT'S *GETTING LATE* ANYWAY...WHY DON'T YOU TAKE OFF...
Earl
MISTER BEAR
IT'S CUDDLIN' TIME!
MMMMMMMMMMM
MMMMMMMMMM
"He's gonna take care of you **forever**."
HMMMMMMMMMM
MMMMMMMMMMM
MMMMMMMMMM
MMMMMMMMMM
"MY THOUGHTS ARE GROWN UNEAGER AND DEPRESSED
SPLASSSSSHHH..

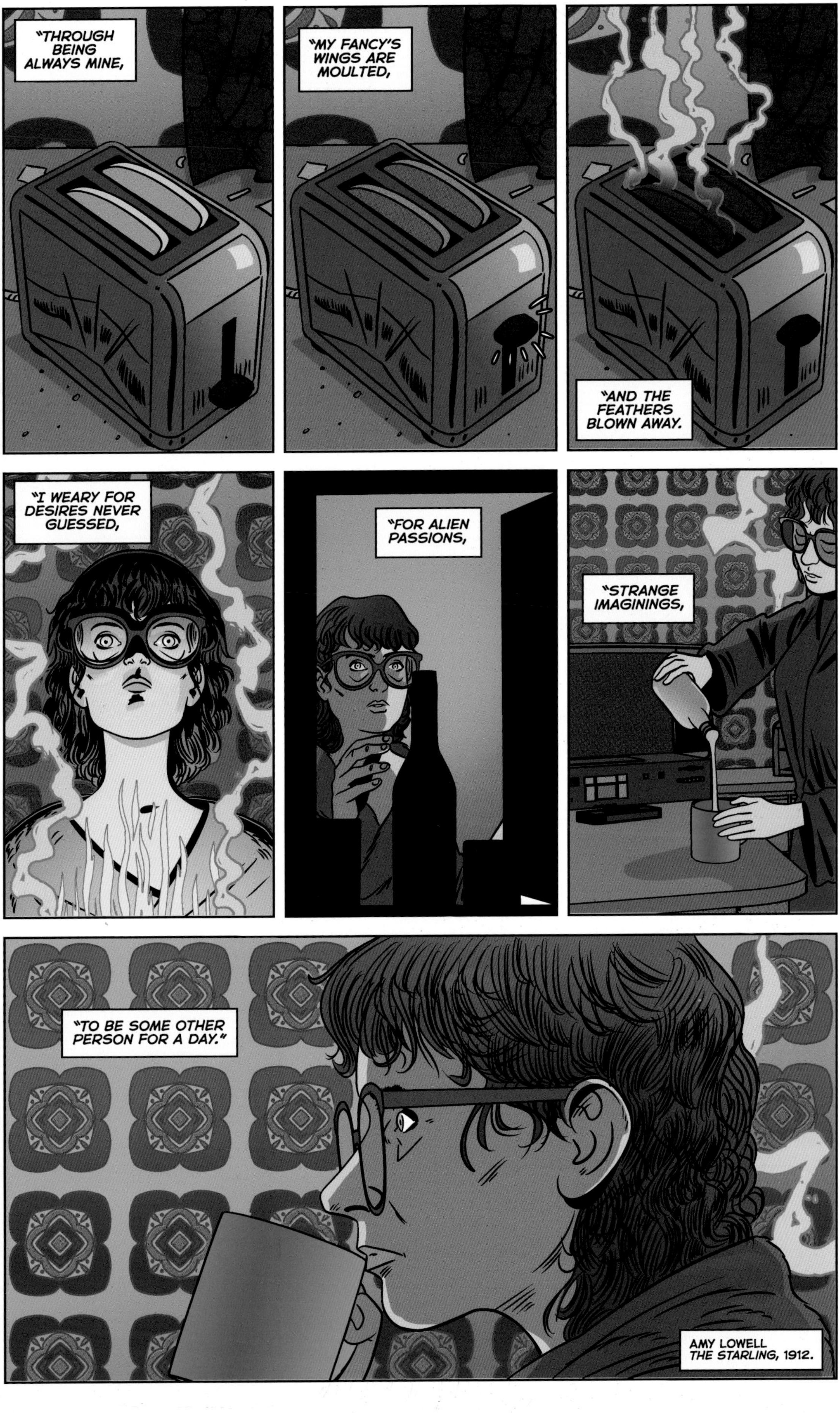
"THROUGH BEING ALWAYS MINE,
"MY FANCY'S WINGS ARE MOULTED,
"AND THE FEATHERS BLOWN AWAY.
"I WEARY FOR DESIRES NEVER GUESSED,
"FOR ALIEN PASSIONS,
"STRANGE IMAGININGS,
"TO BE SOME OTHER PERSON FOR A DAY."
AMY LOWELL
THE STARLING, 1912.

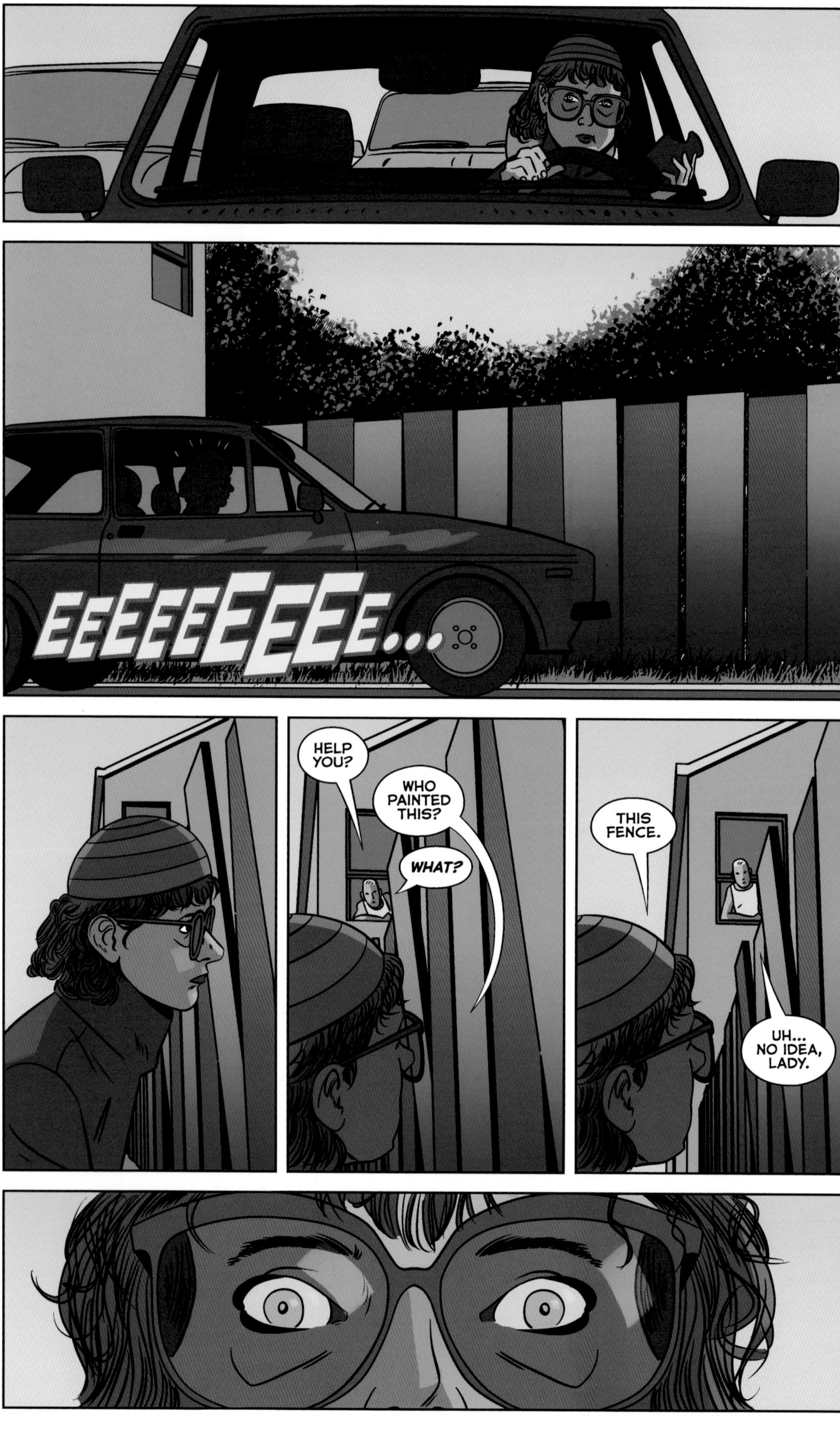
EEEEEEEEE...
HELP YOU?
WHO PAINTED THIS?
WHAT?
THIS FENCE.
UH... NO IDEA, LADY.

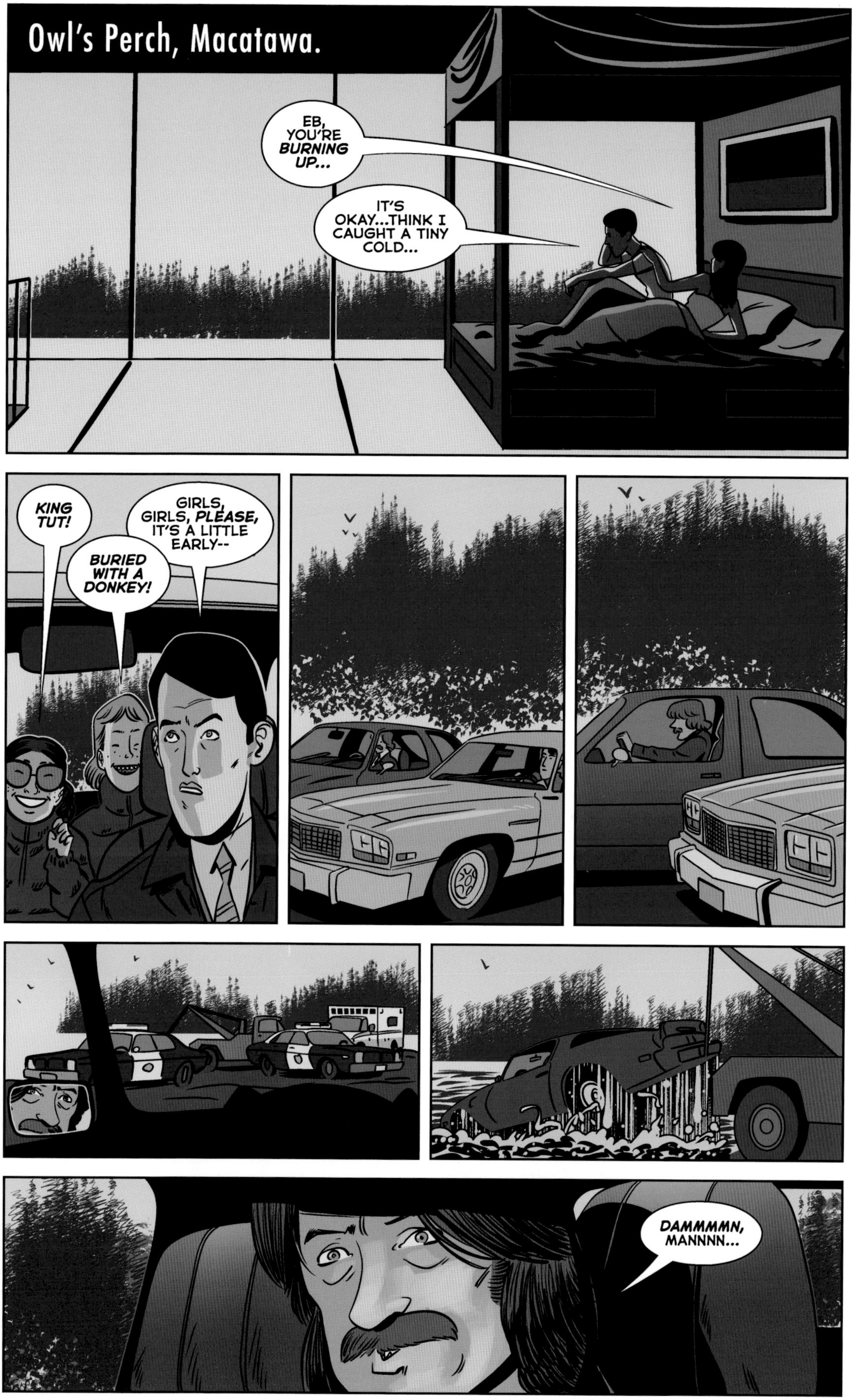
Owl's Perch, Macatawa.
EB, YOU'RE *BURNING* UP...
IT'S OKAY...THINK I CAUGHT A TINY COLD...
KING TUT!
BURIED WITH A DONKEY!
GIRLS, GIRLS, *PLEASE,* IT'S A LITTLE EARLY--
DAMMMMN, MANNNN...

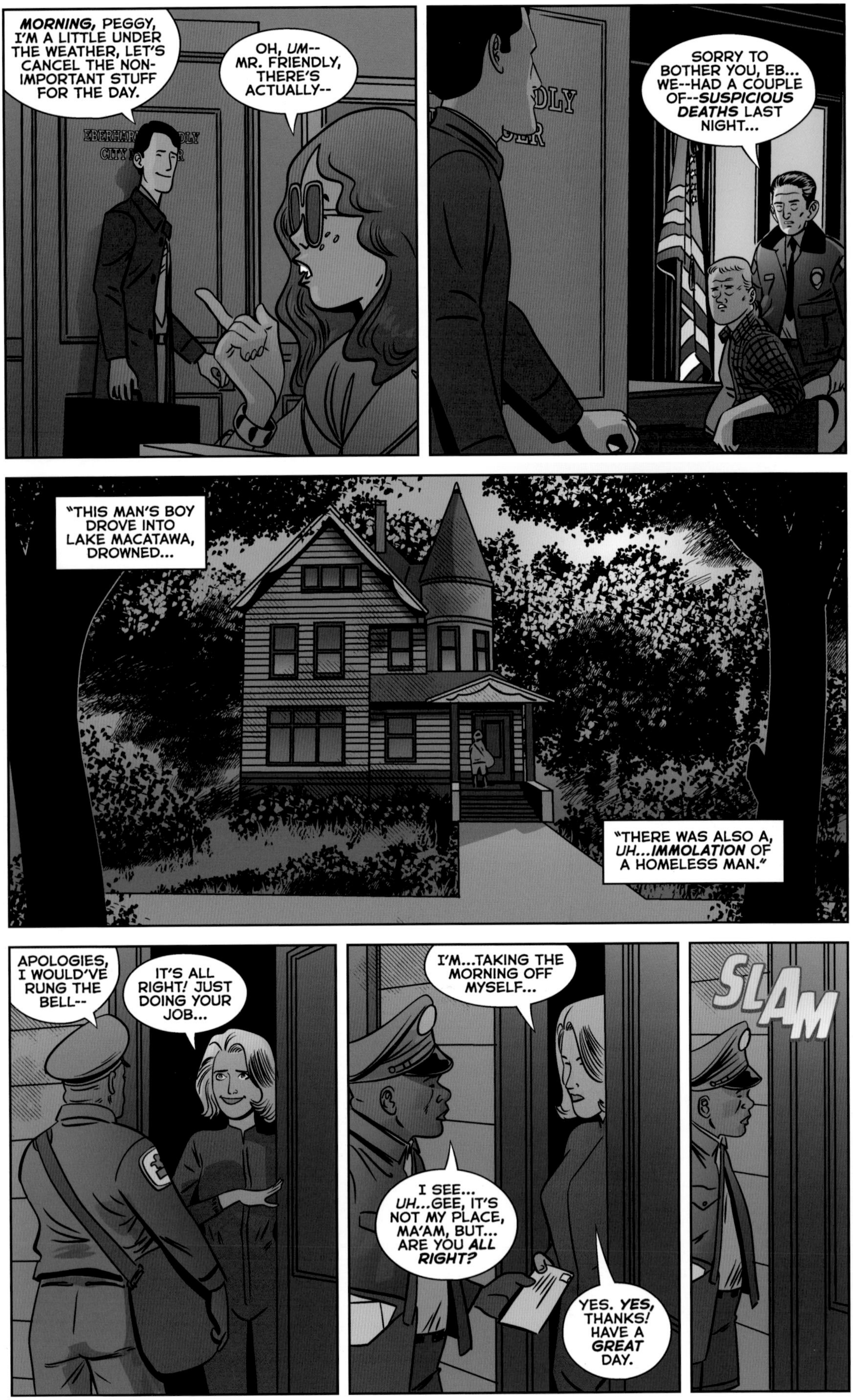
EBERHARDT FRIENDLY
CITY MANAGER
MORNING, PEGGY, I'M A LITTLE UNDER THE WEATHER, LET'S CANCEL THE NON-IMPORTANT STUFF FOR THE DAY.
OH, UM-- MR. FRIENDLY, THERE'S ACTUALLY--
SORRY TO BOTHER YOU, EB... WE--HAD A COUPLE OF--SUSPICIOUS DEATHS LAST NIGHT...
"THIS MAN'S BOY DROVE INTO LAKE MACATAWA, DROWNED...
"THERE WAS ALSO A, UH...IMMOLATION OF A HOMELESS MAN."
APOLOGIES, I WOULD'VE RUNG THE BELL--
IT'S ALL RIGHT! JUST DOING YOUR JOB...
I'M...TAKING THE MORNING OFF MYSELF...
I SEE... UH...GEE, IT'S NOT MY PLACE, MA'AM, BUT... ARE YOU ALL RIGHT?
YES. YES, THANKS! HAVE A GREAT DAY.
SLAM

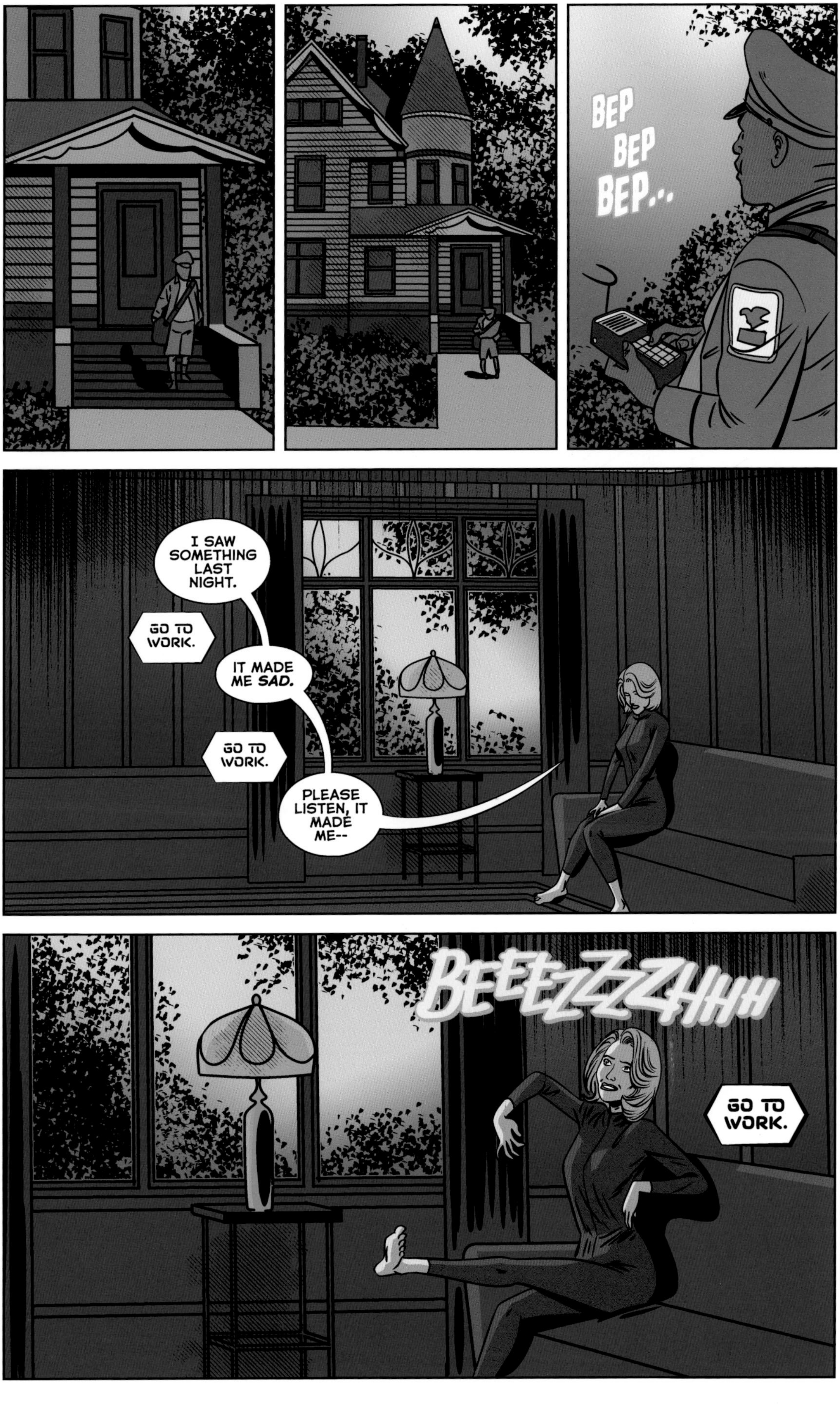
BEP
BEP
BEP...
I SAW SOMETHING LAST NIGHT.
GO TO WORK.
IT MADE ME SAD.
GO TO WORK.
PLEASE LISTEN, IT MADE ME--
BEEEZZZZHHH
GO TO WORK.

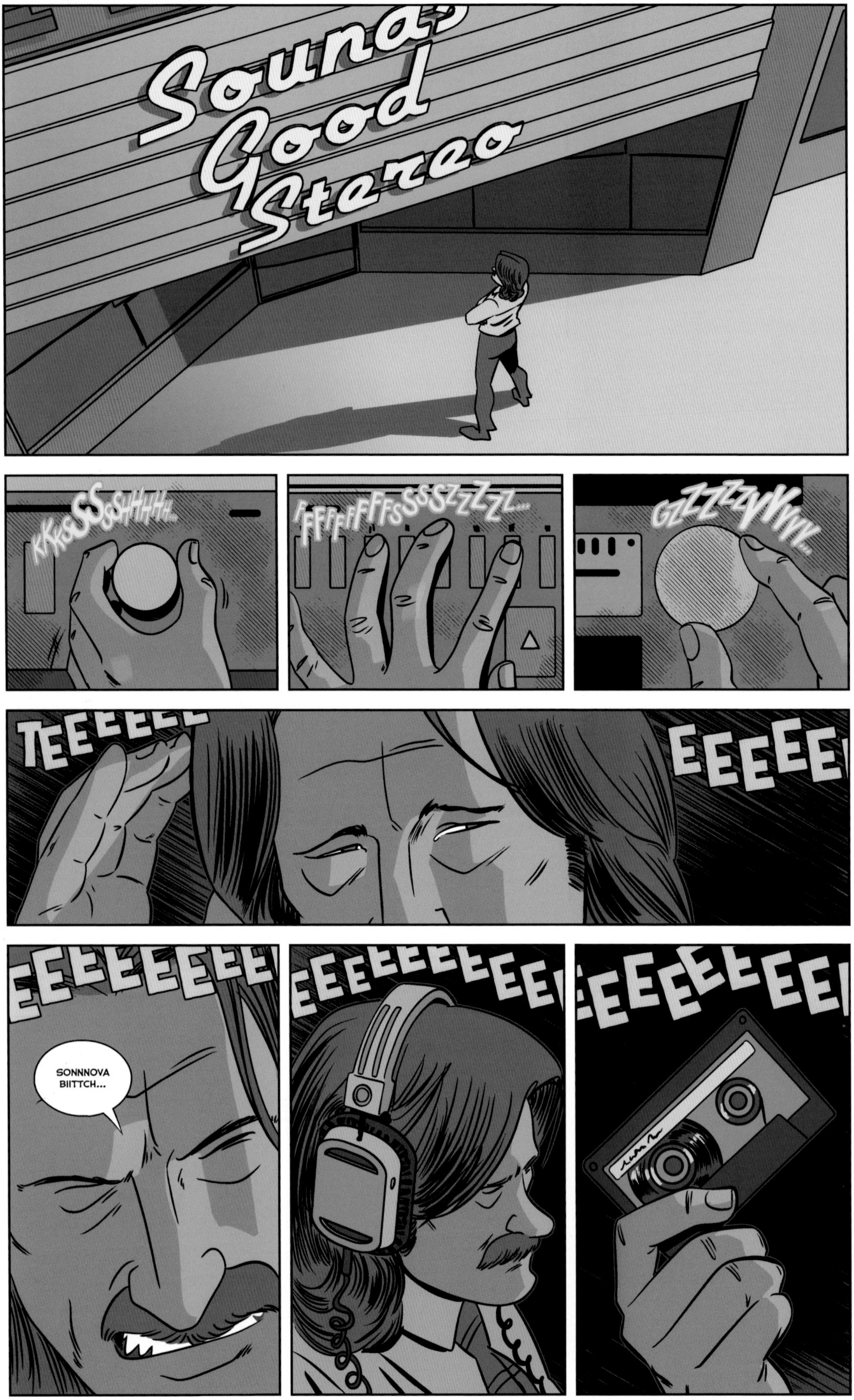
Sounds Good Stereo
KKKSSSSSHHHHHH...
FFFFFFFFFSSSSZZZZZZ...
GZZZZZVVVVVV...
TEEEEEE
EEEEE
EEEEEEEEE
SONNNOVA BIITTCH...
EEEEEEEEEEEE
EEEEEEEEEEE

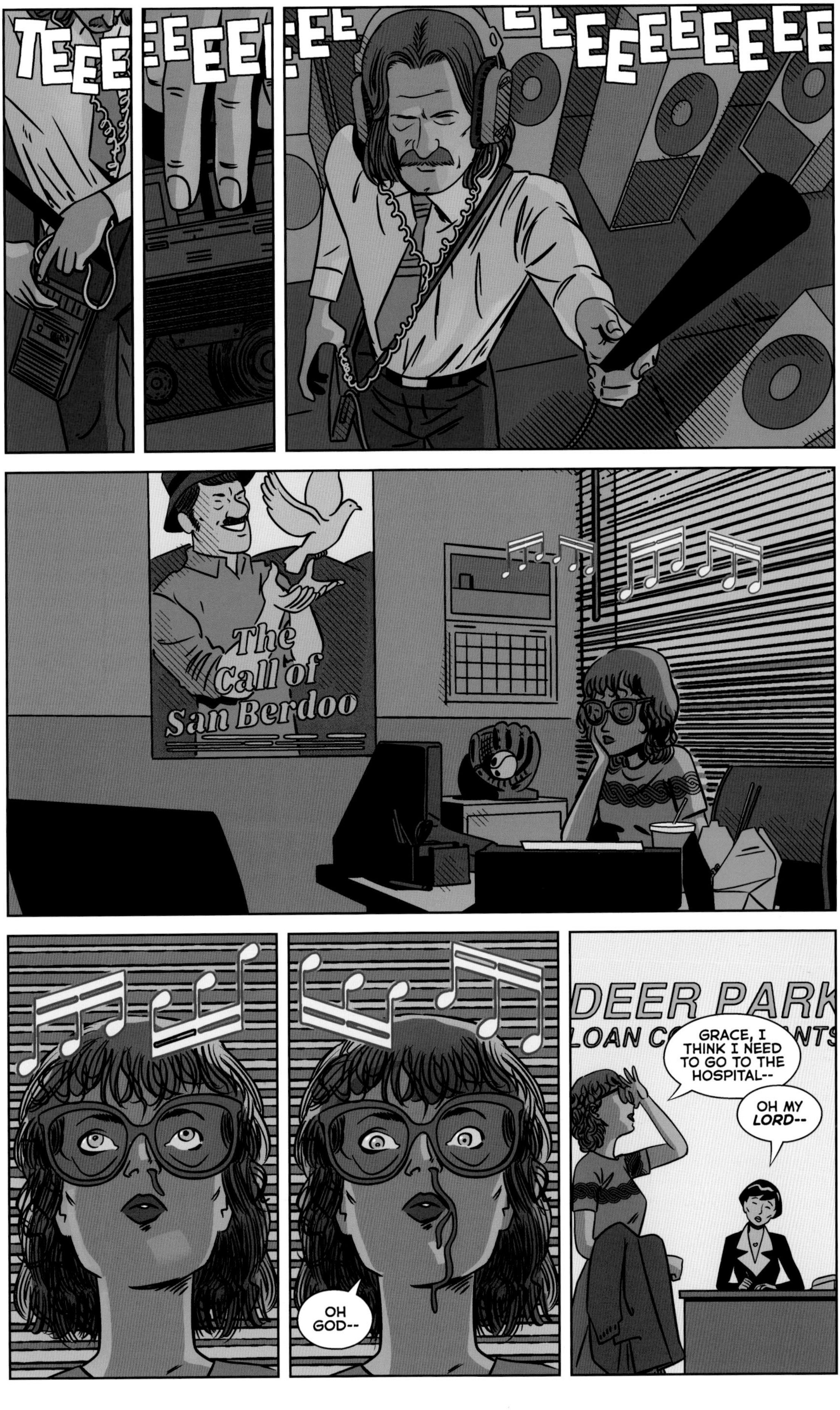
TEEEEEEEEEEEEEEEEEEEE
The Call of San Berdoo
OH GOD--
DEER PARK LOAN CO NTS
GRACE, I THINK I NEED TO GO TO THE HOSPITAL--
OH MY LORD--

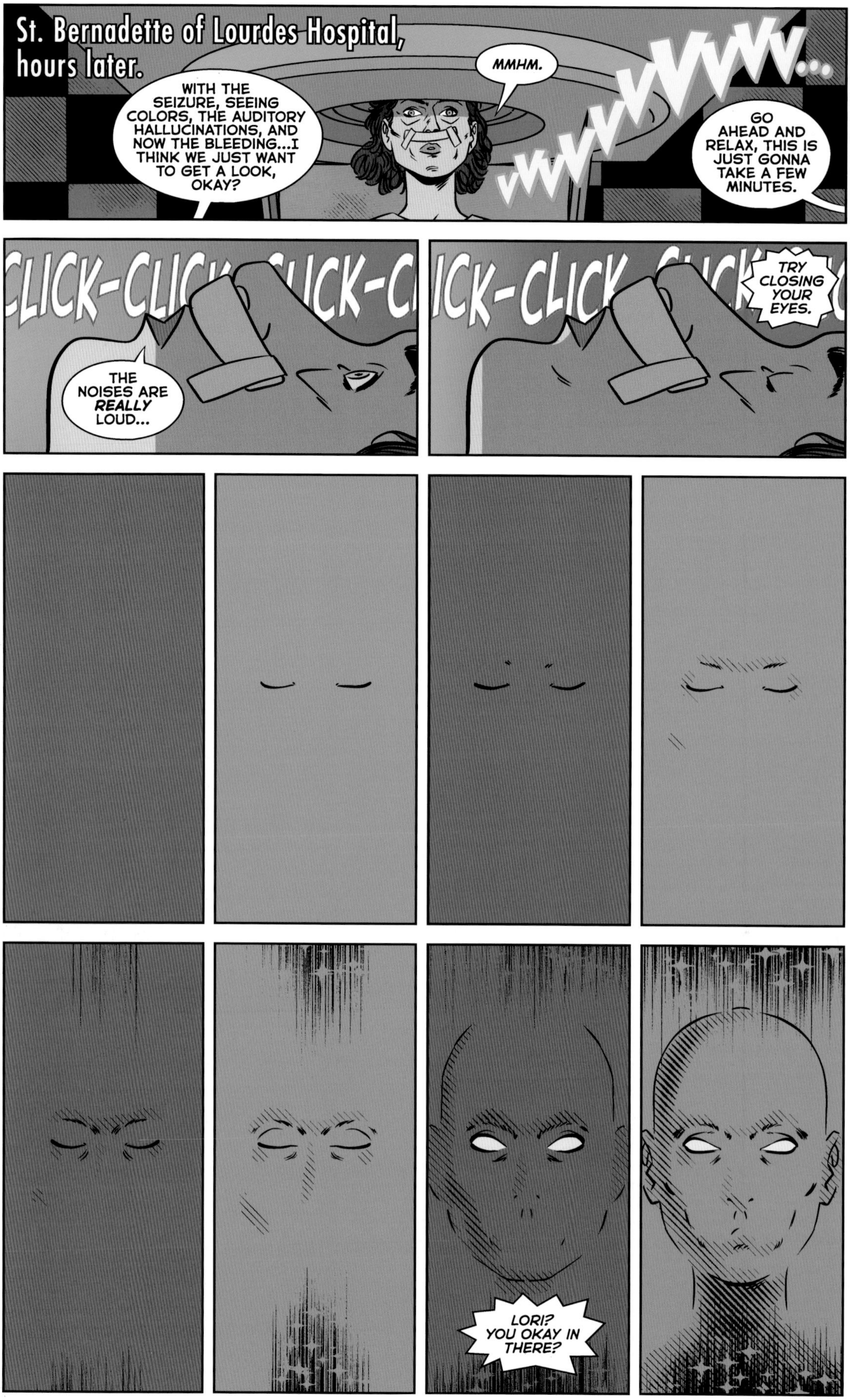

St. Bernadette of Lourdes Hospital, hours later.
WITH THE SEIZURE, SEEING COLORS, THE AUDITORY HALLUCINATIONS, AND NOW THE BLEEDING...I THINK WE JUST WANT TO GET A LOOK, OKAY?
MMHM.
VVVVVVVVVVVVV...
GO AHEAD AND RELAX, THIS IS JUST GONNA TAKE A FEW MINUTES.
CLICK-CLICK
THE NOISES ARE REALLY LOUD...
CLICK-CLICK
TRY CLOSING YOUR EYES.
LORI? YOU OKAY IN THERE?

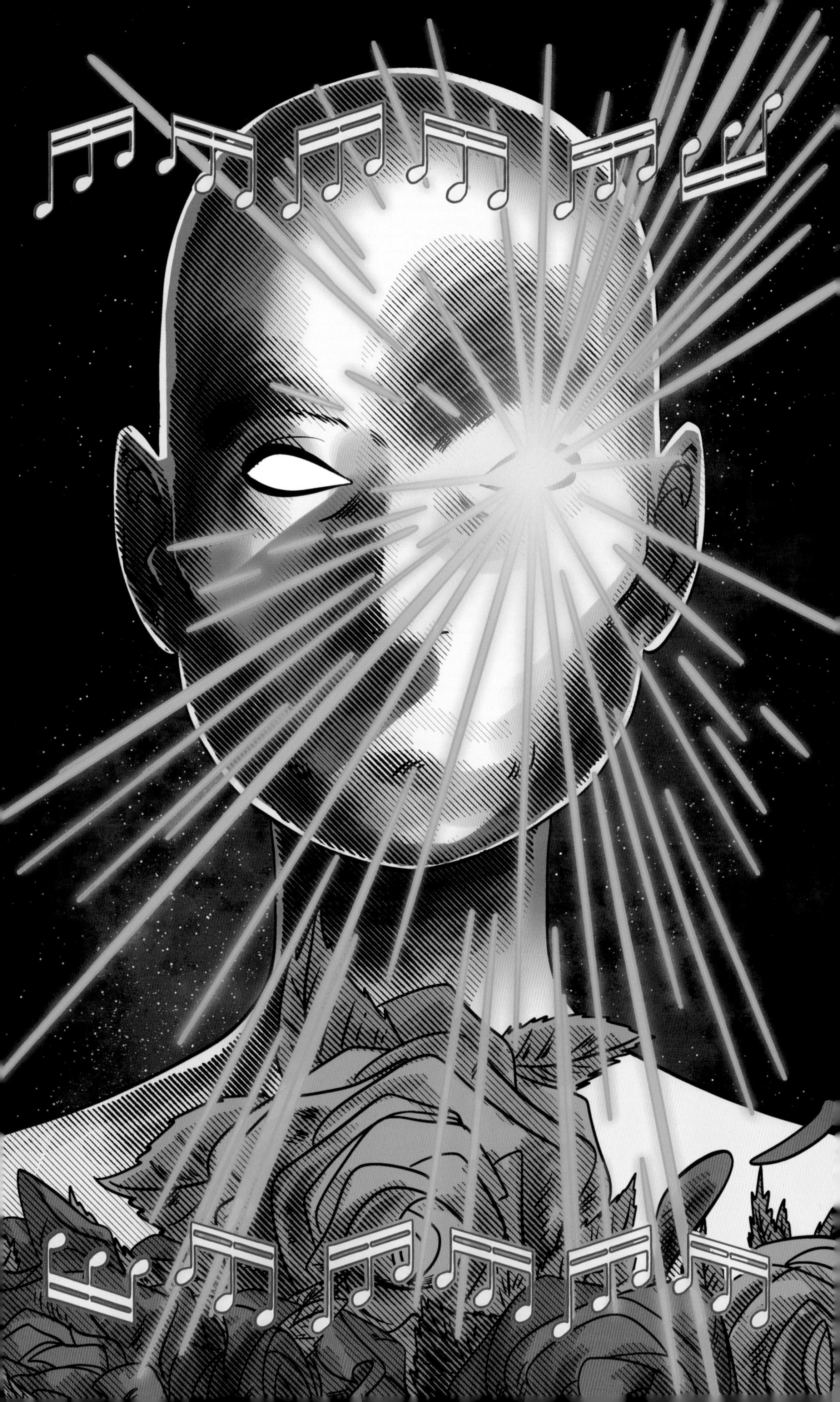

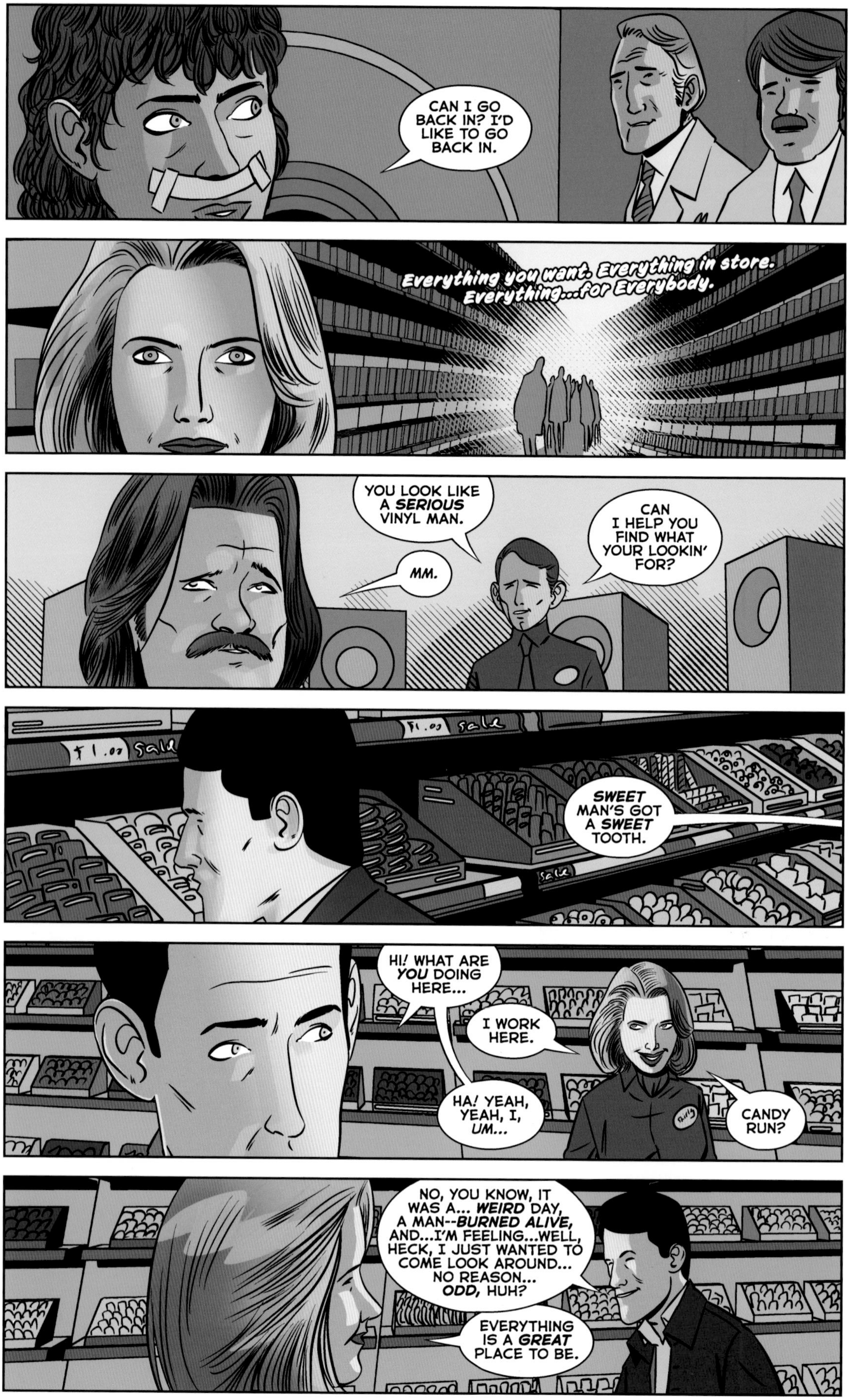
CAN I GO BACK IN? I'D LIKE TO GO BACK IN.
Everything you want. Everything in store.
Everything...for Everybody.
YOU LOOK LIKE A SERIOUS VINYL MAN.
MM.
CAN I HELP YOU FIND WHAT YOUR LOOKIN' FOR?
SWEET MAN'S GOT A SWEET TOOTH.
HI! WHAT ARE YOU DOING HERE...
I WORK HERE.
HA! YEAH, YEAH, I, UM...
CANDY RUN?
NO, YOU KNOW, IT WAS A... WEIRD DAY, A MAN--BURNED ALIVE, AND...I'M FEELING...WELL, HECK, I JUST WANTED TO COME LOOK AROUND... NO REASON... ODD, HUH?
EVERYTHING IS A GREAT PLACE TO BE.

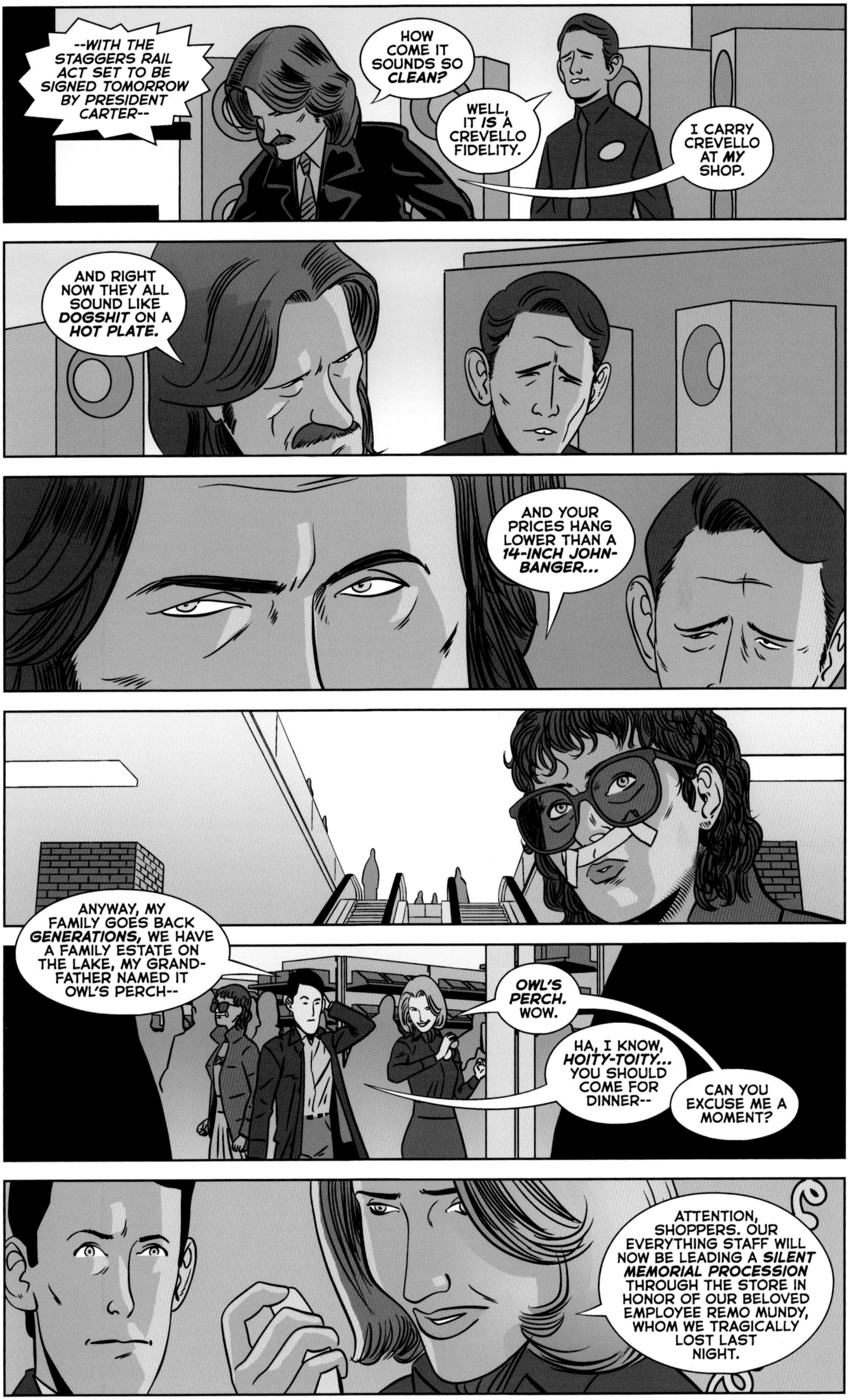
--WITH THE STAGGERS RAIL ACT SET TO BE SIGNED TOMORROW BY PRESIDENT CARTER--
HOW COME IT SOUNDS SO *CLEAN?*
WELL, IT *IS* A CREVELLO FIDELITY.
I CARRY CREVELLO AT *MY* SHOP.
AND RIGHT NOW THEY ALL SOUND LIKE *DOGSHIT* ON A *HOT PLATE.*
AND YOUR PRICES HANG LOWER THAN A *14-INCH JOHN-BANGER...*
ANYWAY, MY FAMILY GOES BACK *GENERATIONS,* WE HAVE A FAMILY ESTATE ON THE LAKE, MY GRAND-FATHER NAMED IT OWL'S PERCH--
OWL'S PERCH. WOW.
HA, I KNOW, *HOITY-TOITY...* YOU SHOULD COME FOR DINNER--
CAN YOU EXCUSE ME A MOMENT?
ATTENTION, SHOPPERS. OUR EVERYTHING STAFF WILL NOW BE LEADING A *SILENT MEMORIAL PROCESSION* THROUGH THE STORE IN HONOR OF OUR BELOVED EMPLOYEE REMO MUNDY, WHOM WE TRAGICALLY LOST LAST NIGHT.

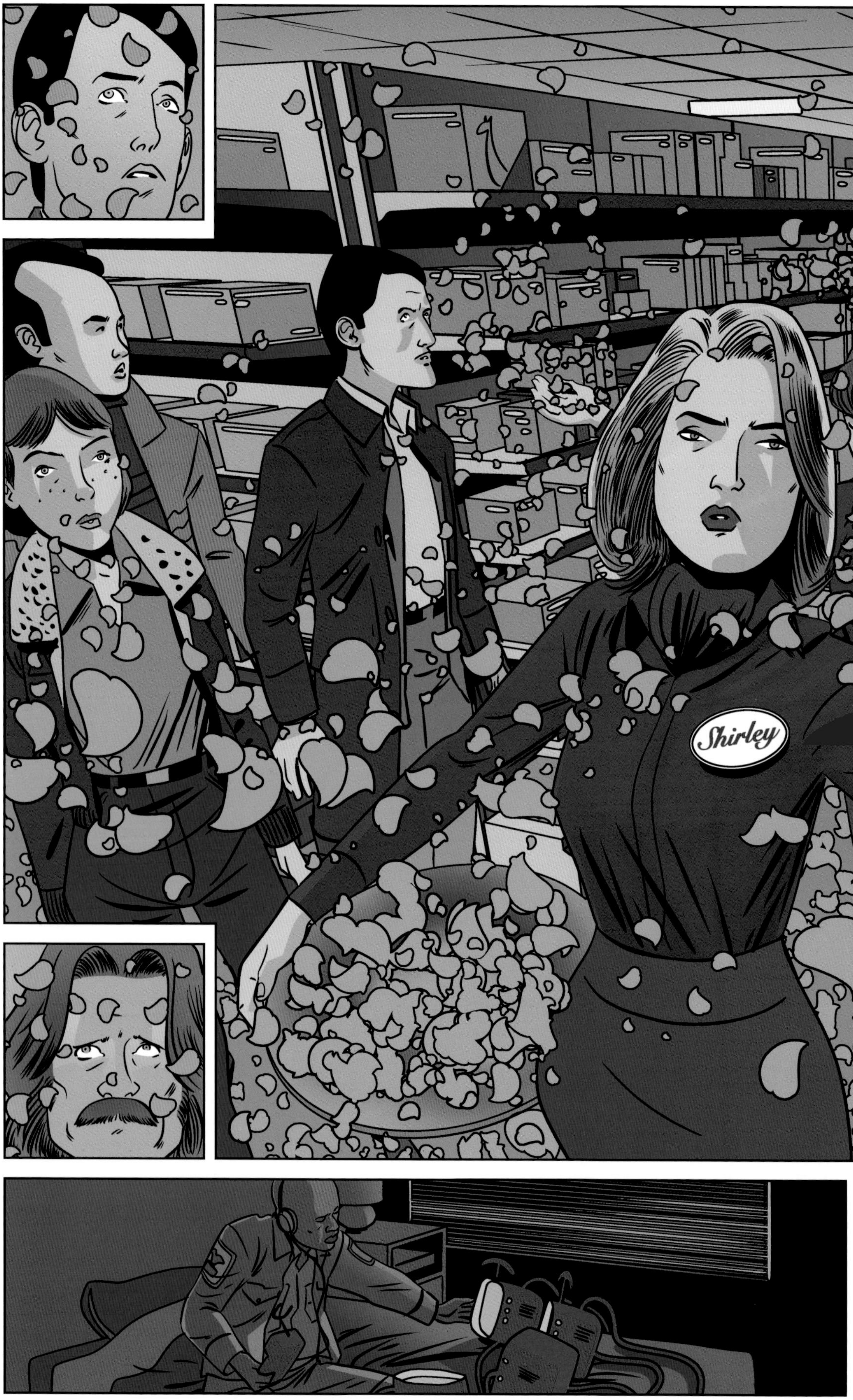
Shirley

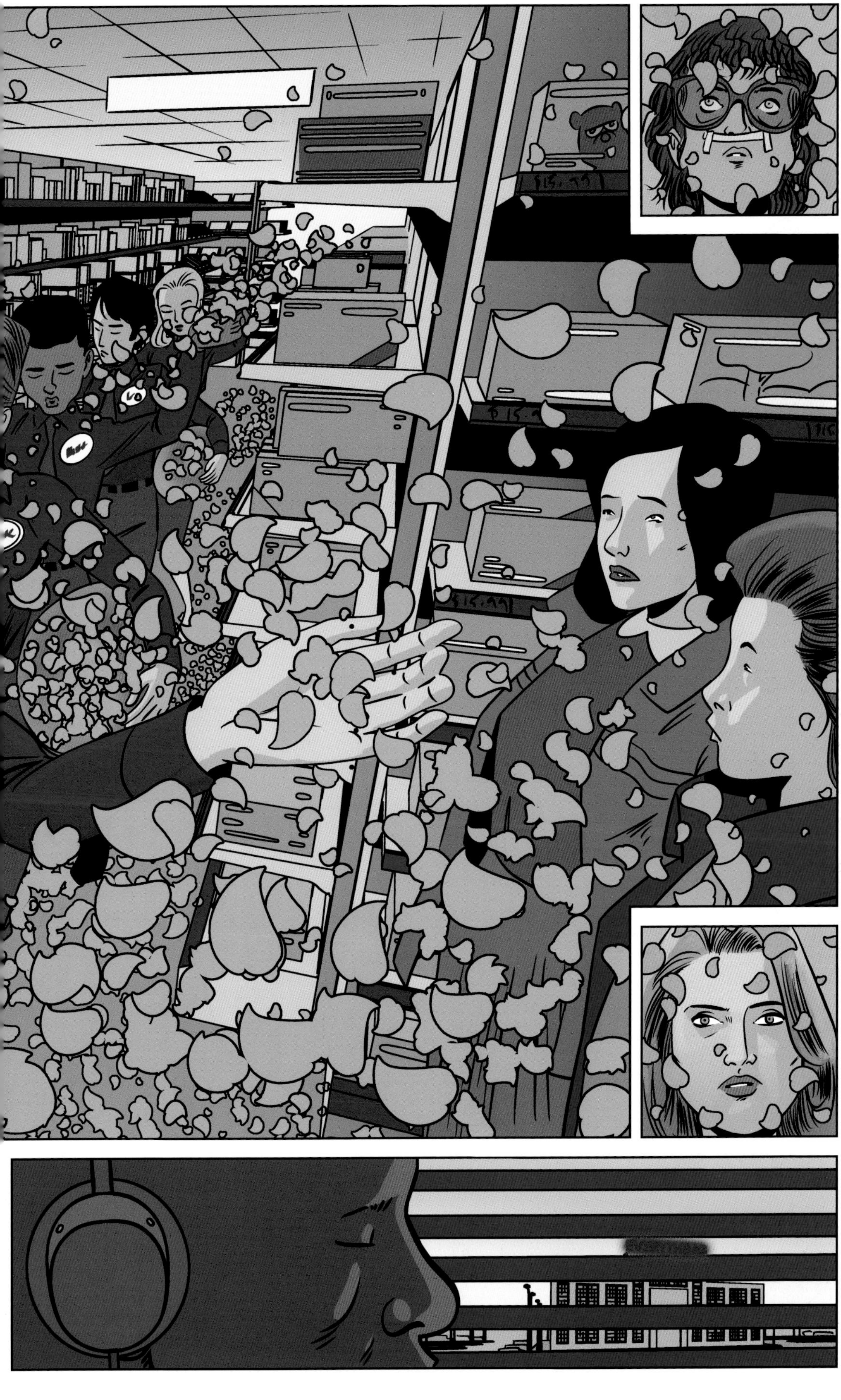

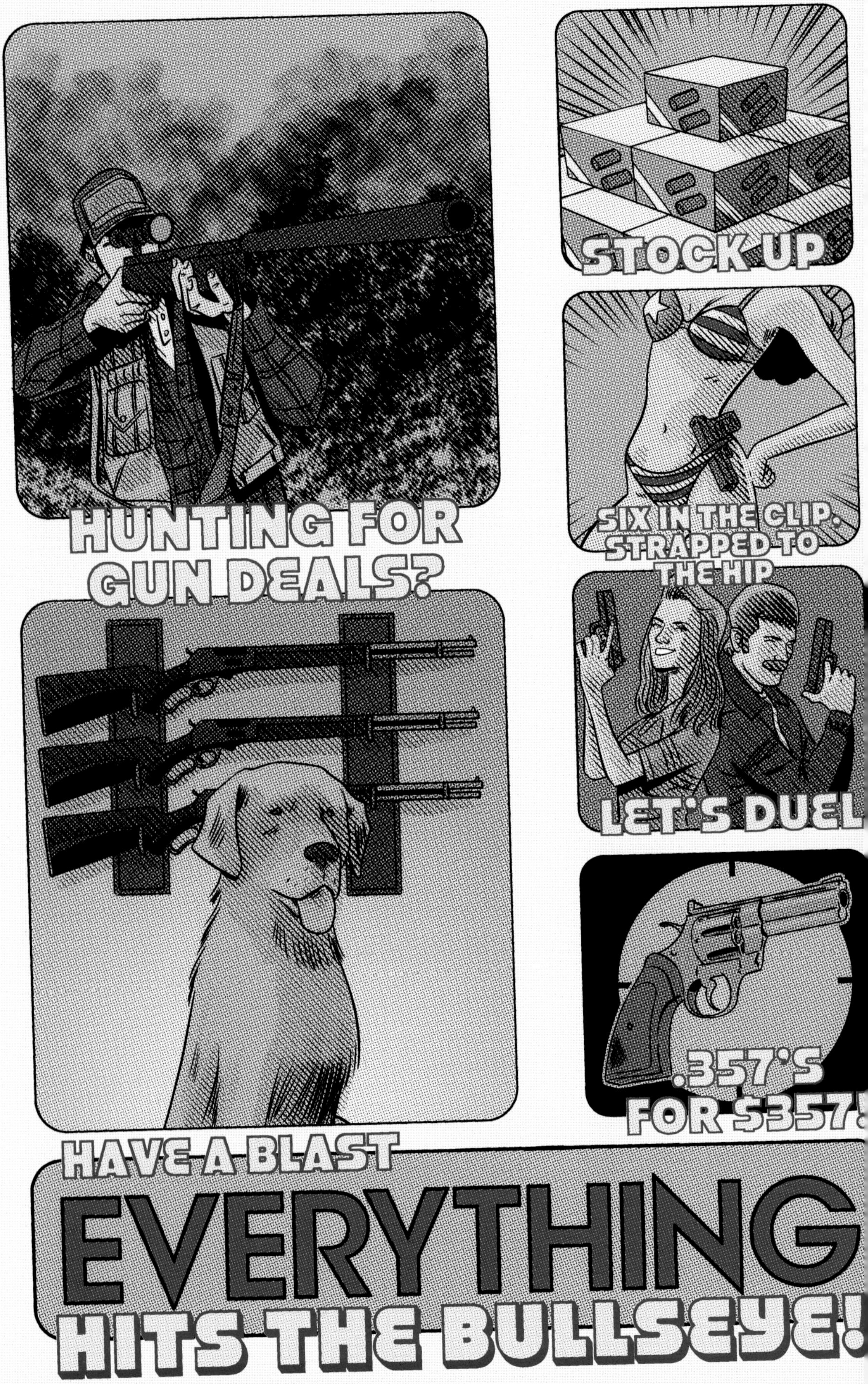
HUNTING FOR GUN DEALS?
STOCK UP
SIX IN THE CLIP, STRAPPED TO THE HIP
LET'S DUEL
.357'S FOR $357
HAVE A BLAST
EVERYTHING
HITS THE BULLSEYE!

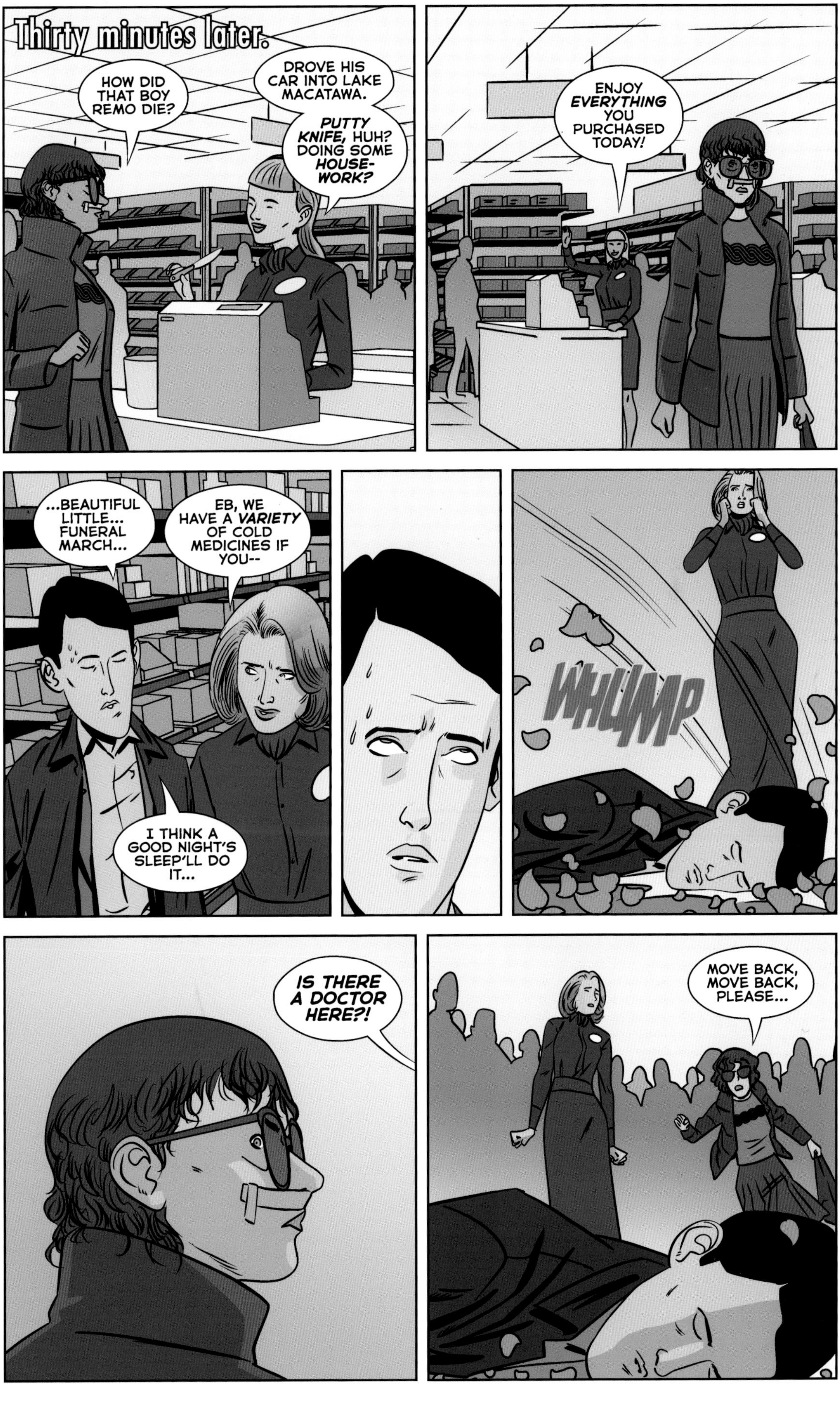
Thirty minutes later.
HOW DID THAT BOY REMO DIE?
DROVE HIS CAR INTO LAKE MACATAWA.
PUTTY KNIFE, HUH? DOING SOME HOUSE-WORK?
ENJOY EVERYTHING YOU PURCHASED TODAY!
...BEAUTIFUL LITTLE... FUNERAL MARCH...
EB, WE HAVE A VARIETY OF COLD MEDICINES IF YOU--
I THINK A GOOD NIGHT'S SLEEP'LL DO IT...
WHUMP
IS THERE A DOCTOR HERE?!
MOVE BACK, MOVE BACK, PLEASE...

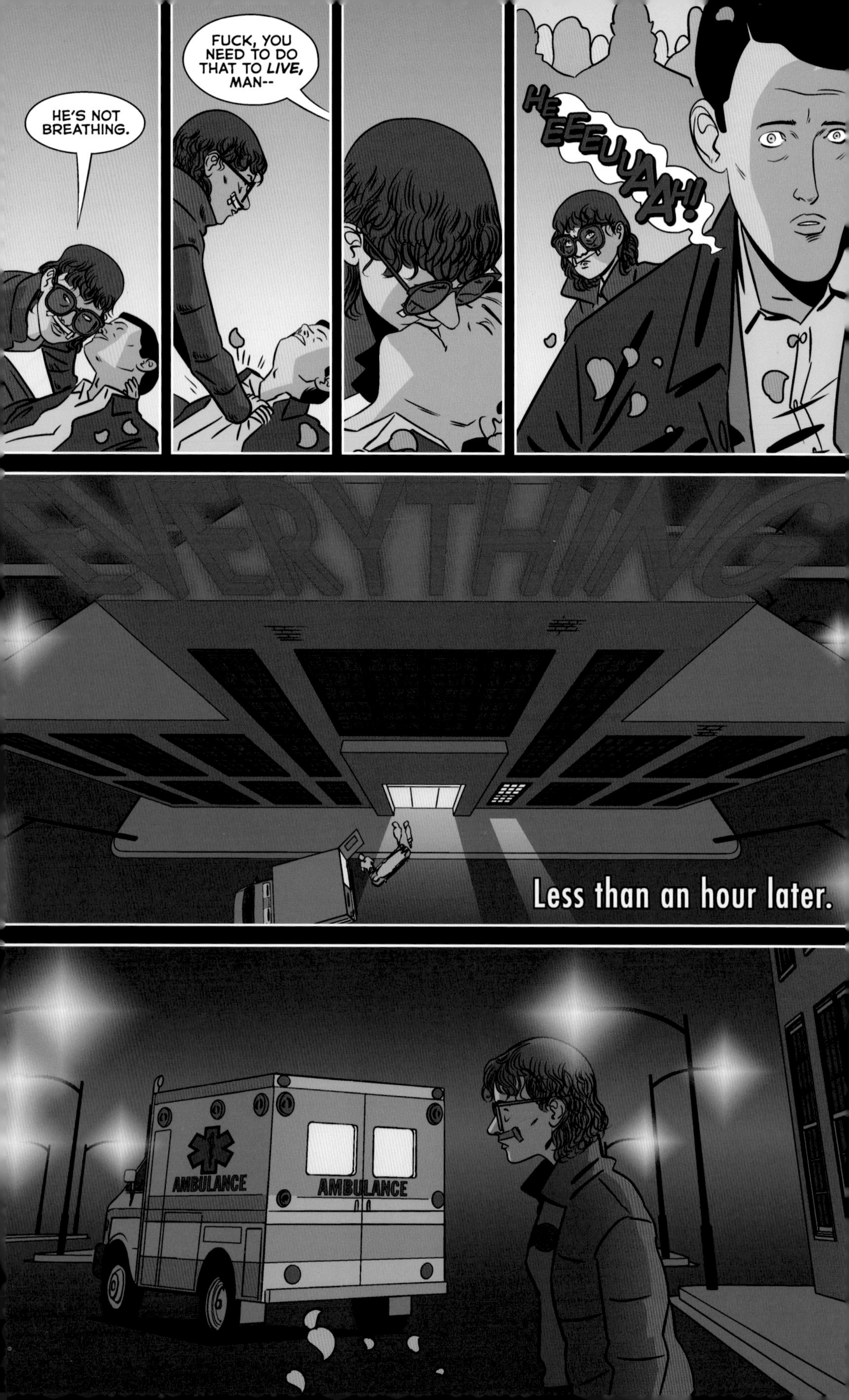

HE'S NOT BREATHING.
FUCK, YOU NEED TO DO THAT TO *LIVE,* MAN--
HEEEEUUAAH!
EVERYTHING
Less than an hour later.
AMBULANCE
AMBULANCE

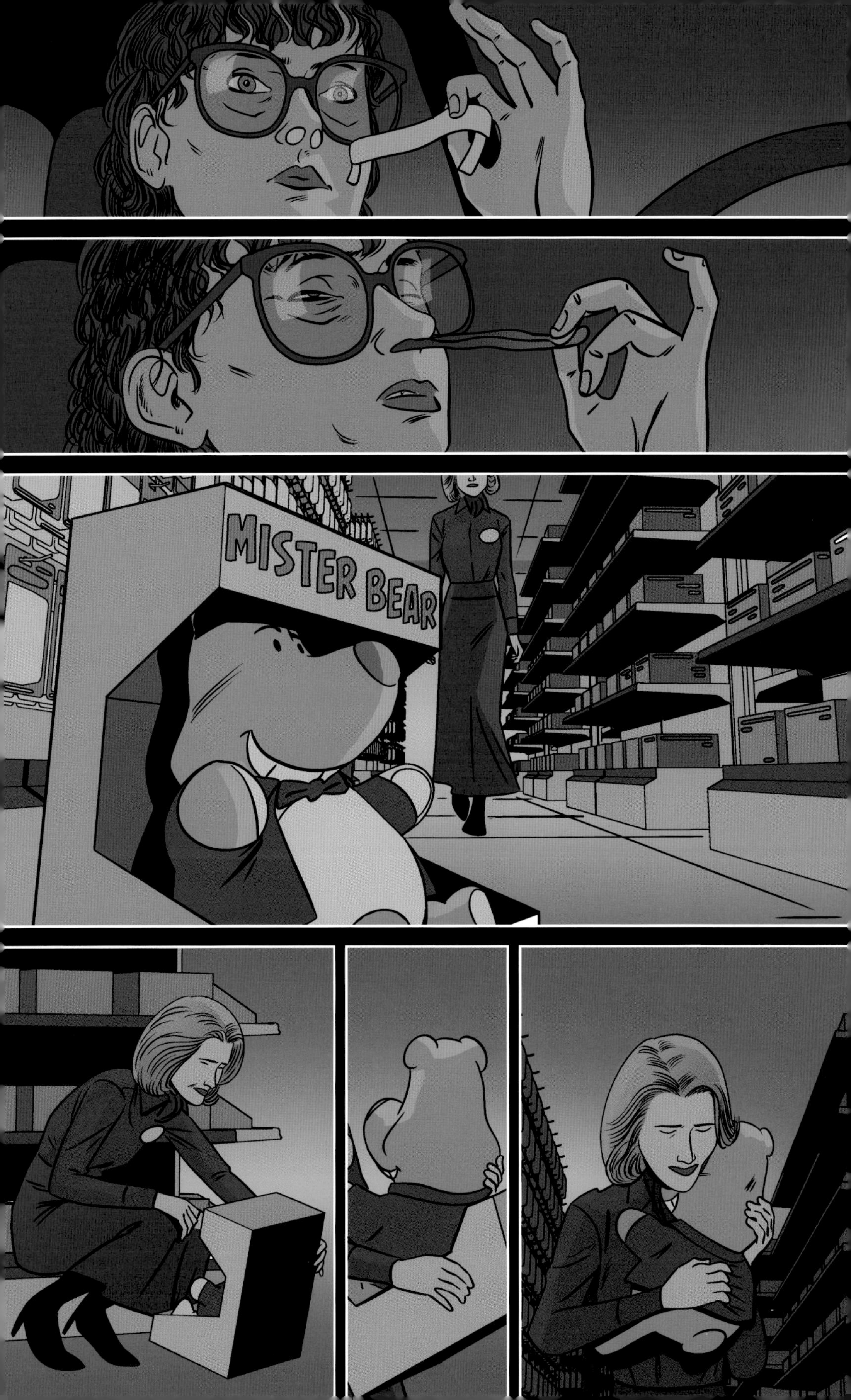
MISTER BEAR

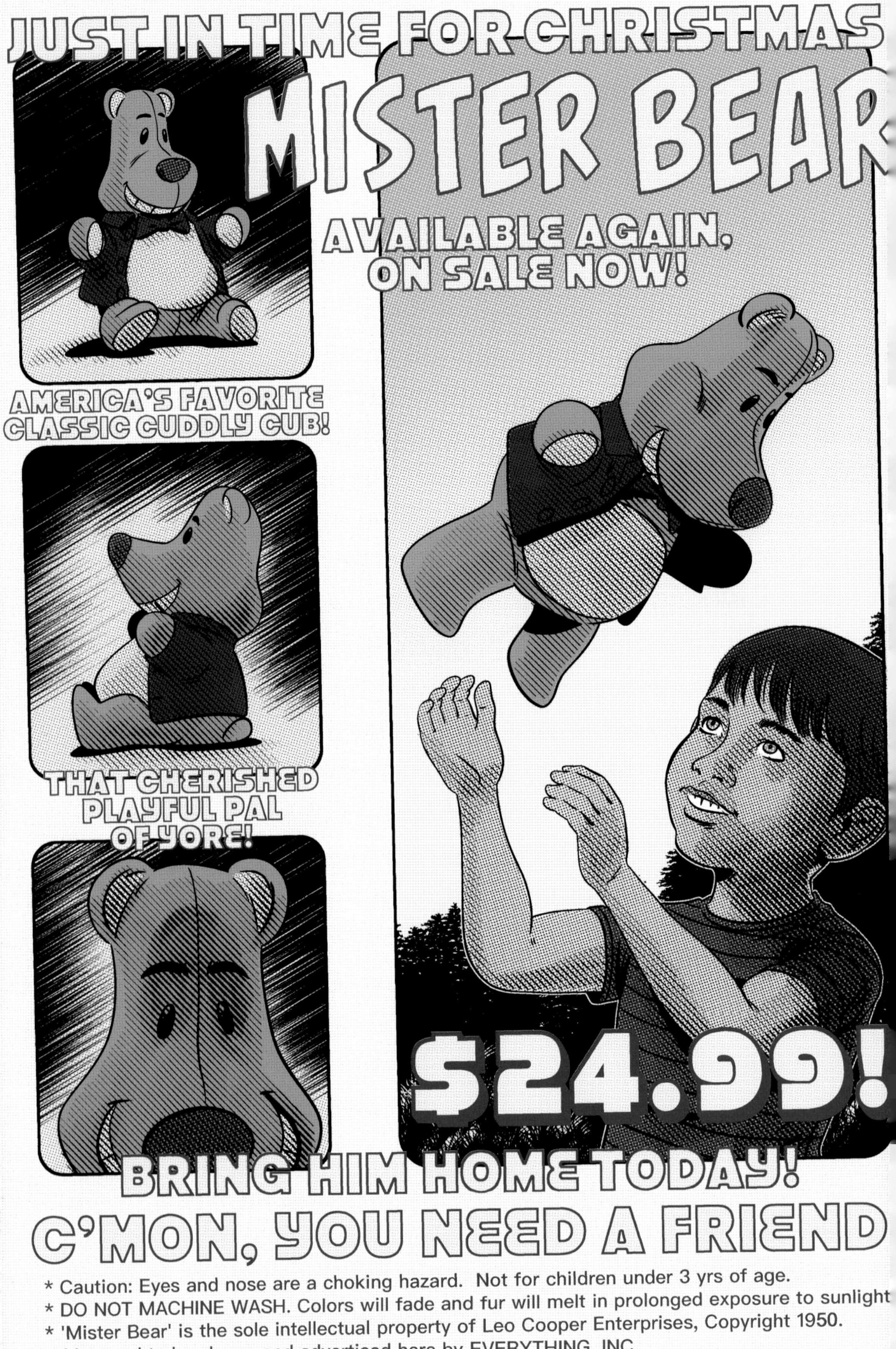
JUST IN TIME FOR CHRISTMAS
MISTER BEAR
AVAILABLE AGAIN,
ON SALE NOW!
AMERICA'S FAVORITE
CLASSIC CUDDLY CUB!
THAT CHERISHED
PLAYFUL PAL
OF YORE!
$24.99!
BRING HIM HOME TODAY!
C'MON, YOU NEED A FRIEND

* Caution: Eyes and nose are a choking hazard. Not for children under 3 yrs of age.
* DO NOT MACHINE WASH. Colors will fade and fur will melt in prolonged exposure to sunlight
* 'Mister Bear' is the sole intellectual property of Leo Cooper Enterprises, Copyright 1950. Licensed to be shown and advertised here by EVERYTHING, INC.
* Made in Boring, Kansas, USA.

Chapter 3:
"See Everything as a Dream"

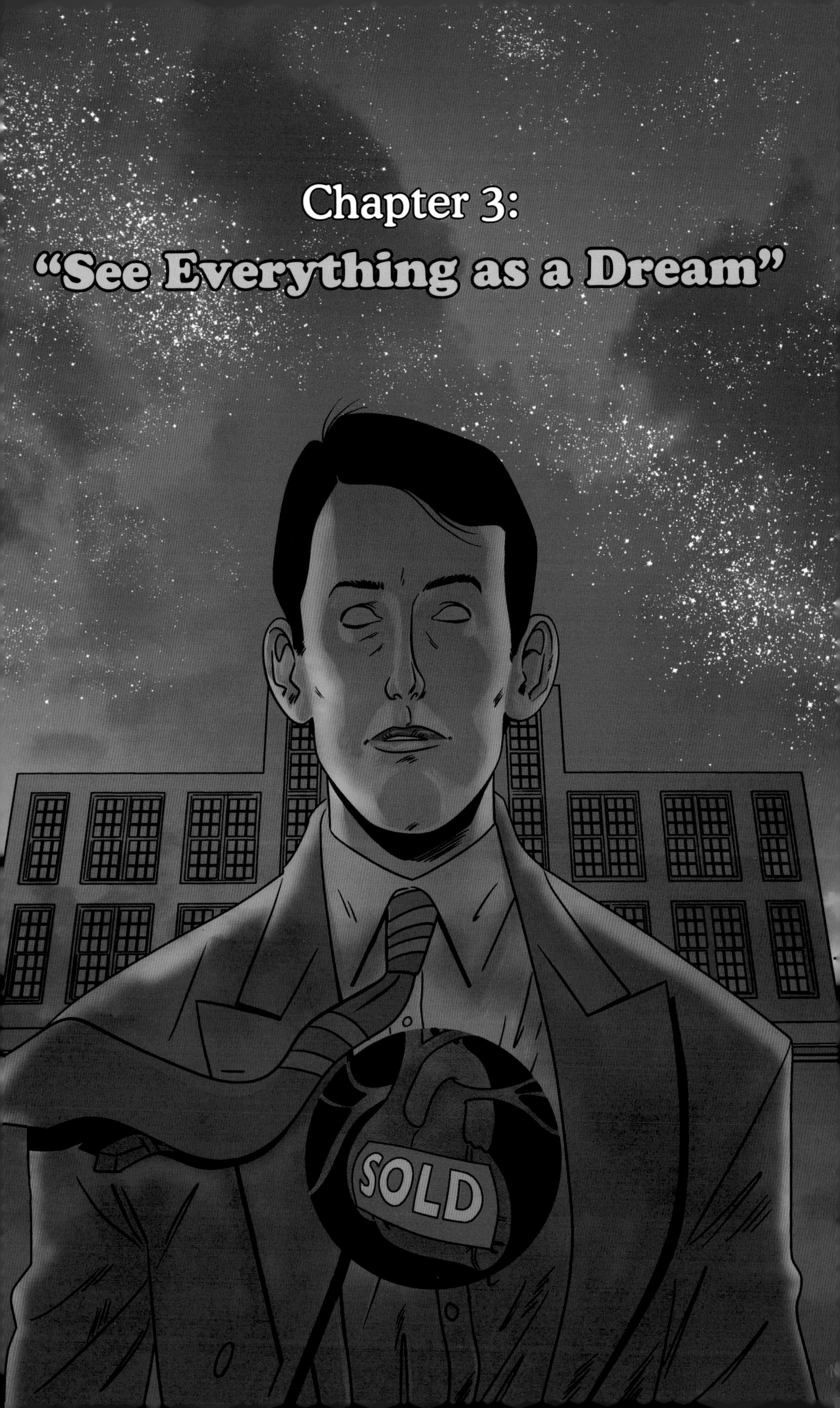
SOLD

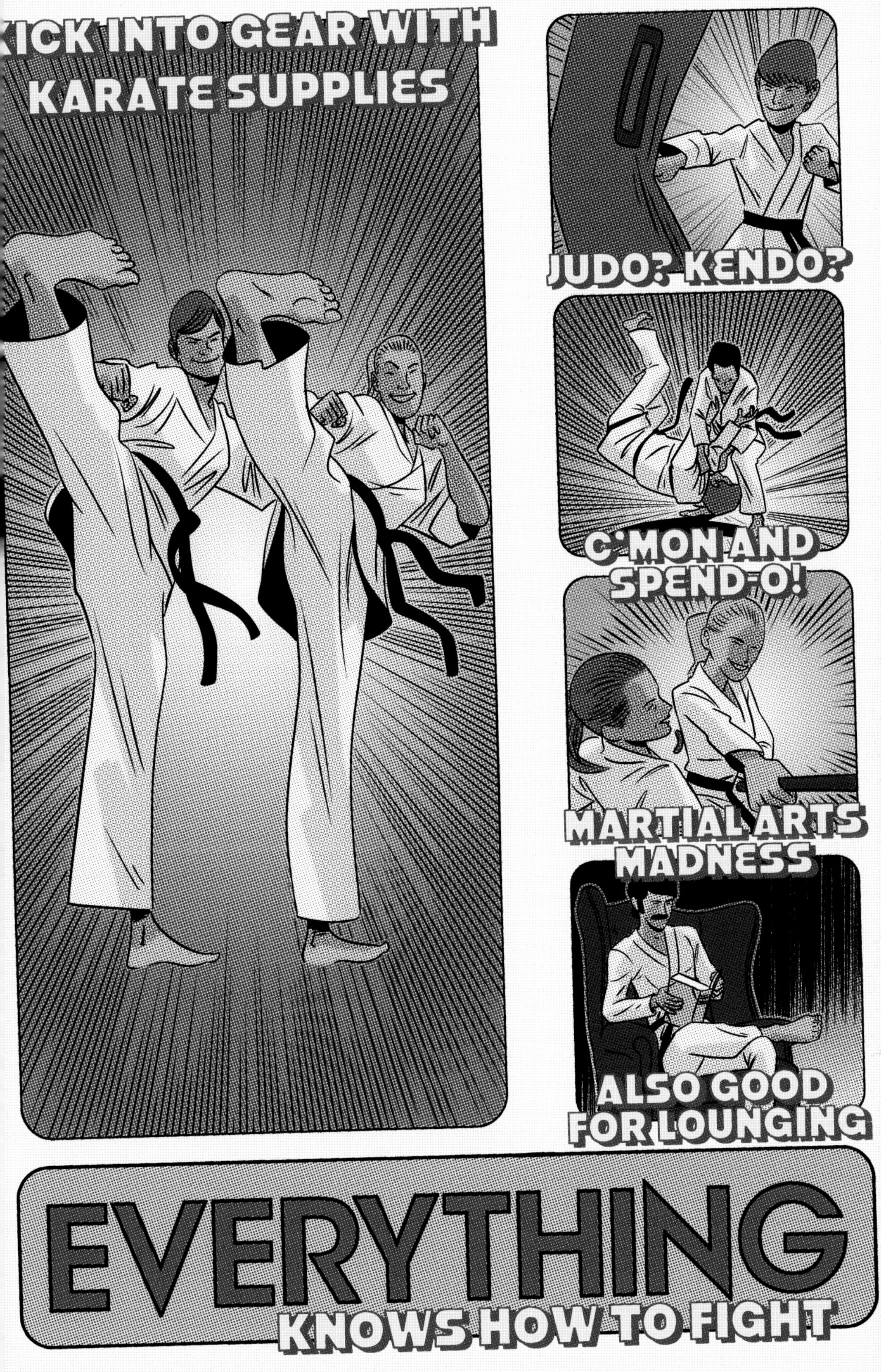
ICK INTO GEAR WITH KARATE SUPPLIES
JUDO? KENDO?
C'MON AND SPEND-O!
MARTIAL ARTS MADNESS
ALSO GOOD FOR LOUNGING
EVERYTHING KNOWS HOW TO FIGHT

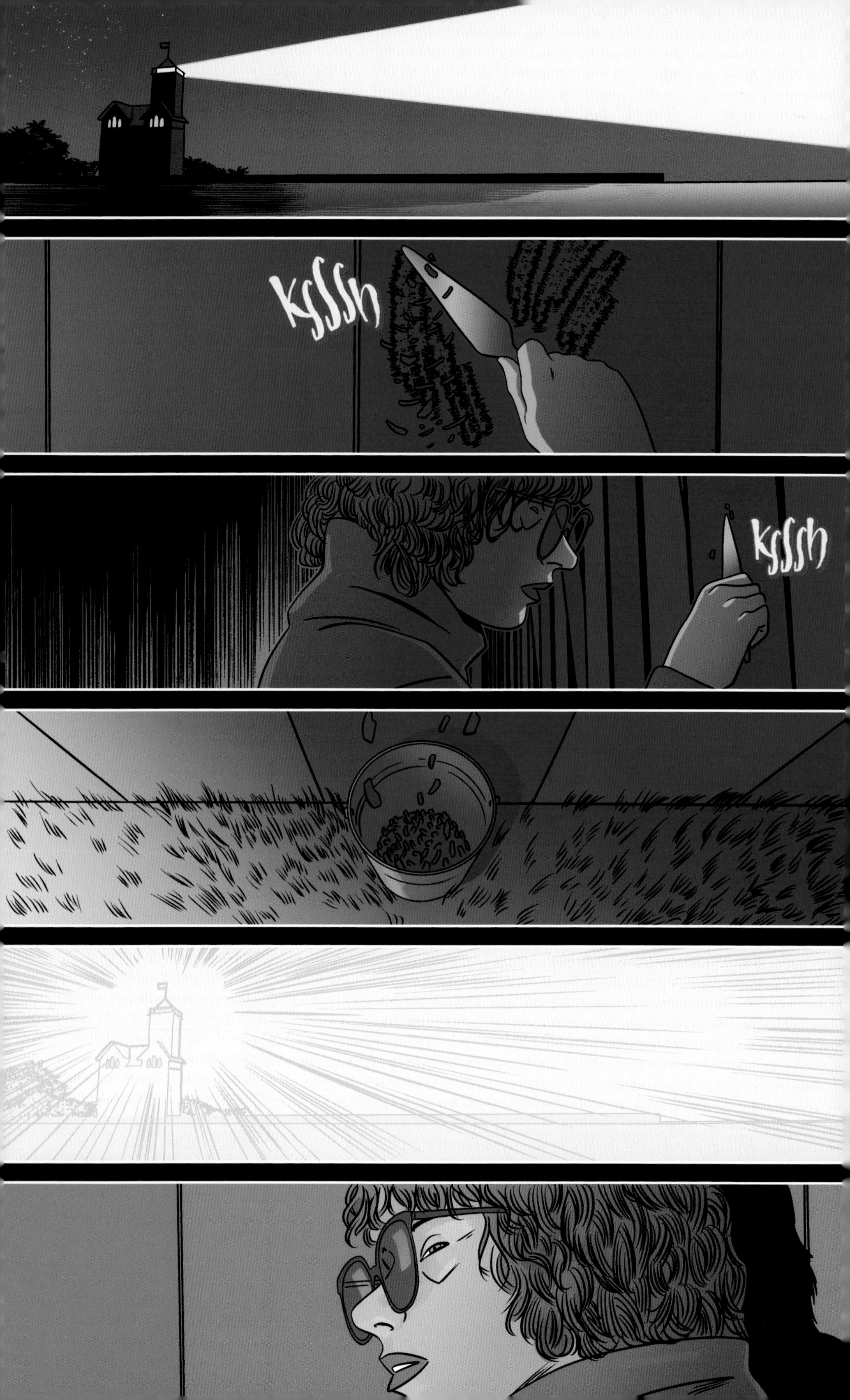
KSSSH
KSSSH

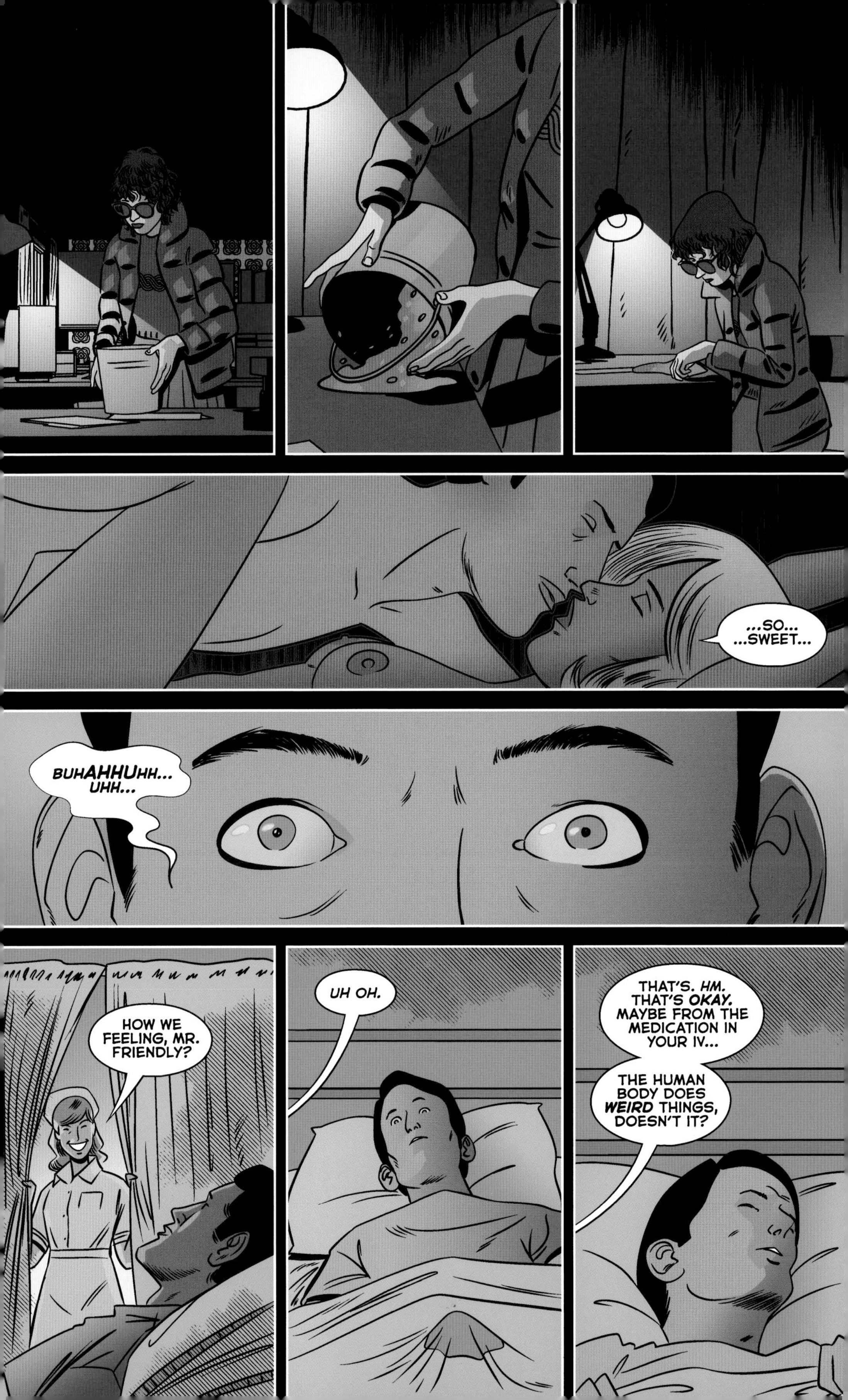
...SO...
...SWEET...
BUHAHHUHH...
UHH...
HOW WE FEELING, MR. FRIENDLY?
UH OH.
THAT'S. HM. THAT'S OKAY. MAYBE FROM THE MEDICATION IN YOUR IV...
THE HUMAN BODY DOES WEIRD THINGS, DOESN'T IT?

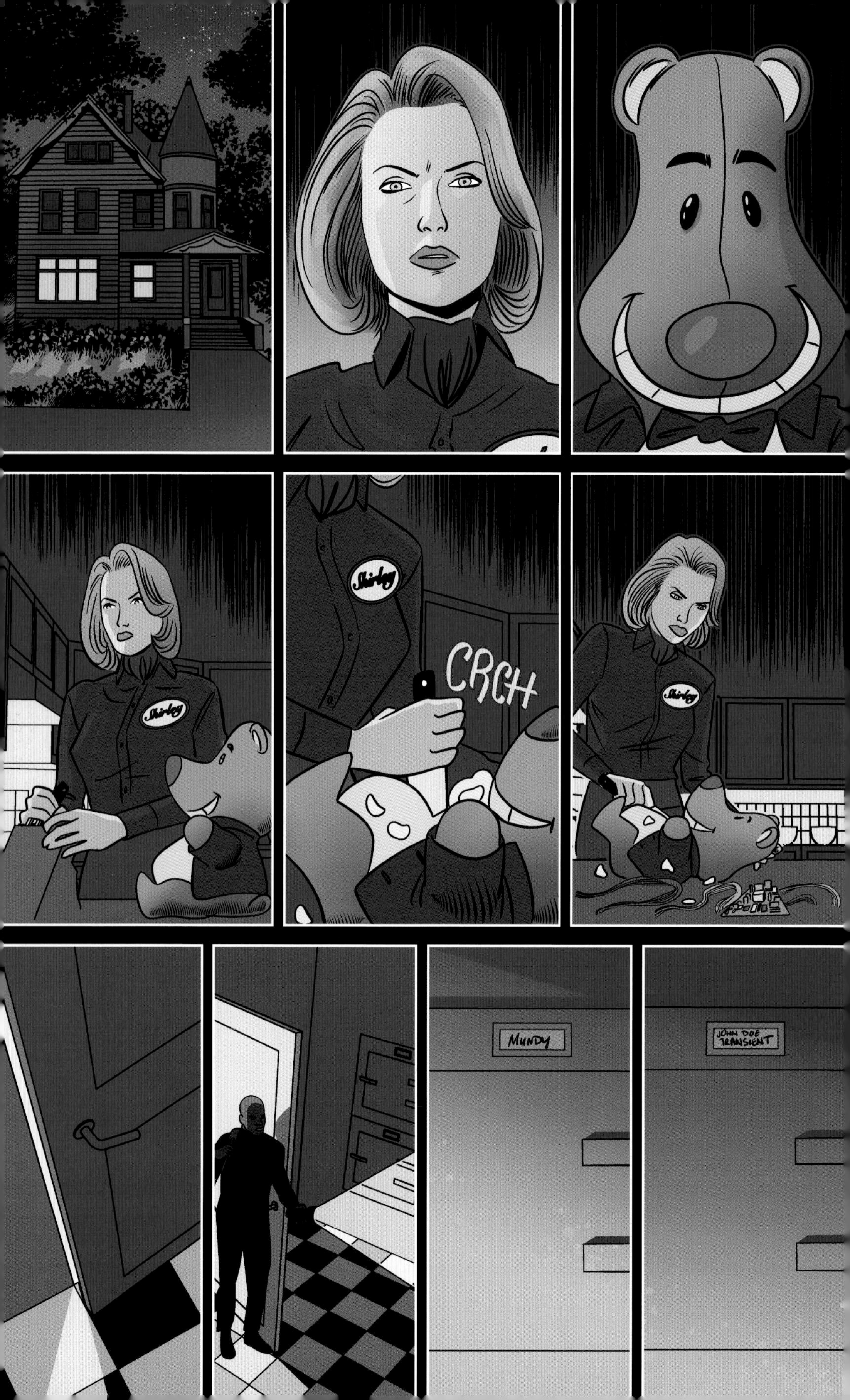

Shirley
CRCH
MUNDY
JOHN DOE
TRANSIENT

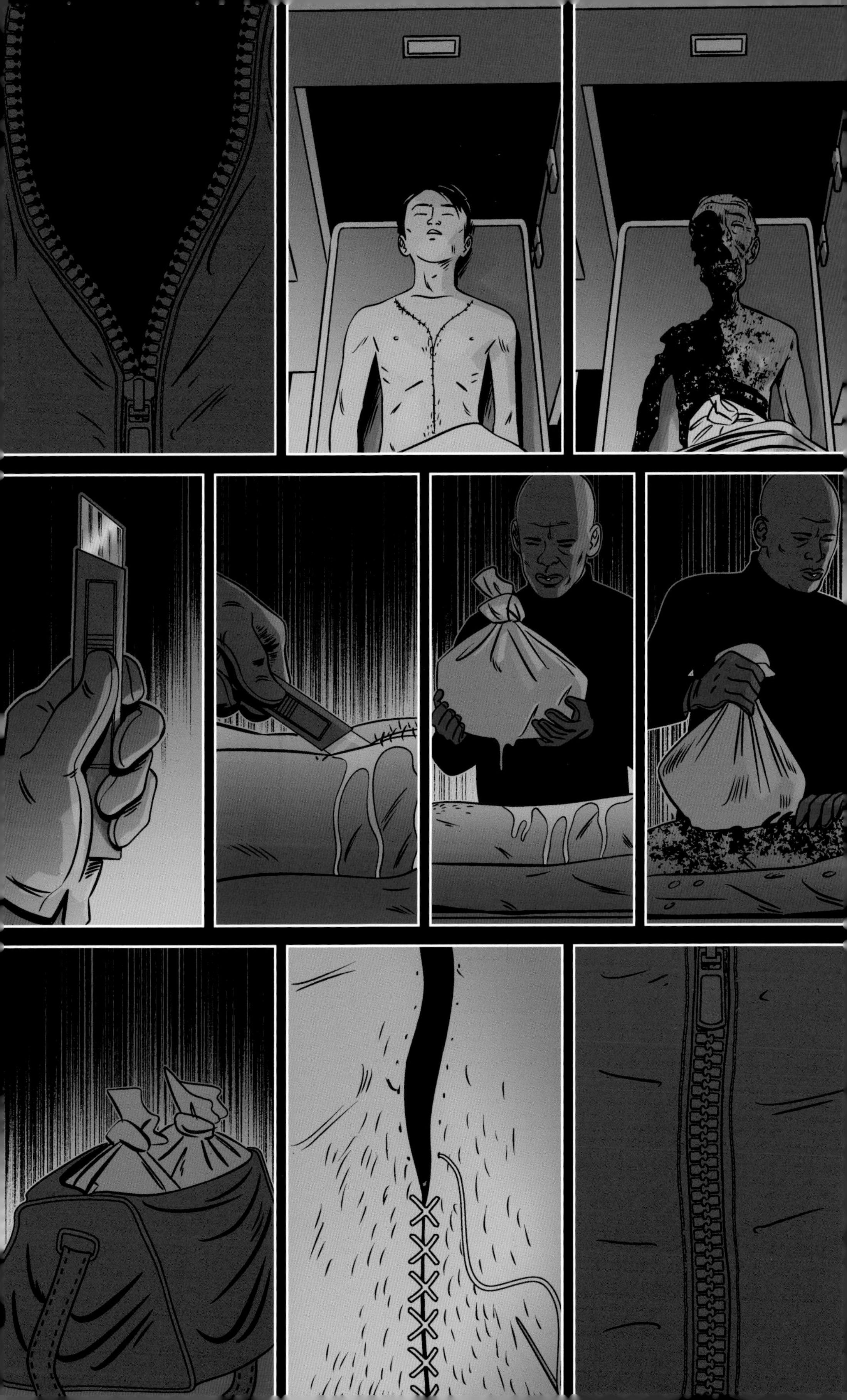

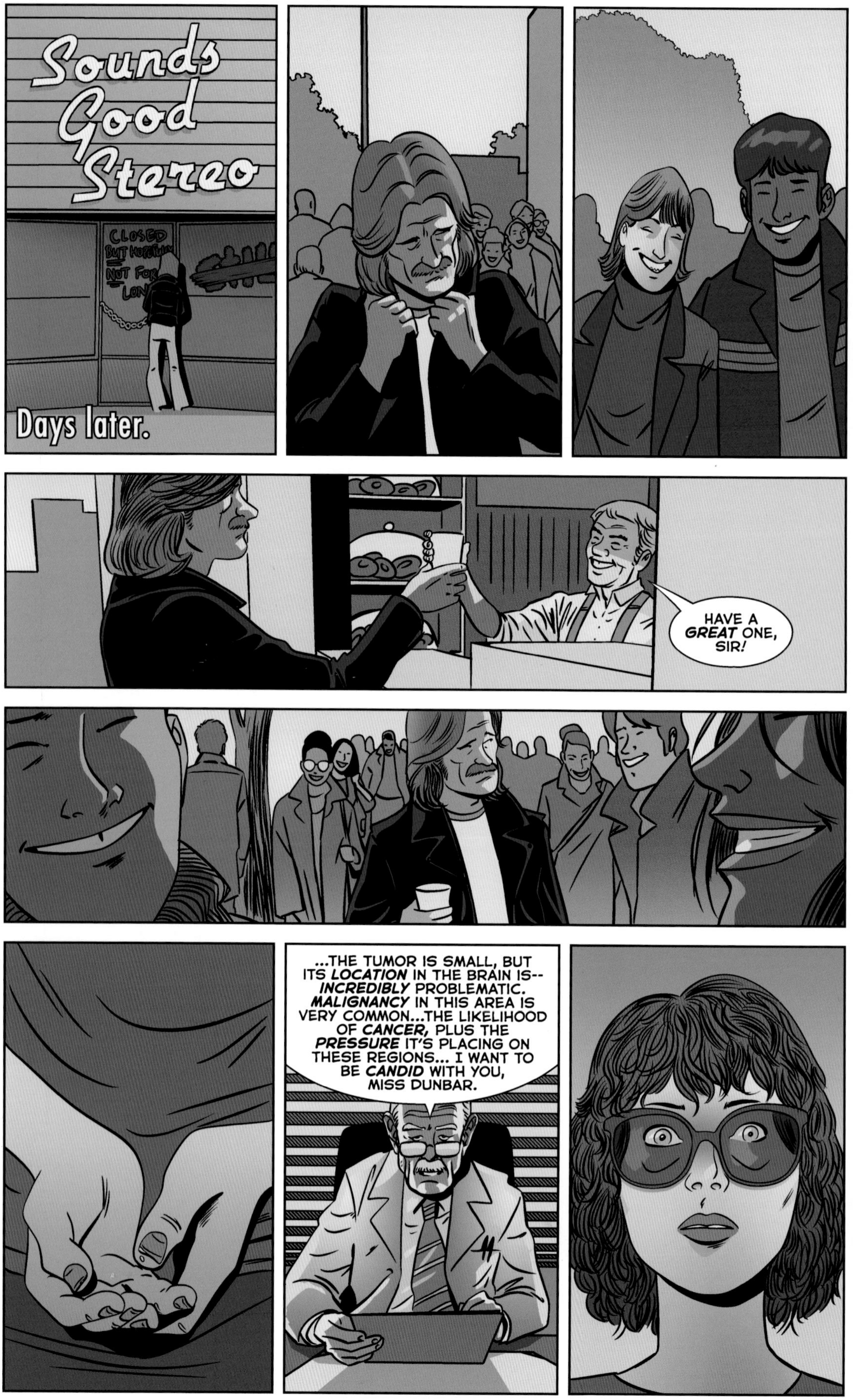
Sounds Good Stereo
CLOSED
Days later.
HAVE A GREAT ONE, SIR!
...THE TUMOR IS SMALL, BUT ITS LOCATION IN THE BRAIN IS-- INCREDIBLY PROBLEMATIC. MALIGNANCY IN THIS AREA IS VERY COMMON...THE LIKELIHOOD OF CANCER, PLUS THE PRESSURE IT'S PLACING ON THESE REGIONS... I WANT TO BE CANDID WITH YOU, MISS DUNBAR.

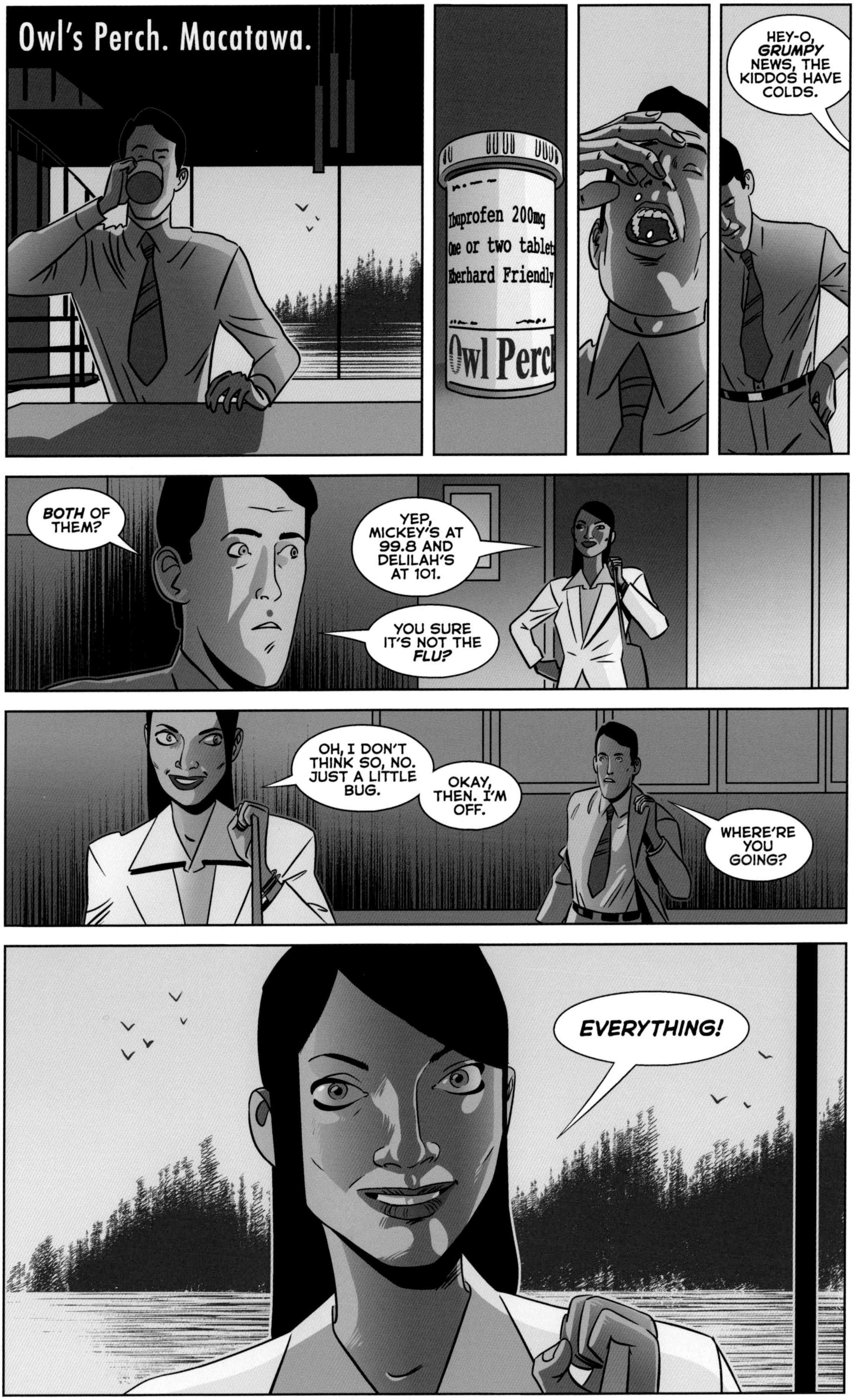
Owl's Perch. Macatawa.
Ibuprofen 200mg
One or two tablets
Eberhard Friendly
Owl Perch
HEY-O, GRUMPY NEWS, THE KIDDOS HAVE COLDS.
BOTH OF THEM?
YEP, MICKEY'S AT 99.8 AND DELILAH'S AT 101.
YOU SURE IT'S NOT THE FLU?
OH, I DON'T THINK SO, NO. JUST A LITTLE BUG.
OKAY, THEN. I'M OFF.
WHERE'RE YOU GOING?
EVERYTHING!

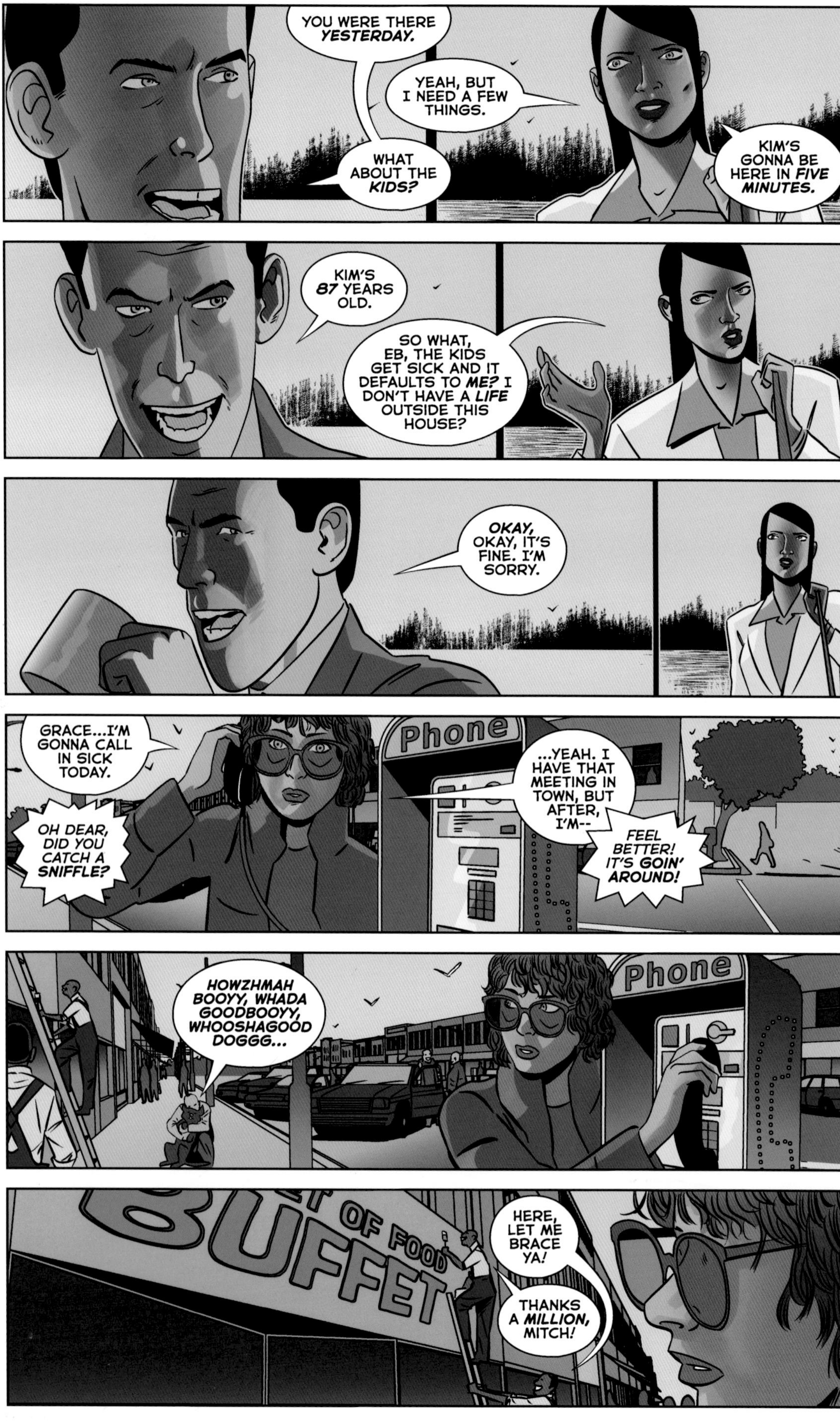

YOU WERE THERE *YESTERDAY.*
YEAH, BUT I NEED A FEW THINGS.
WHAT ABOUT THE *KIDS?*
KIM'S GONNA BE HERE IN *FIVE MINUTES.*
KIM'S *87* YEARS OLD.
SO WHAT, EB, THE KIDS GET SICK AND IT DEFAULTS TO *ME?* I DON'T HAVE A *LIFE* OUTSIDE THIS HOUSE?
OKAY, OKAY, IT'S FINE. I'M SORRY.
GRACE...I'M GONNA CALL IN SICK TODAY.
OH DEAR, DID YOU CATCH A SNIFFLE?
Phone
...YEAH. I HAVE THAT MEETING IN TOWN, BUT AFTER, I'M--
FEEL BETTER! IT'S GOIN' AROUND!
HOWZHMAH BOOYY, WHADA GOODBOOYY, WHOOSHAGOOD DOGGG...
Phone
OF FOOD BUFFET
HERE, LET ME BRACE YA!
THANKS A *MILLION,* MITCH!

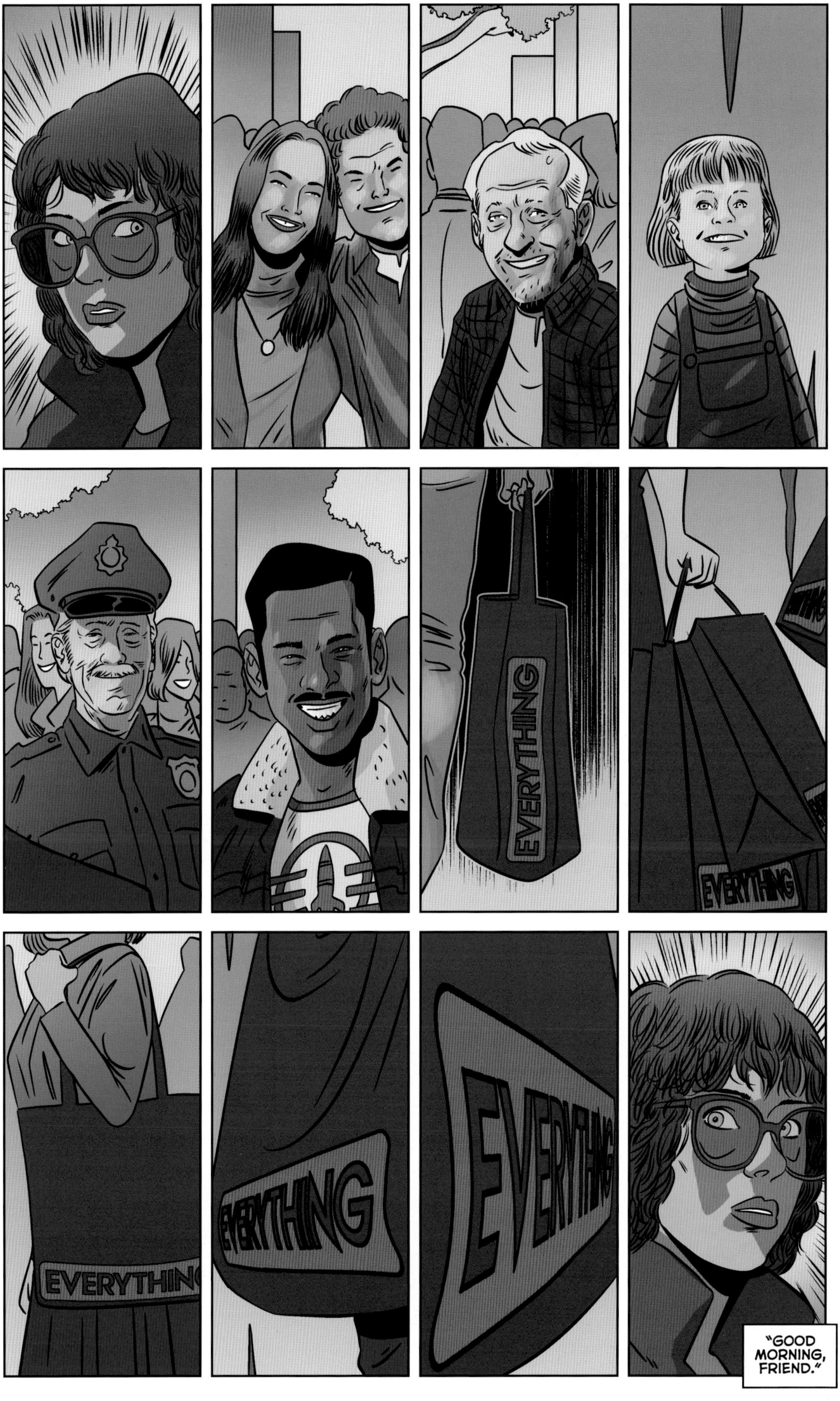
EVERYTHING
EVERYTHING
EVERYTHING
EVERYTHING
EVERYTHING
EVERYTHING
"GOOD MORNING, FRIEND."

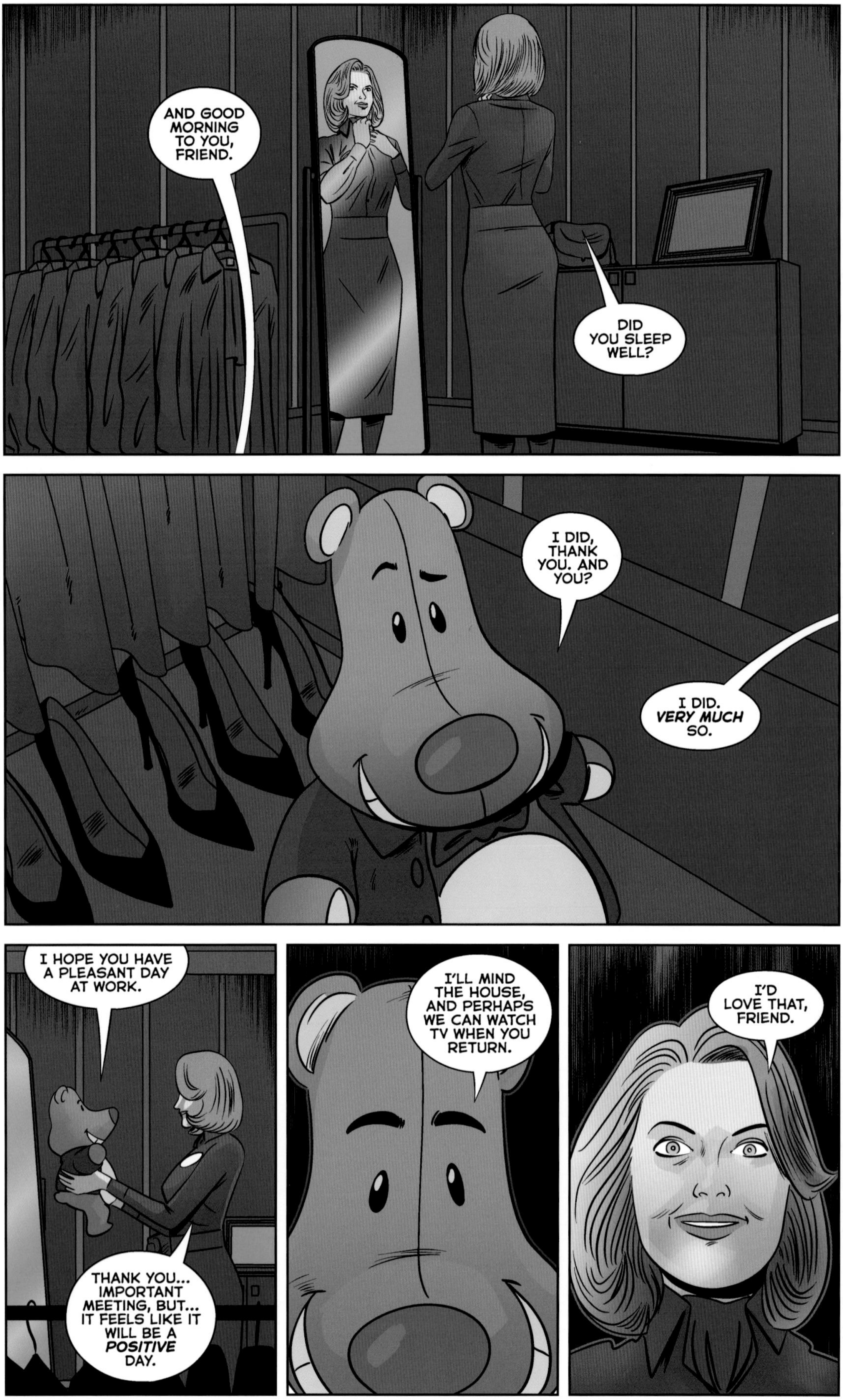
AND GOOD MORNING TO YOU, FRIEND.
DID YOU SLEEP WELL?
I DID, THANK YOU. AND YOU?
I DID. *VERY MUCH* SO.
I HOPE YOU HAVE A PLEASANT DAY AT WORK.
THANK YOU... IMPORTANT MEETING, BUT... IT FEELS LIKE IT WILL BE A *POSITIVE* DAY.
I'LL MIND THE HOUSE, AND PERHAPS WE CAN WATCH TV WHEN YOU RETURN.
I'D LOVE THAT, FRIEND.

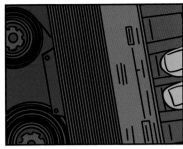

PILGRIM HOME CEMETERY, ONE MILE EAST OF DOWNTOWN, 10:33 A.M.

BOY SUSTAINED A HEAD INJURY *WELL BEFORE* THE CRASH. AND THE TRANSIENT... NO ACCELERANT WAS USED TO BURN HIM.

WHAT'S THAT *MEAN*, THEN?

IT MEANS THE GUY *SOMEHOW* BURNED ON HIS OWN WITHOUT GASOLINE OR EXPOSURE TO FLAMES OR... *ANYTHING.*

EXCUSE ME, MISTER FRIENDLY, YOUR ELEVEN O'CLOCK IS HERE.

OKAY, THANKS, PEGGY. ROPER, LET'S CHAT MORE LATER.

SURE THING. AND I'M GLAD YOU'RE OKAY, EB.

THANK YOU KINDLY...

MISS DUNBAR, *HELLO!*

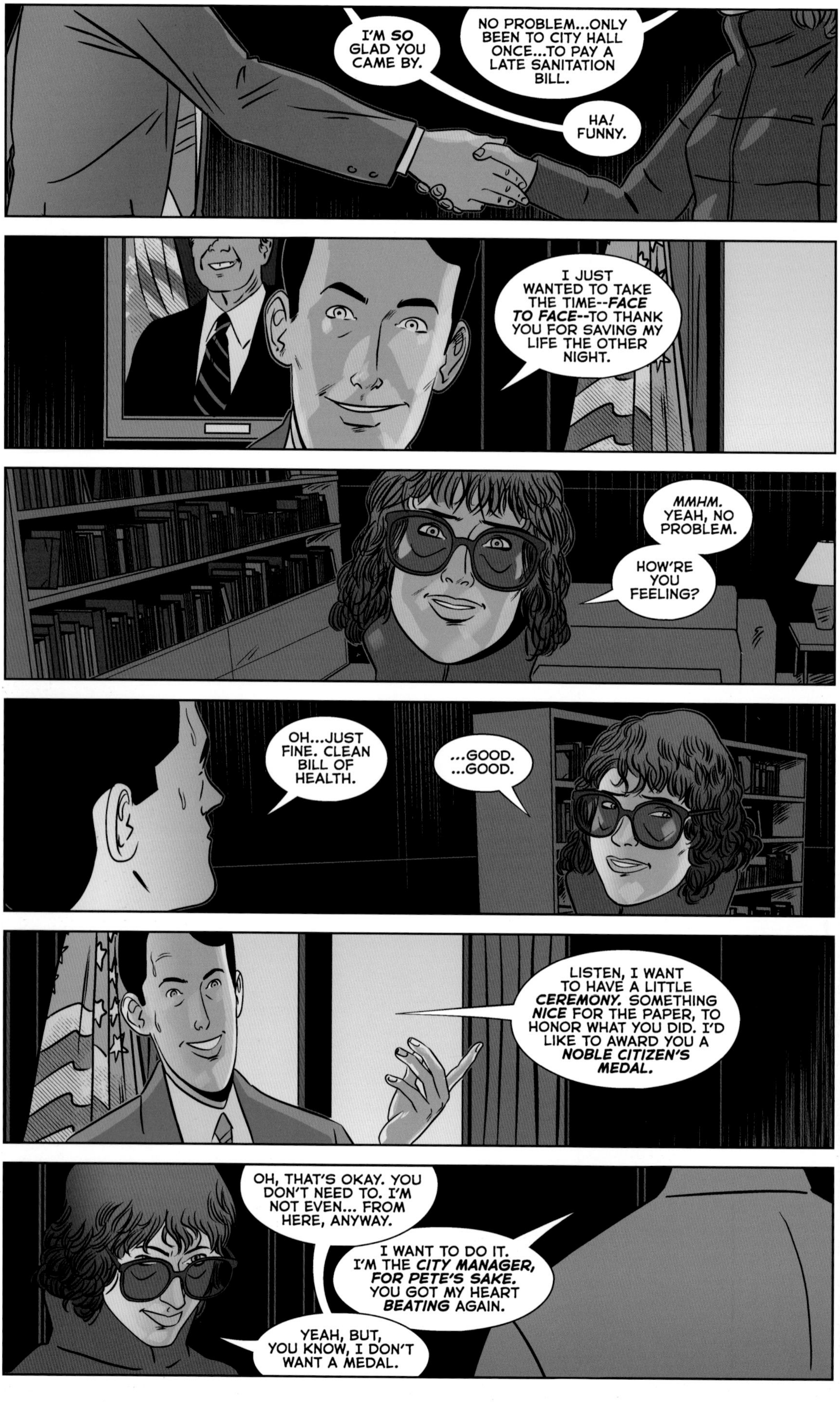

I'M SO GLAD YOU CAME BY.
NO PROBLEM...ONLY BEEN TO CITY HALL ONCE...TO PAY A LATE SANITATION BILL.
HA! FUNNY.
I JUST WANTED TO TAKE THE TIME--FACE TO FACE--TO THANK YOU FOR SAVING MY LIFE THE OTHER NIGHT.
MMHM. YEAH, NO PROBLEM.
HOW'RE YOU FEELING?
OH...JUST FINE. CLEAN BILL OF HEALTH.
...GOOD. ...GOOD.
LISTEN, I WANT TO HAVE A LITTLE CEREMONY. SOMETHING NICE FOR THE PAPER, TO HONOR WHAT YOU DID. I'D LIKE TO AWARD YOU A NOBLE CITIZEN'S MEDAL.
OH, THAT'S OKAY. YOU DON'T NEED TO. I'M NOT EVEN... FROM HERE, ANYWAY.
I WANT TO DO IT. I'M THE CITY MANAGER, FOR PETE'S SAKE. YOU GOT MY HEART BEATING AGAIN.
YEAH, BUT, YOU KNOW, I DON'T WANT A MEDAL.

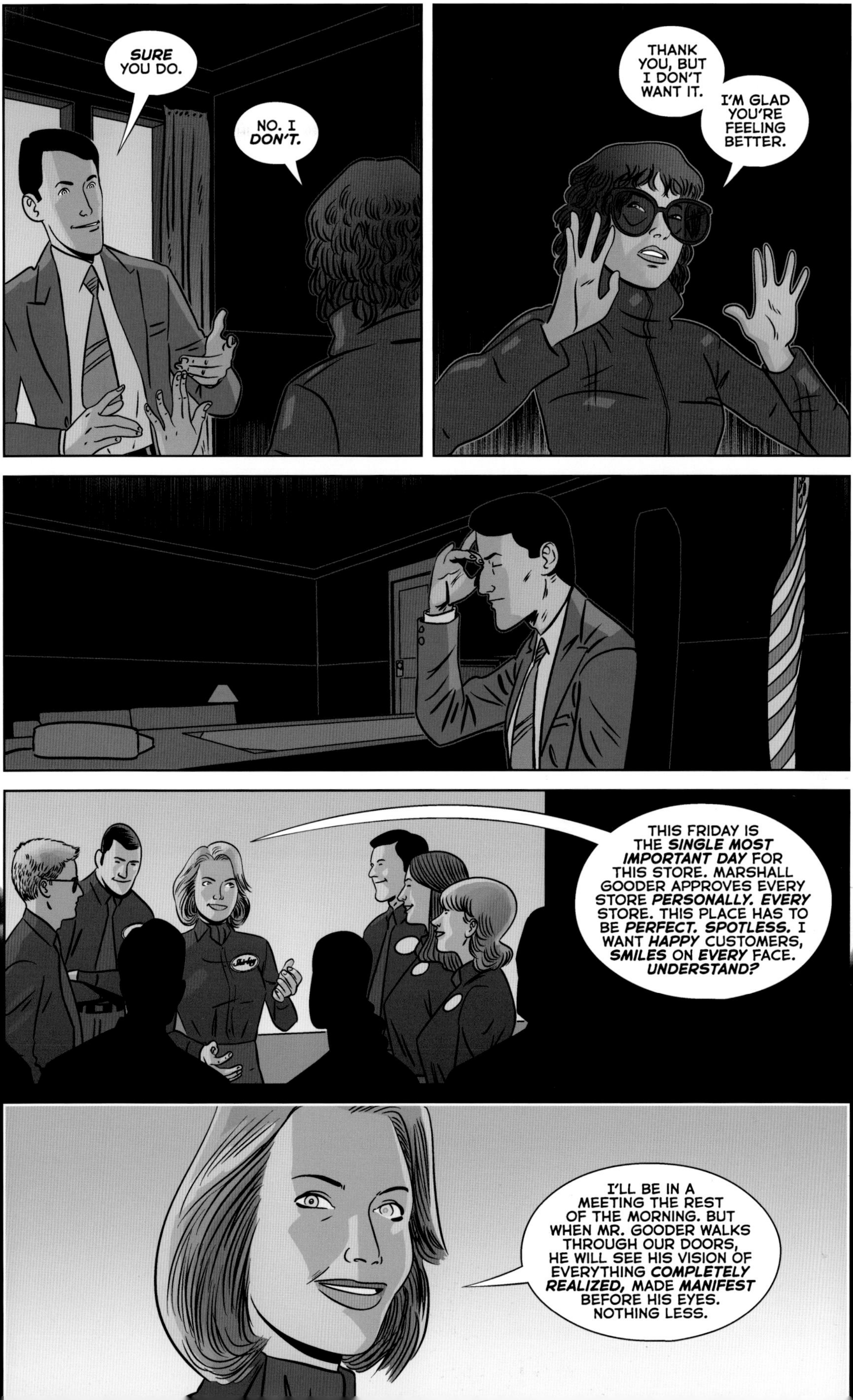
SURE YOU DO.
NO. I DON'T.
THANK YOU, BUT I DON'T WANT IT.
I'M GLAD YOU'RE FEELING BETTER.
THIS FRIDAY IS THE SINGLE MOST IMPORTANT DAY FOR THIS STORE. MARSHALL GOODER APPROVES EVERY STORE PERSONALLY. EVERY STORE. THIS PLACE HAS TO BE PERFECT. SPOTLESS. I WANT HAPPY CUSTOMERS, SMILES ON EVERY FACE. UNDERSTAND?
I'LL BE IN A MEETING THE REST OF THE MORNING. BUT WHEN MR. GOODER WALKS THROUGH OUR DOORS, HE WILL SEE HIS VISION OF EVERYTHING COMPLETELY REALIZED, MADE MANIFEST BEFORE HIS EYES. NOTHING LESS.

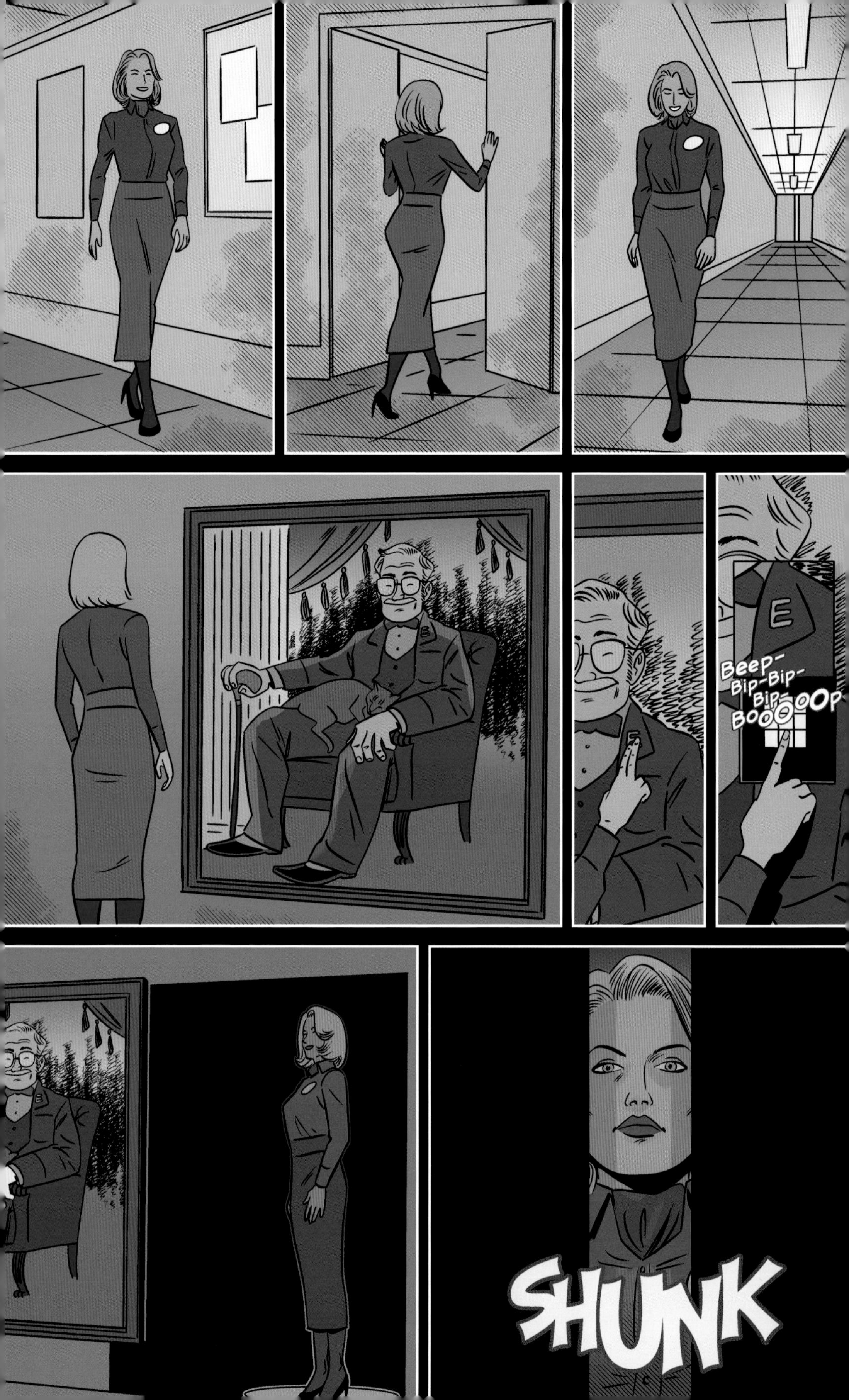
Beep-Bip-Bip-Bip-BoOOOOOp
SHUNK

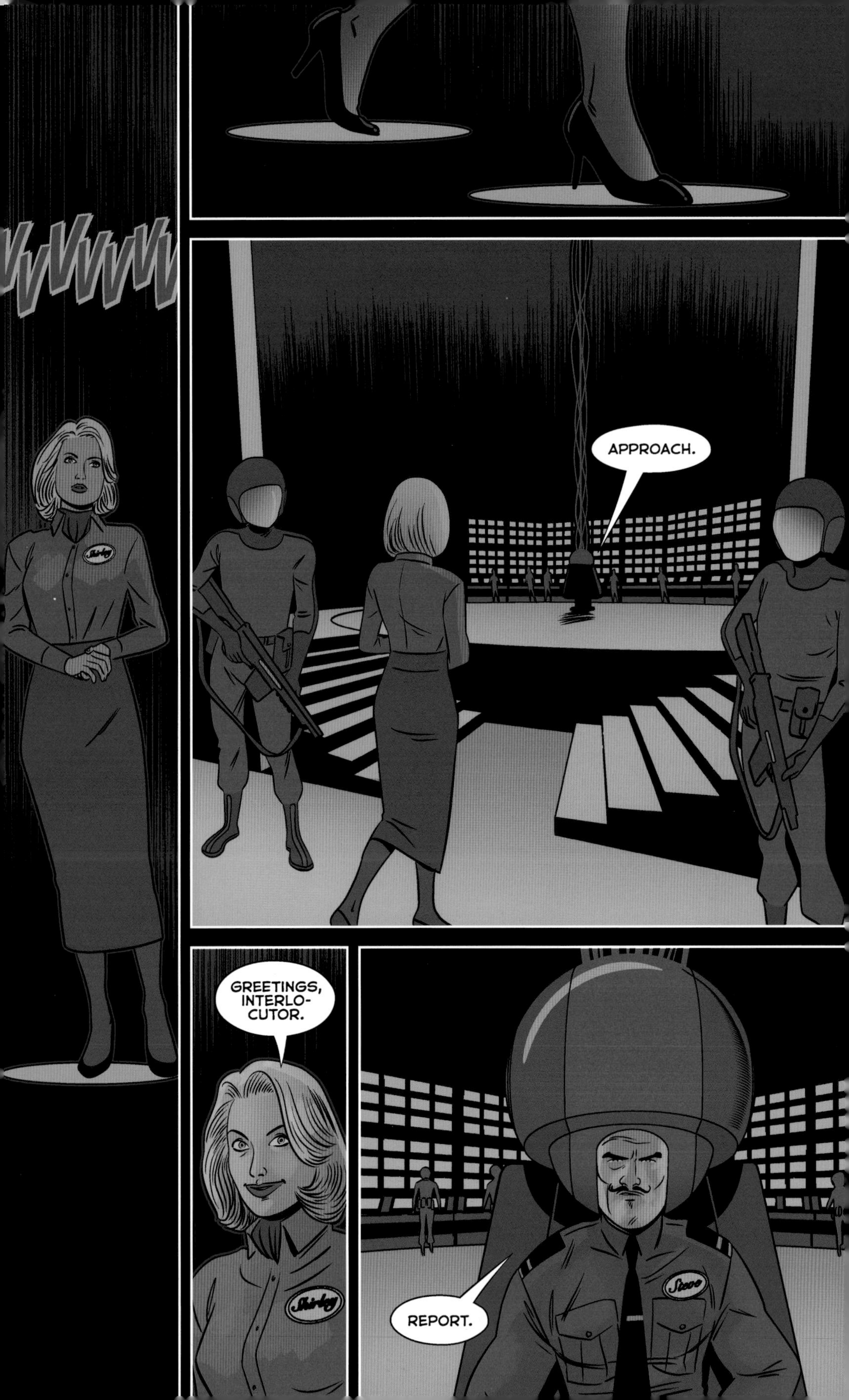
VVVVVVV
APPROACH.
GREETINGS, INTERLOCUTOR.
REPORT.
Shirley
Steve

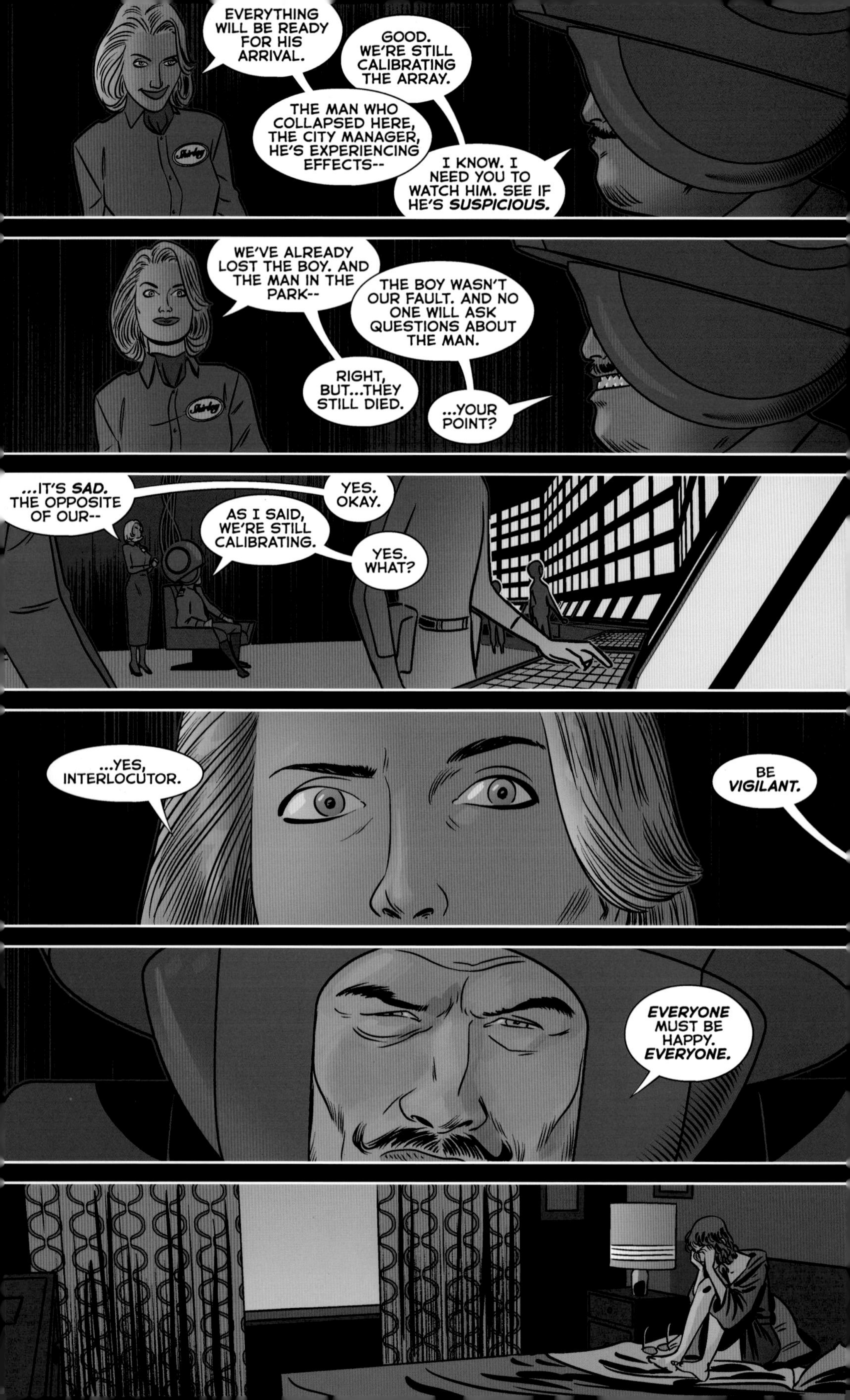
EVERYTHING WILL BE READY FOR HIS ARRIVAL.
GOOD. WE'RE STILL CALIBRATING THE ARRAY.
THE MAN WHO COLLAPSED HERE, THE CITY MANAGER, HE'S EXPERIENCING EFFECTS--
I KNOW. I NEED YOU TO WATCH HIM. SEE IF HE'S *SUSPICIOUS.*
WE'VE ALREADY LOST THE BOY. AND THE MAN IN THE PARK--
THE BOY WASN'T OUR FAULT. AND NO ONE WILL ASK QUESTIONS ABOUT THE MAN.
RIGHT, BUT...THEY STILL DIED.
...YOUR POINT?
...IT'S *SAD.* THE OPPOSITE OF OUR--
YES. OKAY.
AS I SAID, WE'RE STILL CALIBRATING.
YES. WHAT?
...YES, INTERLOCUTOR.
BE *VIGILANT.*
EVERYONE MUST BE HAPPY. *EVERYONE.*

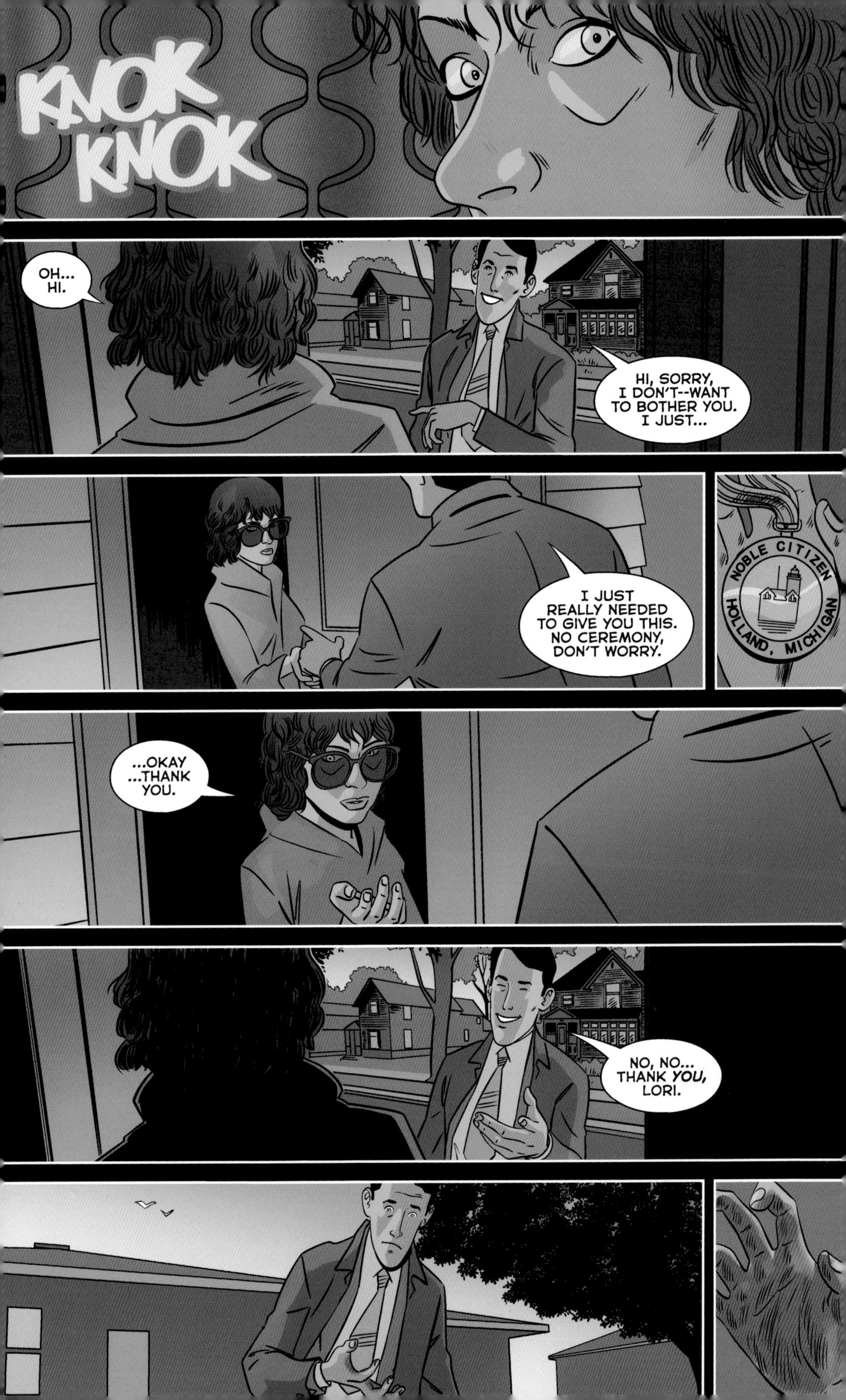
KNOK KNOK
OH... HI.
HI, SORRY, I DON'T--WANT TO BOTHER YOU. I JUST...
I JUST REALLY NEEDED TO GIVE YOU THIS. NO CEREMONY, DON'T WORRY.
NOBLE CITIZEN HOLLAND, MICHIGAN
...OKAY ...THANK YOU.
NO, NO... THANK YOU, LORI.

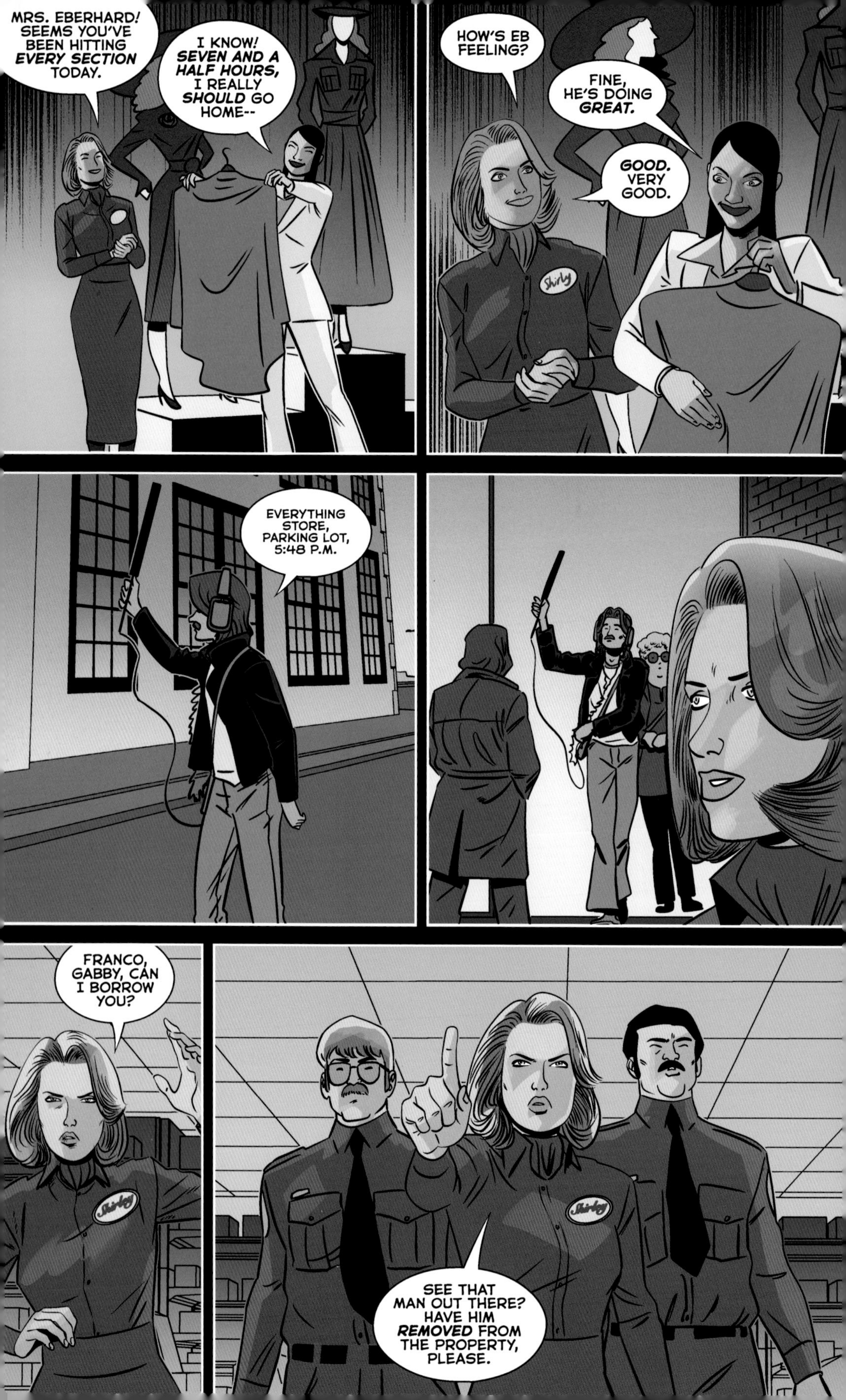
MRS. EBERHARD! SEEMS YOU'VE BEEN HITTING EVERY SECTION TODAY.
I KNOW! SEVEN AND A HALF HOURS, I REALLY SHOULD GO HOME--
HOW'S EB FEELING?
FINE, HE'S DOING GREAT.
GOOD. VERY GOOD.
Shirly
EVERYTHING STORE, PARKING LOT, 5:48 P.M.
FRANCO, GABBY, CAN I BORROW YOU?
Shirley
Shirley
SEE THAT MAN OUT THERE? HAVE HIM REMOVED FROM THE PROPERTY, PLEASE.

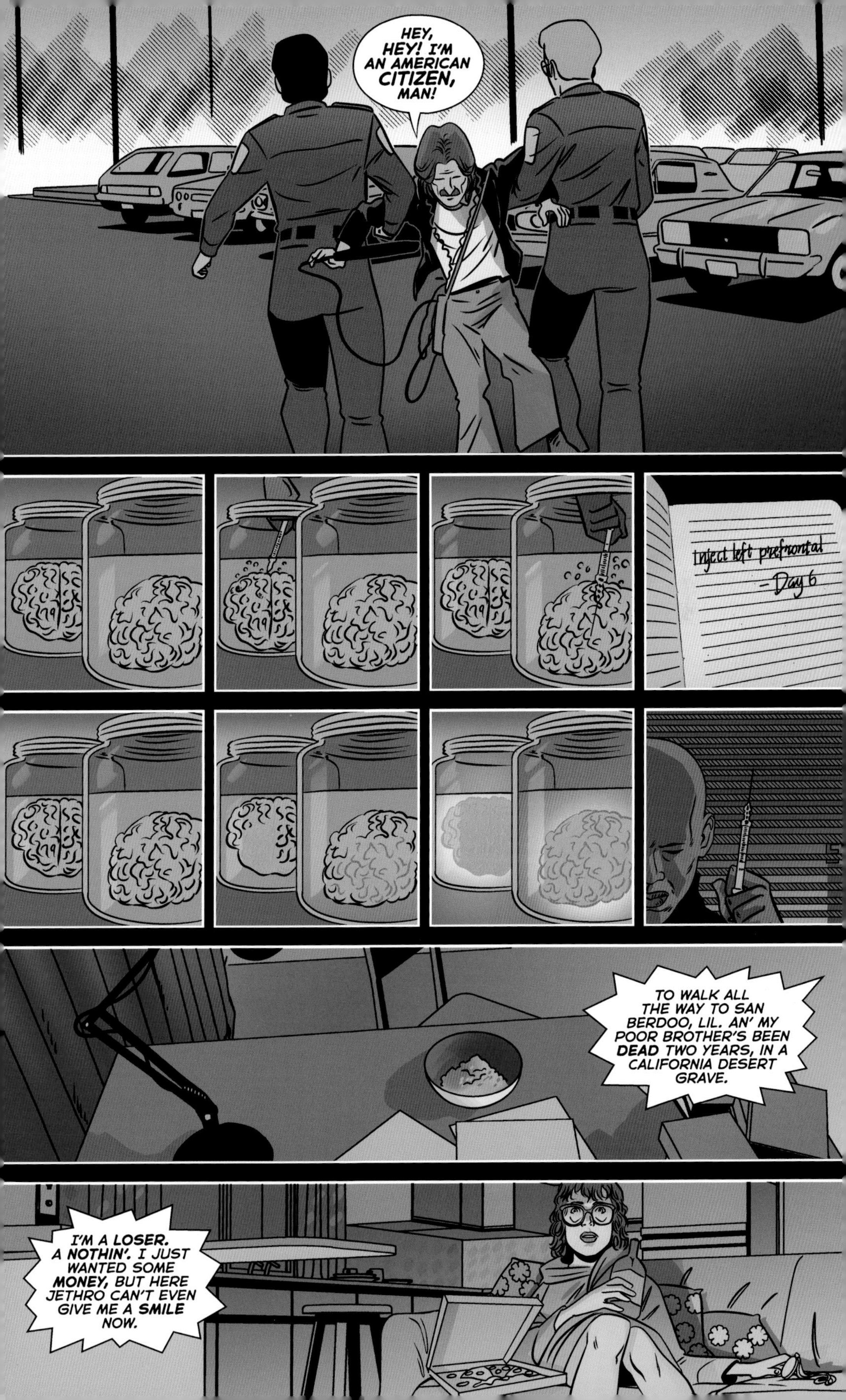
HEY, HEY! I'M AN AMERICAN CITIZEN, MAN!
Inject left prefrontal
-Day 6
TO WALK ALL THE WAY TO SAN BERDOO, LIL. AN' MY POOR BROTHER'S BEEN DEAD TWO YEARS, IN A CALIFORNIA DESERT GRAVE.
I'M A LOSER. A NOTHIN'. I JUST WANTED SOME MONEY, BUT HERE JETHRO CAN'T EVEN GIVE ME A SMILE NOW.

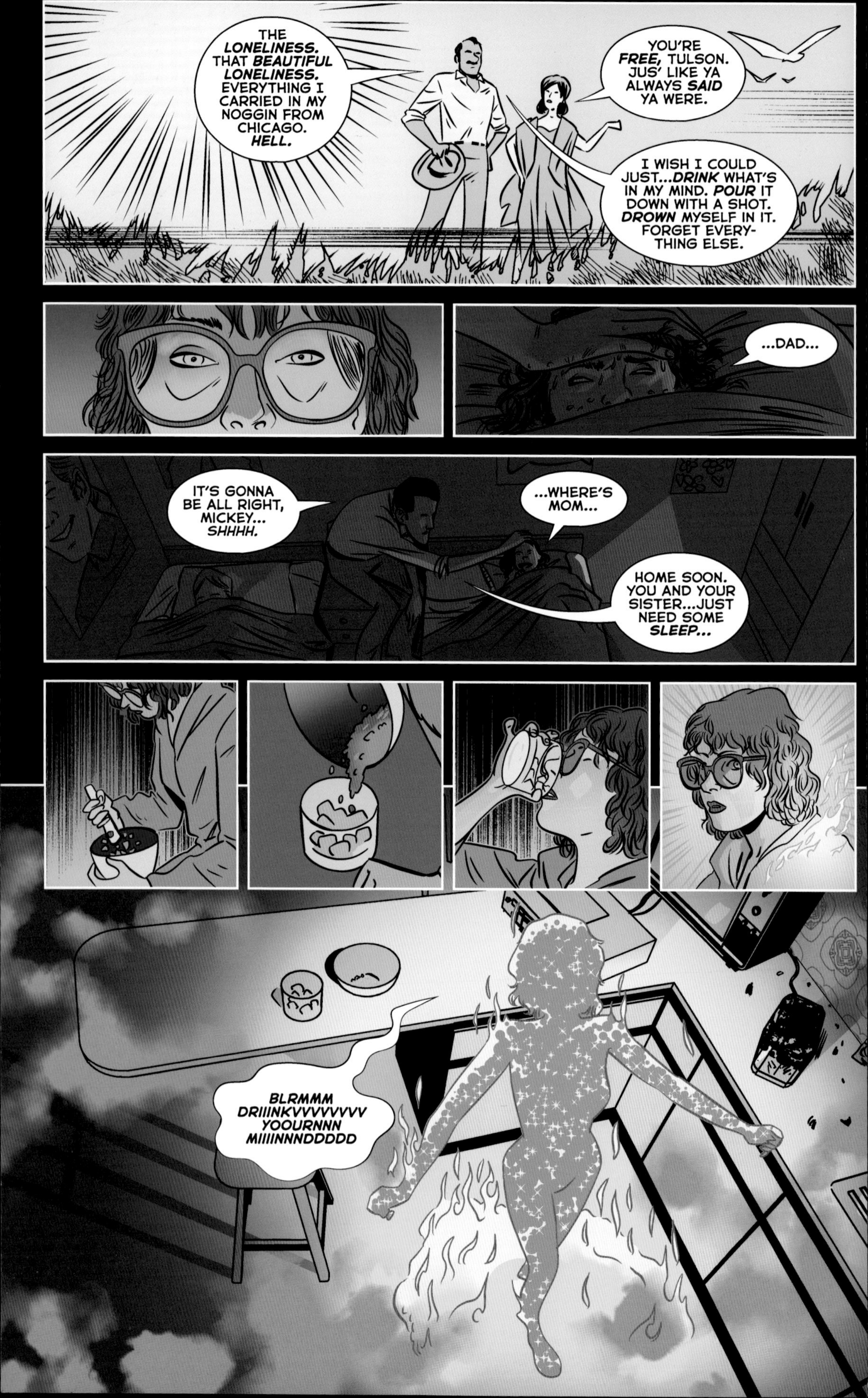
THE LONELINESS. THAT BEAUTIFUL LONELINESS. EVERYTHING I CARRIED IN MY NOGGIN FROM CHICAGO. HELL.
YOU'RE FREE, TULSON. JUS' LIKE YA ALWAYS SAID YA WERE.
I WISH I COULD JUST...DRINK WHAT'S IN MY MIND. POUR IT DOWN WITH A SHOT. DROWN MYSELF IN IT. FORGET EVERY-THING ELSE.
...DAD...
IT'S GONNA BE ALL RIGHT, MICKEY... SHHHH.
...WHERE'S MOM...
HOME SOON. YOU AND YOUR SISTER...JUST NEED SOME SLEEP...
BLRMMM DRIIINKVVVVVVVV YOOURNNN MIIIINNNDDDDD

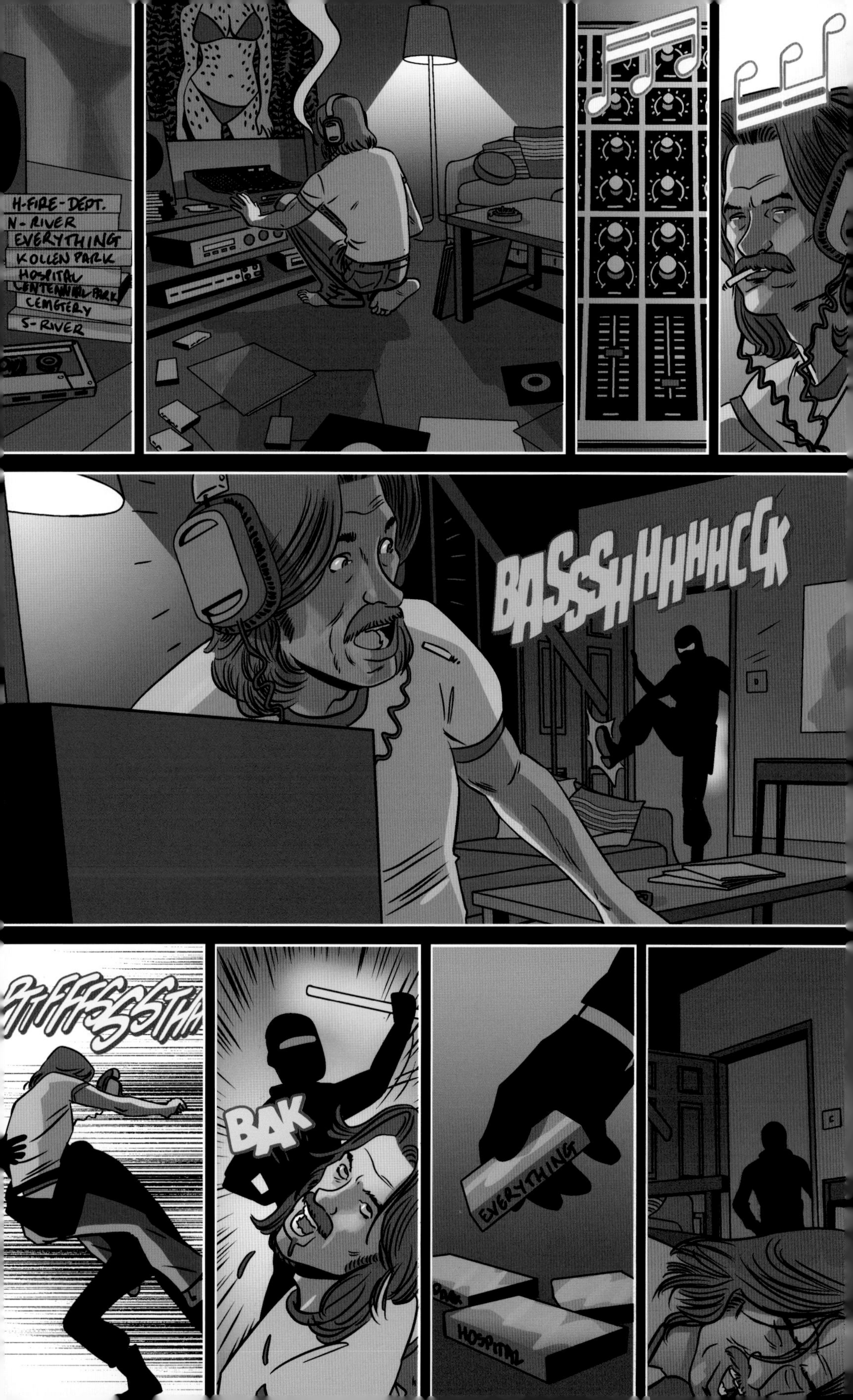
H-FIRE-DEPT.
N-RIVER
EVERYTHING
KOLLEN PARK
HOSPITAL
CENTENNIAL PARK
CEMETERY
S-RIVER
BASSSHHHHHCCK
BAK
EVERYTHING
HOSPITAL

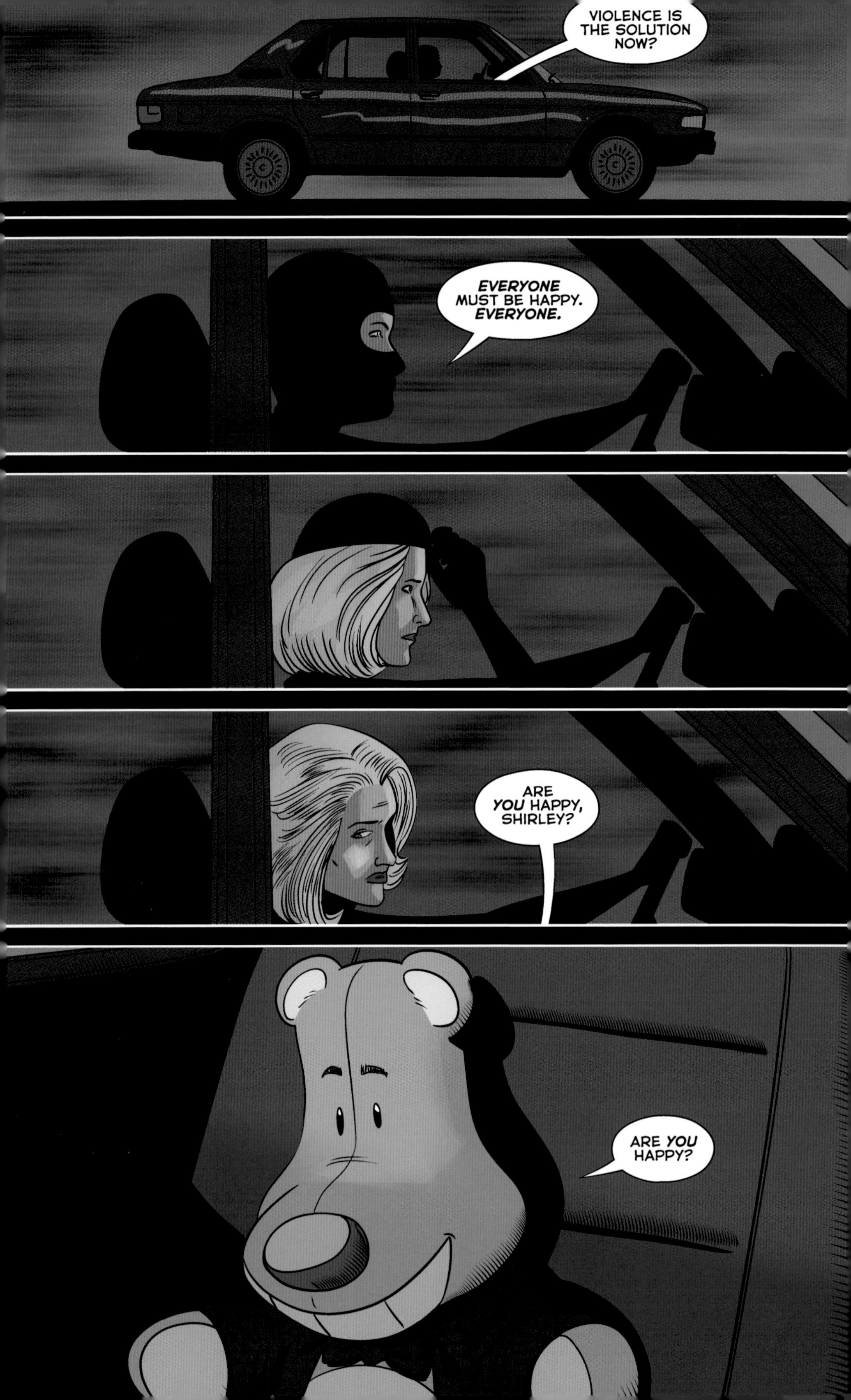
VIOLENCE IS THE SOLUTION NOW?
EVERYONE MUST BE HAPPY. EVERYONE.
ARE YOU HAPPY, SHIRLEY?
ARE YOU HAPPY?

Chapter 4:
"Praxis and Allies"

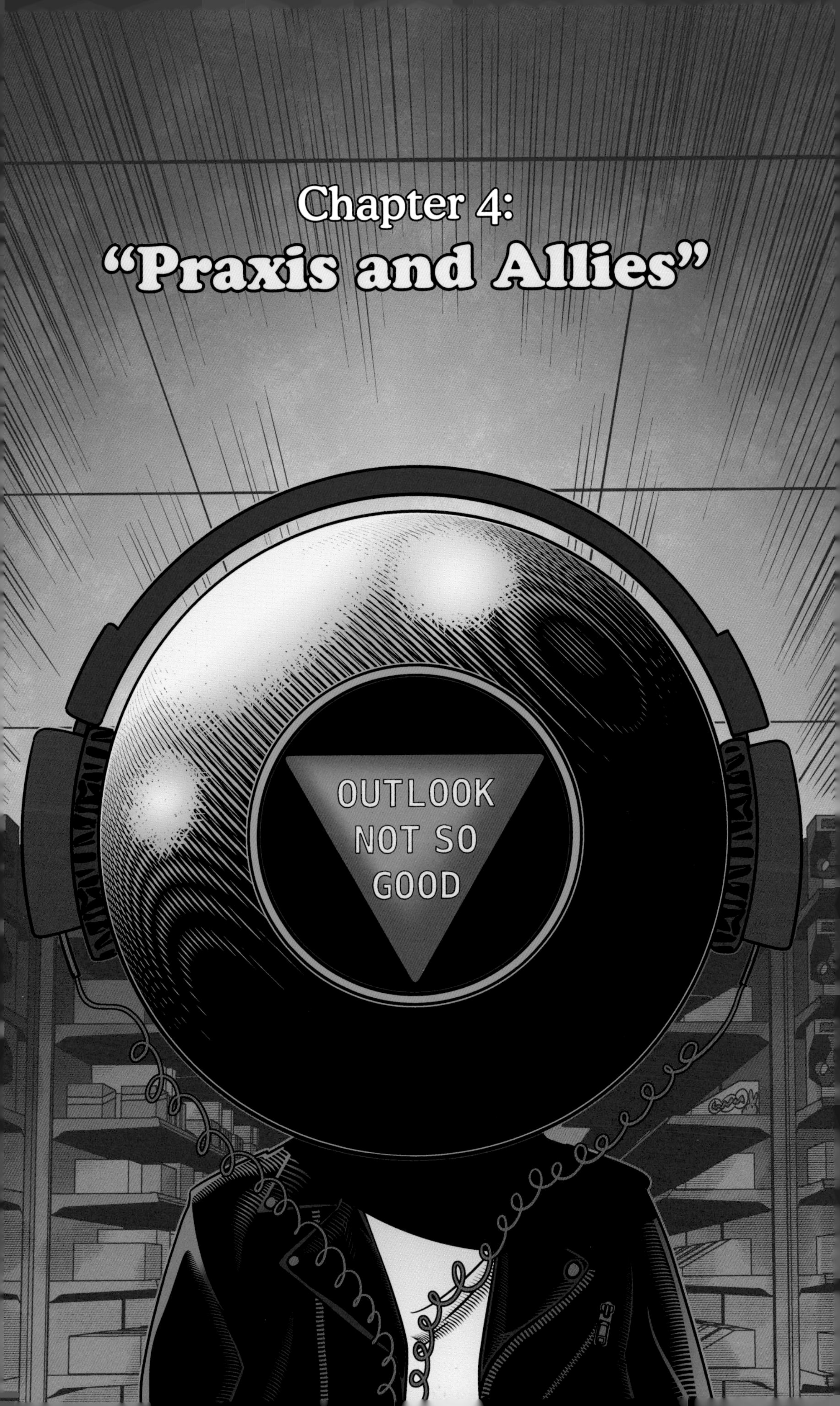
OUTLOOK
NOT SO
GOOD

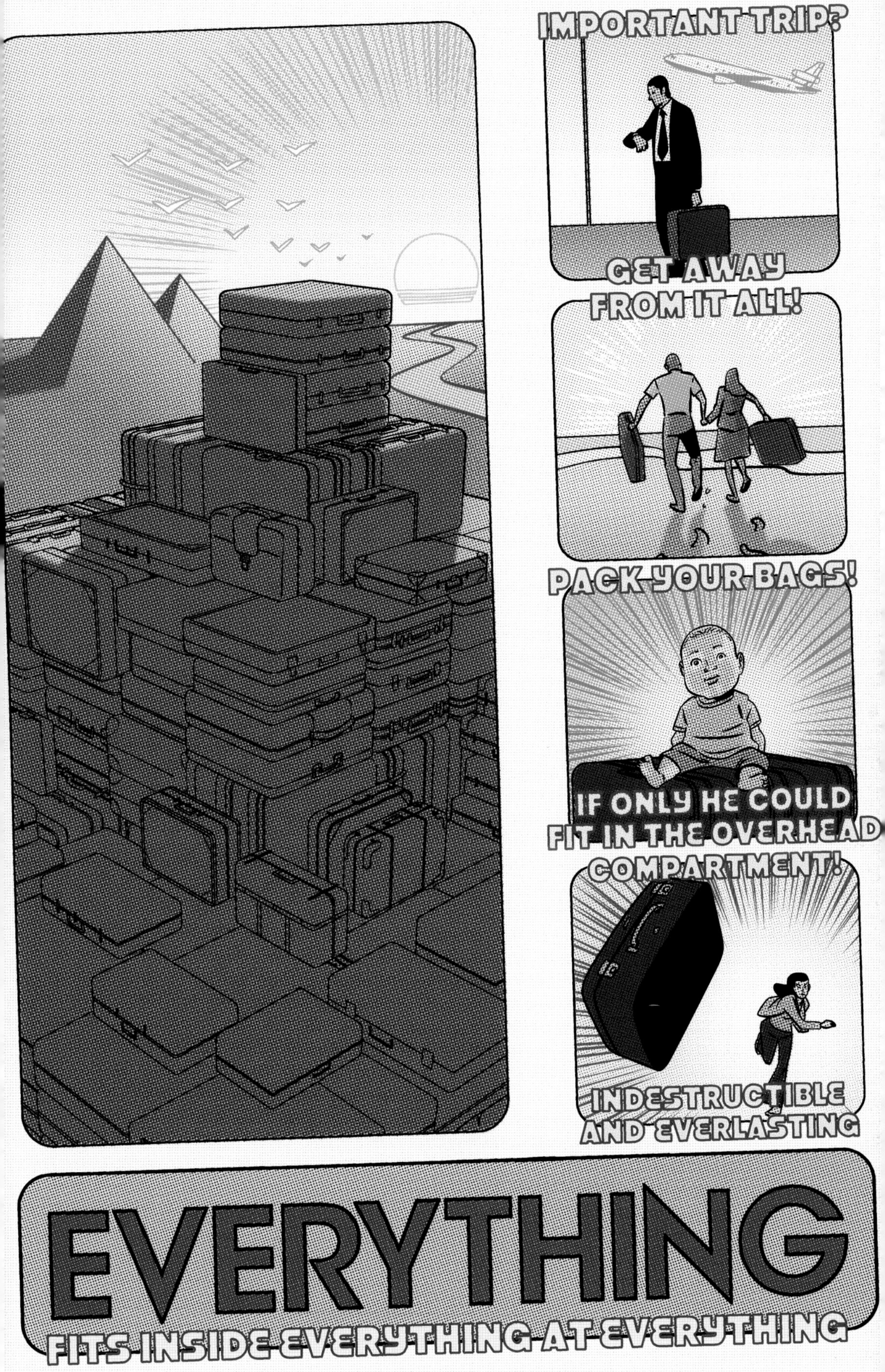

IMPORTANT TRIP?
GET AWAY FROM IT ALL!
PACK YOUR BAGS!
IF ONLY HE COULD FIT IN THE OVERHEAD COMPARTMENT!
INDESTRUCTIBLE AND EVERLASTING
EVERYTHING
FITS INSIDE EVERYTHING AT EVERYTHING

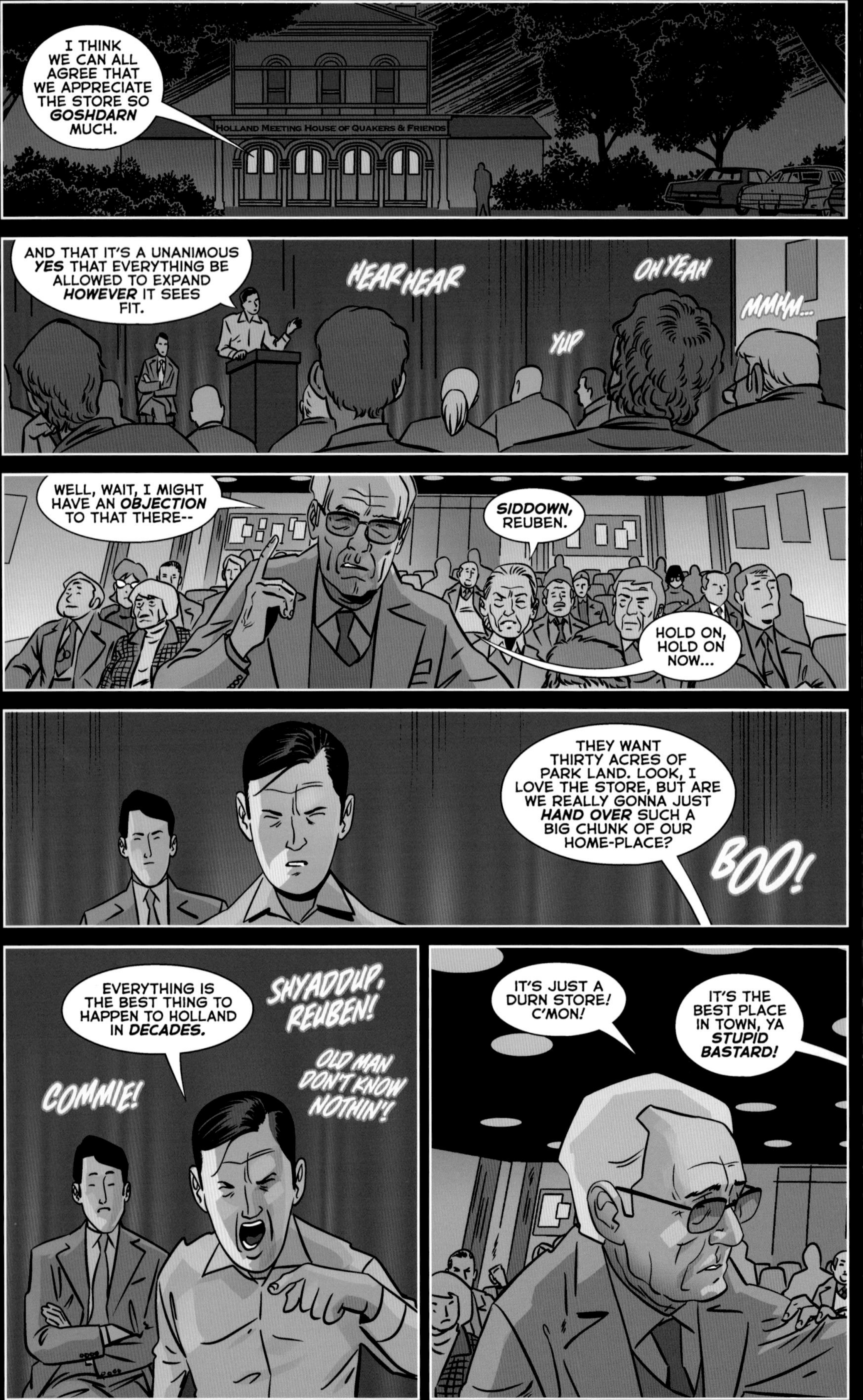

I THINK WE CAN ALL AGREE THAT WE APPRECIATE THE STORE SO GOSHDARN MUCH.
HOLLAND MEETING HOUSE OF QUAKERS & FRIENDS
AND THAT IT'S A UNANIMOUS YES THAT EVERYTHING BE ALLOWED TO EXPAND HOWEVER IT SEES FIT.
HEAR HEAR
YUP
OH YEAH
MMHM...
WELL, WAIT, I MIGHT HAVE AN OBJECTION TO THAT THERE--
SIDDOWN, REUBEN.
HOLD ON, HOLD ON NOW...
THEY WANT THIRTY ACRES OF PARK LAND. LOOK, I LOVE THE STORE, BUT ARE WE REALLY GONNA JUST HAND OVER SUCH A BIG CHUNK OF OUR HOME-PLACE?
BOO!
EVERYTHING IS THE BEST THING TO HAPPEN TO HOLLAND IN DECADES.
SHYADDUP, REUBEN!
COMMIE!
OLD MAN DON'T KNOW NOTHIN'!
IT'S JUST A DURN STORE! C'MON!
IT'S THE BEST PLACE IN TOWN, YA STUPID BASTARD!

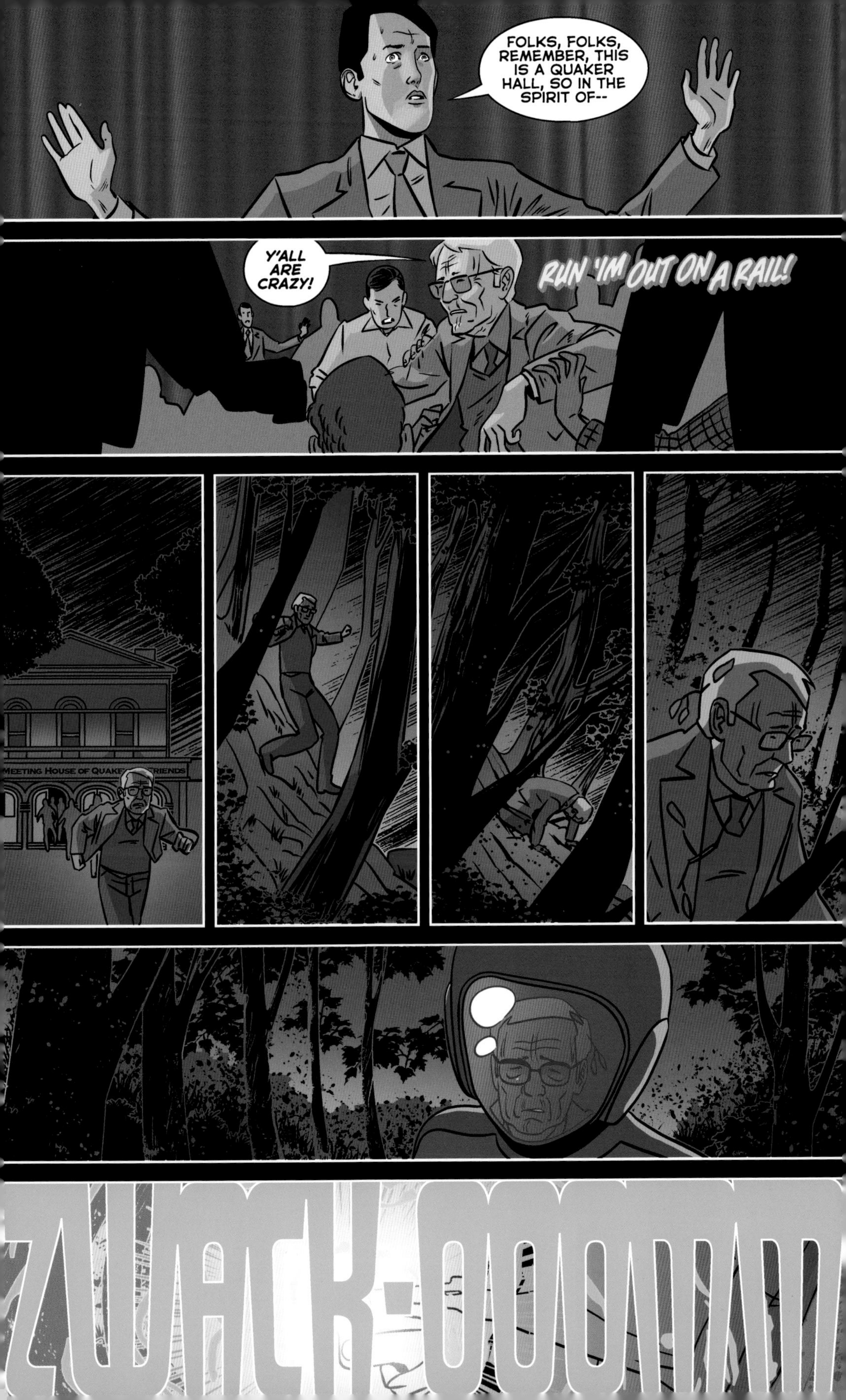

FOLKS, FOLKS, REMEMBER, THIS IS A QUAKER HALL, SO IN THE SPIRIT OF--
Y'ALL ARE CRAZY!
RUN 'IM OUT ON A RAIL!
ZWACK-OOOMM

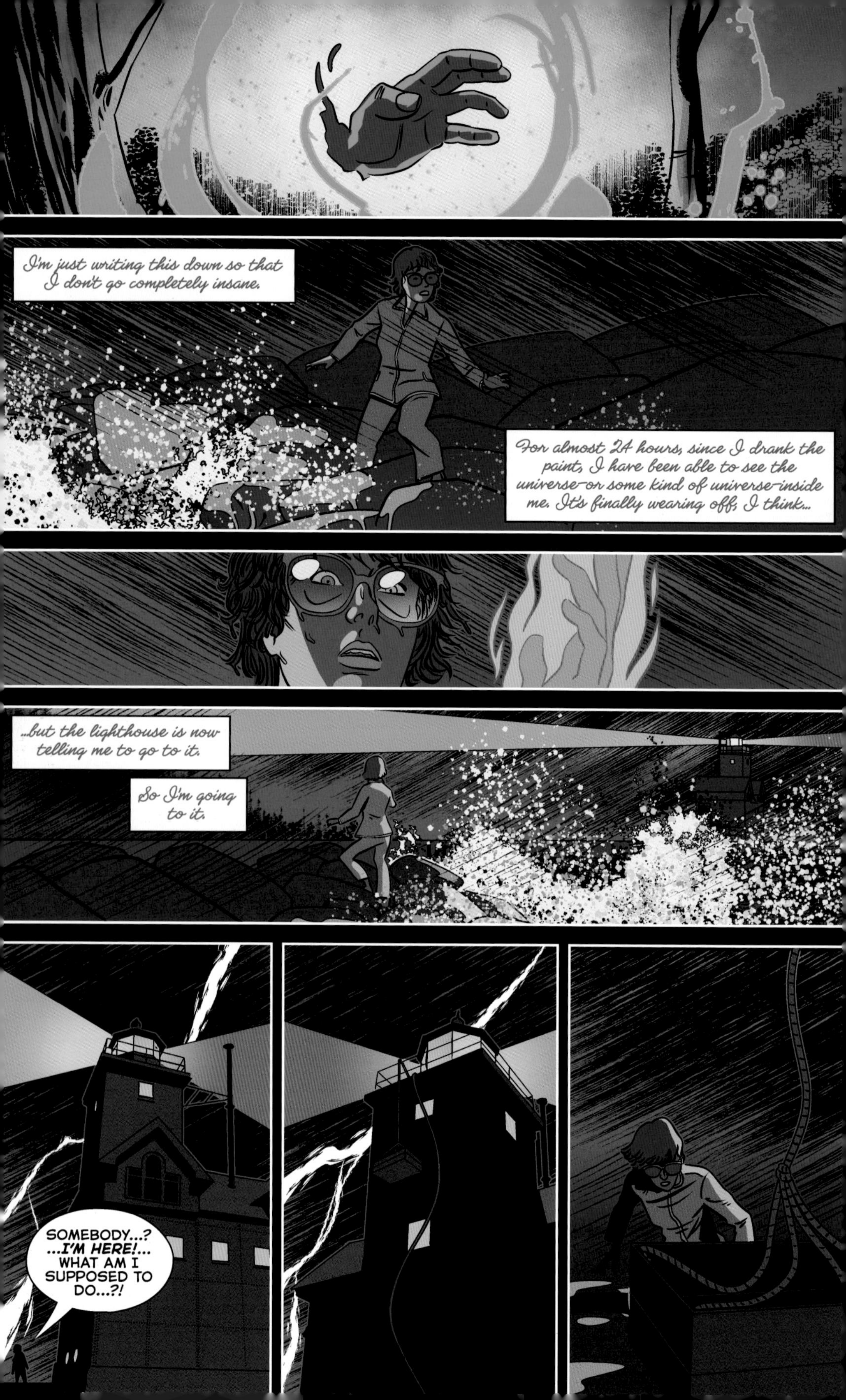
I'm just writing this down so that I don't go completely insane.
For almost 24 hours, since I drank the paint, I have been able to see the universe—or some kind of universe—inside me. It's finally wearing off, I think...
...but the lighthouse is now telling me to go to it.
So I'm going to it.
SOMEBODY...? ...I'M HERE!... WHAT AM I SUPPOSED TO DO...?!

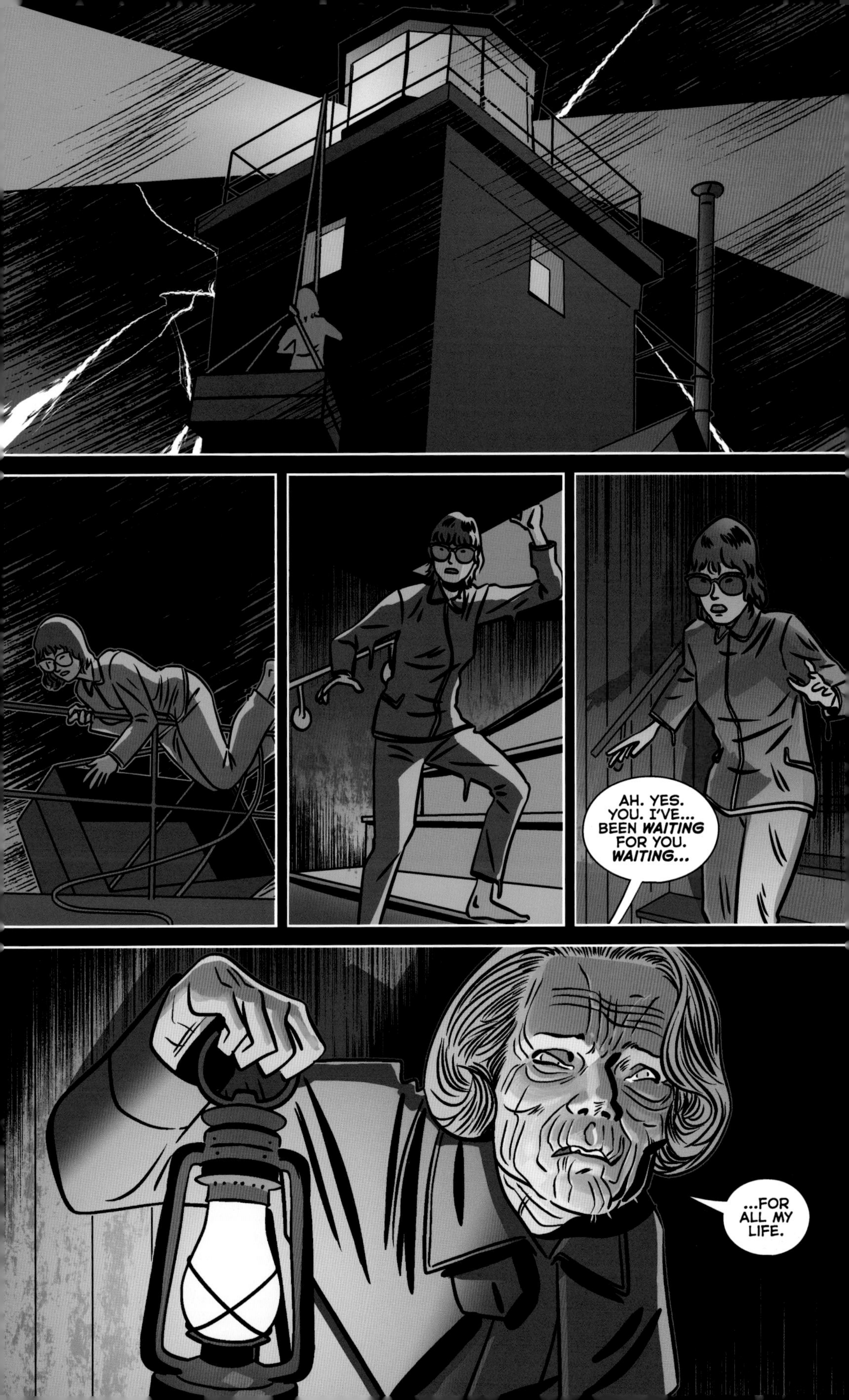
AH. YES. YOU. I'VE... BEEN *WAITING* FOR YOU. *WAITING...*
...FOR ALL MY LIFE.

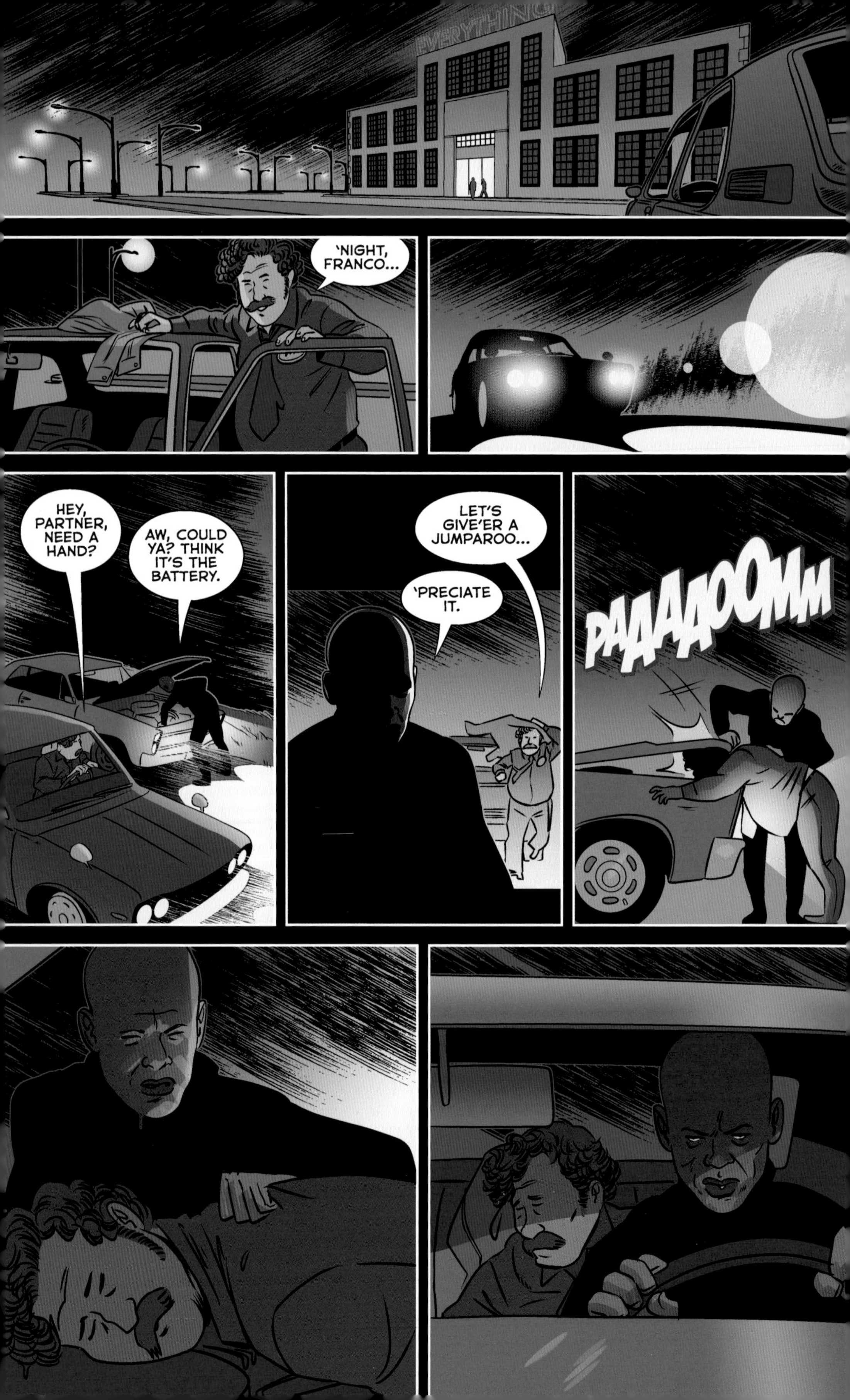
EVERYTHING
'NIGHT, FRANCO...
HEY, PARTNER, NEED A HAND?
AW, COULD YA? THINK IT'S THE BATTERY.
LET'S GIVE'ER A JUMPAROO...
'PRECIATE IT.
PAAAAOOMM

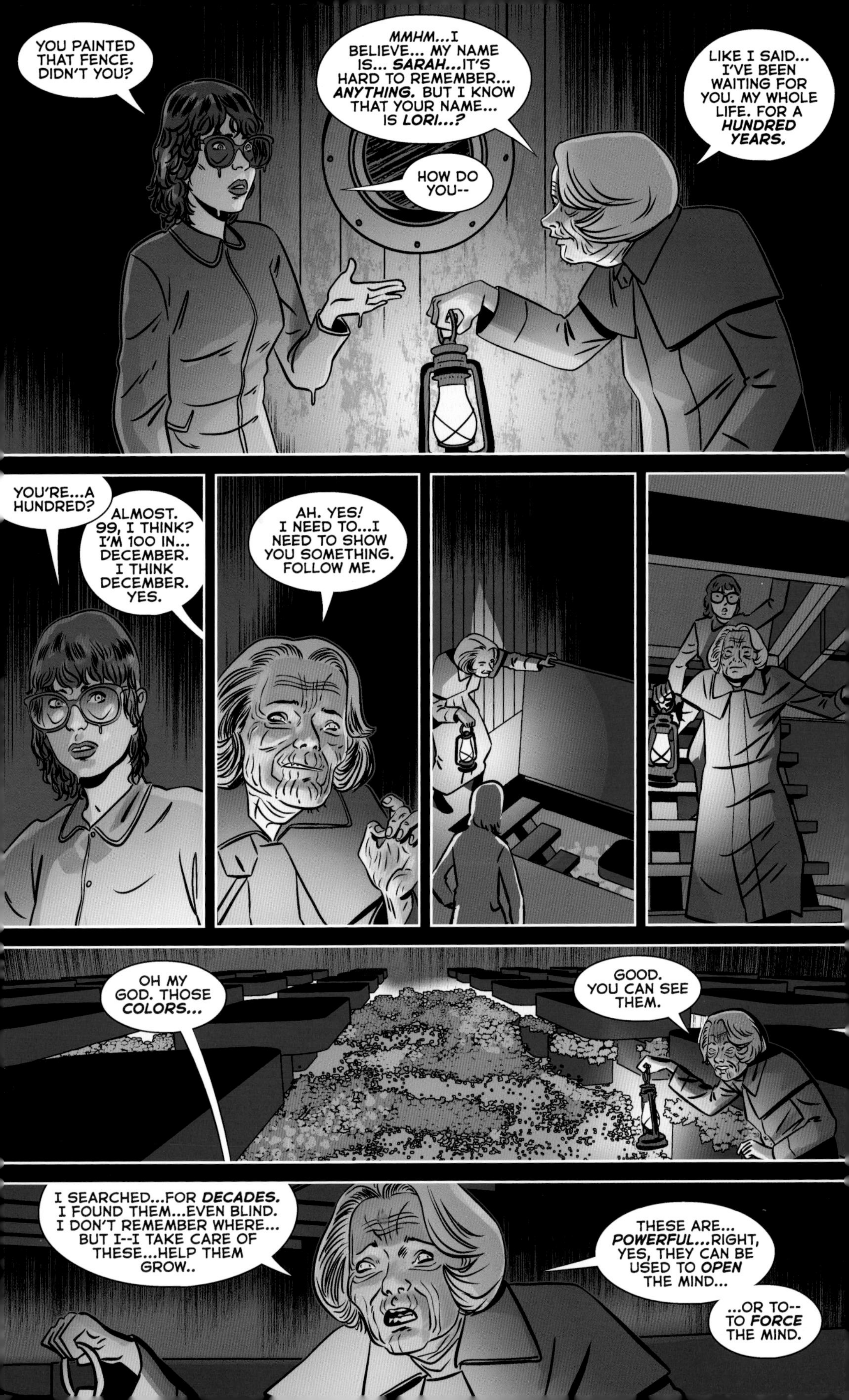
YOU PAINTED THAT FENCE. DIDN'T YOU?
MMHM...I BELIEVE... MY NAME IS... SARAH...IT'S HARD TO REMEMBER... ANYTHING. BUT I KNOW THAT YOUR NAME... IS LORI...?
HOW DO YOU--
LIKE I SAID... I'VE BEEN WAITING FOR YOU. MY WHOLE LIFE. FOR A HUNDRED YEARS.
YOU'RE...A HUNDRED?
ALMOST. 99, I THINK? I'M 100 IN... DECEMBER. I THINK DECEMBER. YES.
AH. YES! I NEED TO...I NEED TO SHOW YOU SOMETHING. FOLLOW ME.
OH MY GOD. THOSE COLORS...
GOOD. YOU CAN SEE THEM.
I SEARCHED...FOR DECADES. I FOUND THEM...EVEN BLIND. I DON'T REMEMBER WHERE... BUT I--I TAKE CARE OF THESE...HELP THEM GROW..
THESE ARE... POWERFUL...RIGHT, YES, THEY CAN BE USED TO OPEN THE MIND...
...OR TO--TO FORCE THE MIND.

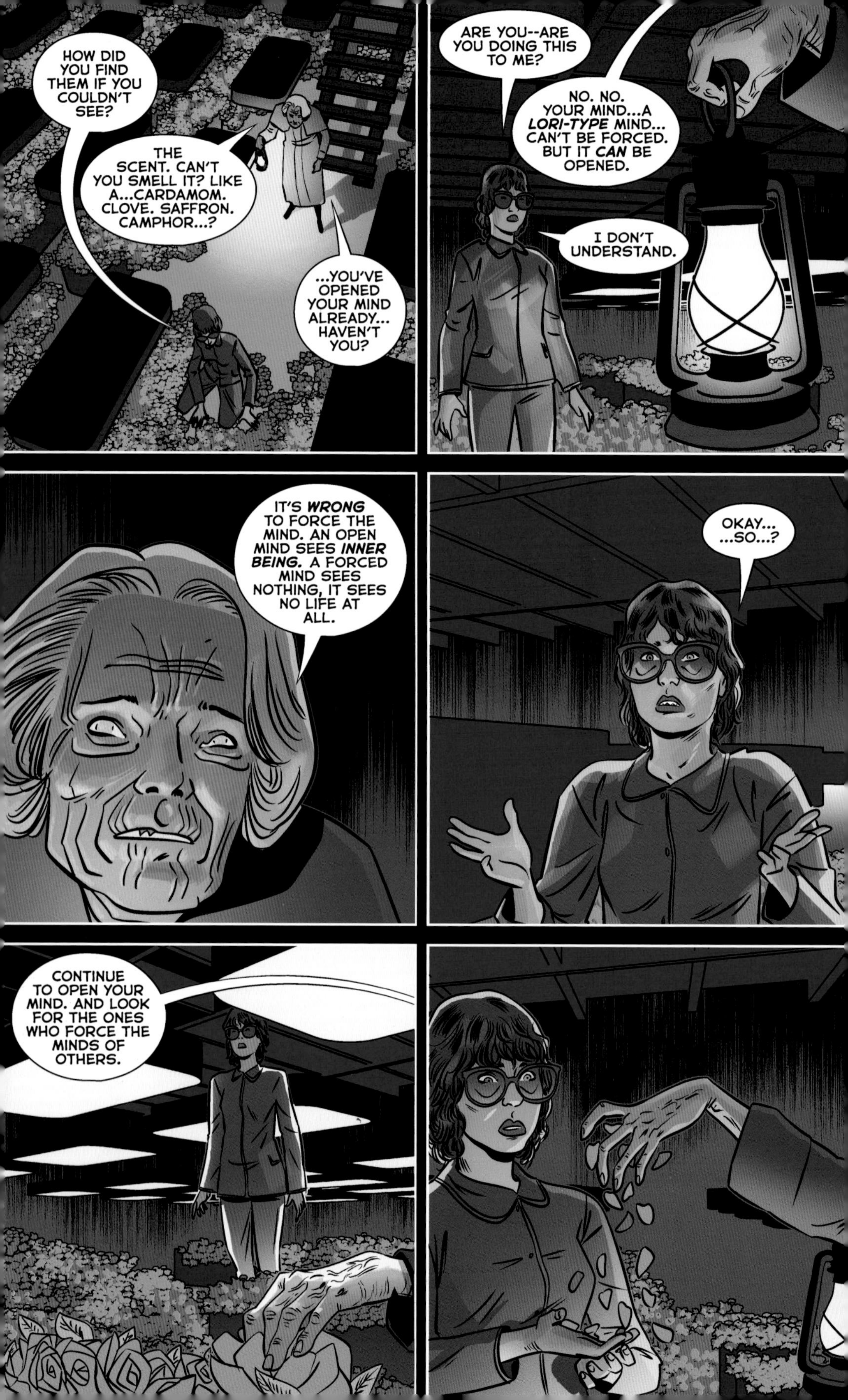
HOW DID YOU FIND THEM IF YOU COULDN'T SEE?
THE SCENT. CAN'T YOU SMELL IT? LIKE A...CARDAMOM. CLOVE. SAFFRON. CAMPHOR...?
...YOU'VE OPENED YOUR MIND ALREADY... HAVEN'T YOU?
ARE YOU--ARE YOU DOING THIS TO ME?
NO. NO. YOUR MIND...A LORI-TYPE MIND... CAN'T BE FORCED. BUT IT CAN BE OPENED.
I DON'T UNDERSTAND.
IT'S WRONG TO FORCE THE MIND. AN OPEN MIND SEES INNER BEING. A FORCED MIND SEES NOTHING, IT SEES NO LIFE AT ALL.
OKAY... ...SO...?
CONTINUE TO OPEN YOUR MIND. AND LOOK FOR THE ONES WHO FORCE THE MINDS OF OTHERS.

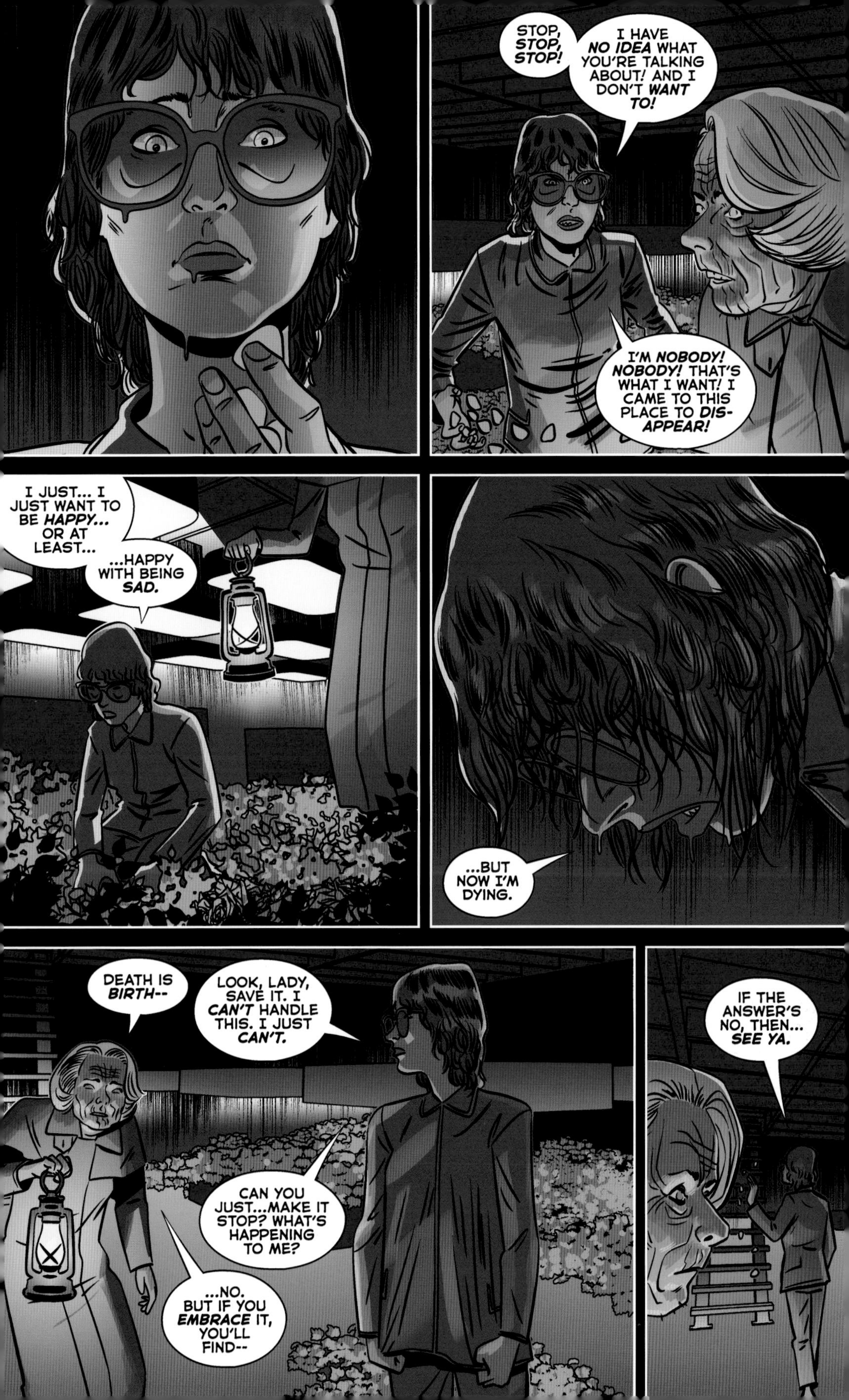

STOP, STOP, STOP!
I HAVE NO IDEA WHAT YOU'RE TALKING ABOUT! AND I DON'T WANT TO!
I'M NOBODY! NOBODY! THAT'S WHAT I WANT! I CAME TO THIS PLACE TO DIS-APPEAR!
I JUST... I JUST WANT TO BE HAPPY... OR AT LEAST...
...HAPPY WITH BEING SAD.
...BUT NOW I'M DYING.
DEATH IS BIRTH--
LOOK, LADY, SAVE IT. I CAN'T HANDLE THIS. I JUST CAN'T.
CAN YOU JUST...MAKE IT STOP? WHAT'S HAPPENING TO ME?
...NO. BUT IF YOU EMBRACE IT, YOU'LL FIND--
IF THE ANSWER'S NO, THEN... SEE YA.

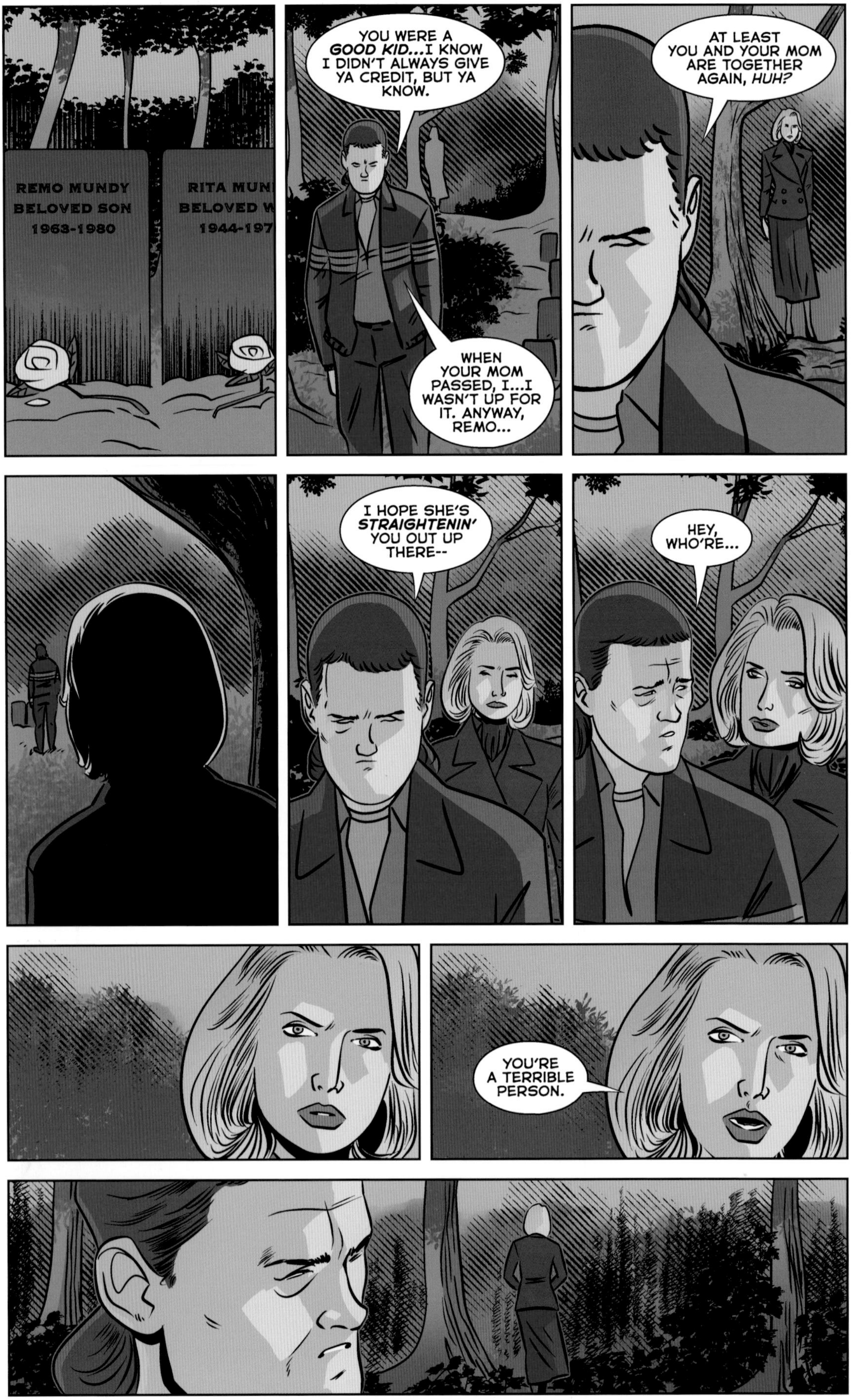
REMO MUNDY
BELOVED SON
1963-1980
RITA MUND
BELOVED W
1944-197
YOU WERE A *GOOD KID*...I KNOW I DIDN'T ALWAYS GIVE YA CREDIT, BUT YA KNOW.
WHEN YOUR MOM PASSED, I...I WASN'T UP FOR IT. ANYWAY, REMO...
AT LEAST YOU AND YOUR MOM ARE TOGETHER AGAIN, *HUH?*
I HOPE SHE'S *STRAIGHTENIN'* YOU OUT UP THERE--
HEY, WHO'RE...
YOU'RE A TERRIBLE PERSON.

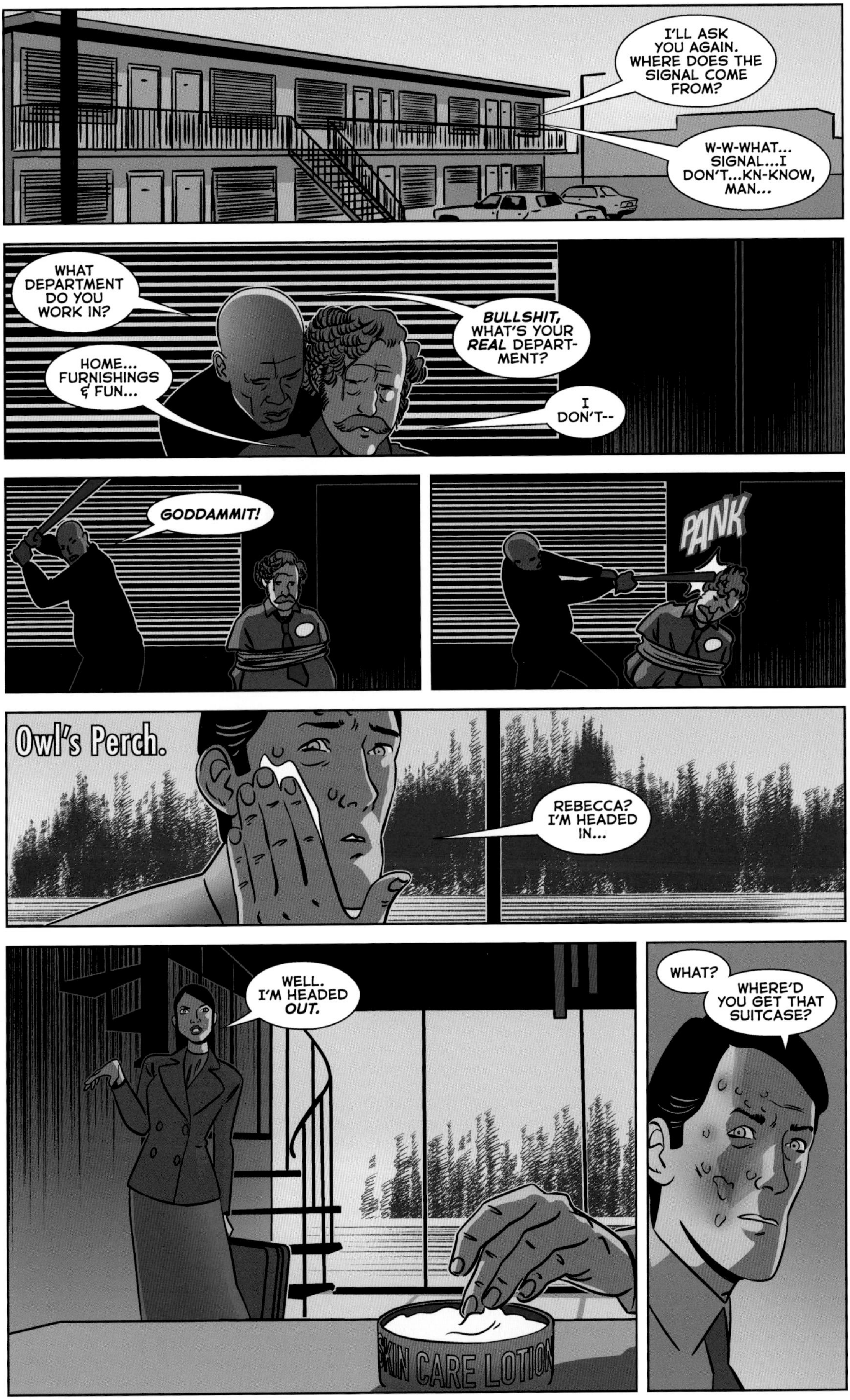
I'LL ASK YOU AGAIN. WHERE DOES THE SIGNAL COME FROM?
W-W-WHAT... SIGNAL...I DON'T...KN-KNOW, MAN...
WHAT DEPARTMENT DO YOU WORK IN?
HOME... FURNISHINGS & FUN...
BULLSHIT, WHAT'S YOUR REAL DEPARTMENT?
I DON'T--
GODDAMMIT!
PANK
Owl's Perch.
REBECCA? I'M HEADED IN...
WELL. I'M HEADED OUT.
WHAT?
WHERE'D YOU GET THAT SUITCASE?
SKIN CARE LOTION

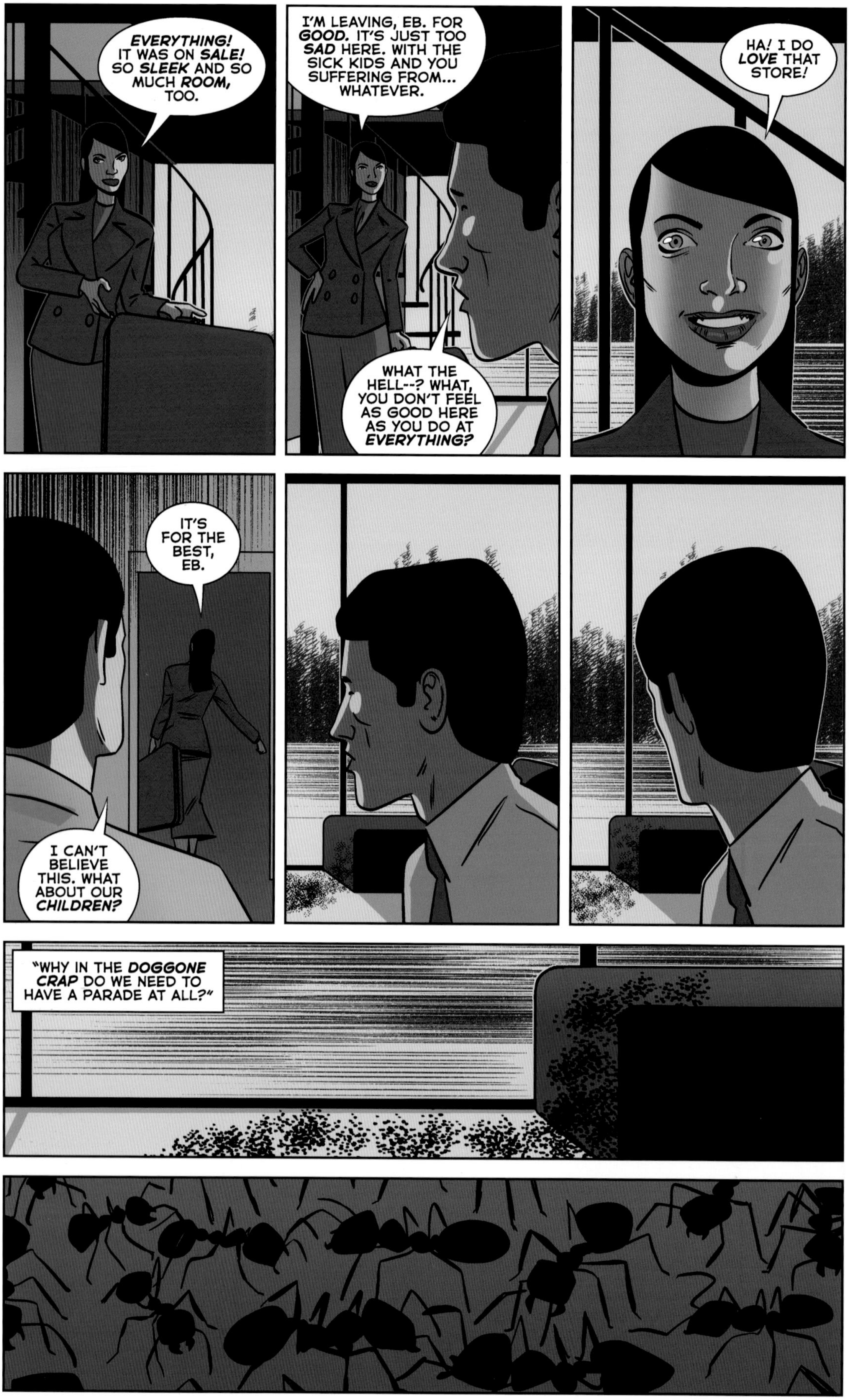
EVERYTHING! IT WAS ON SALE! SO SLEEK AND SO MUCH ROOM, TOO.
I'M LEAVING, EB. FOR GOOD. IT'S JUST TOO SAD HERE. WITH THE SICK KIDS AND YOU SUFFERING FROM... WHATEVER.
WHAT THE HELL--? WHAT, YOU DON'T FEEL AS GOOD HERE AS YOU DO AT EVERYTHING?
HA! I DO LOVE THAT STORE!
IT'S FOR THE BEST, EB.
I CAN'T BELIEVE THIS. WHAT ABOUT OUR CHILDREN?
"WHY IN THE DOGGONE CRAP DO WE NEED TO HAVE A PARADE AT ALL?"

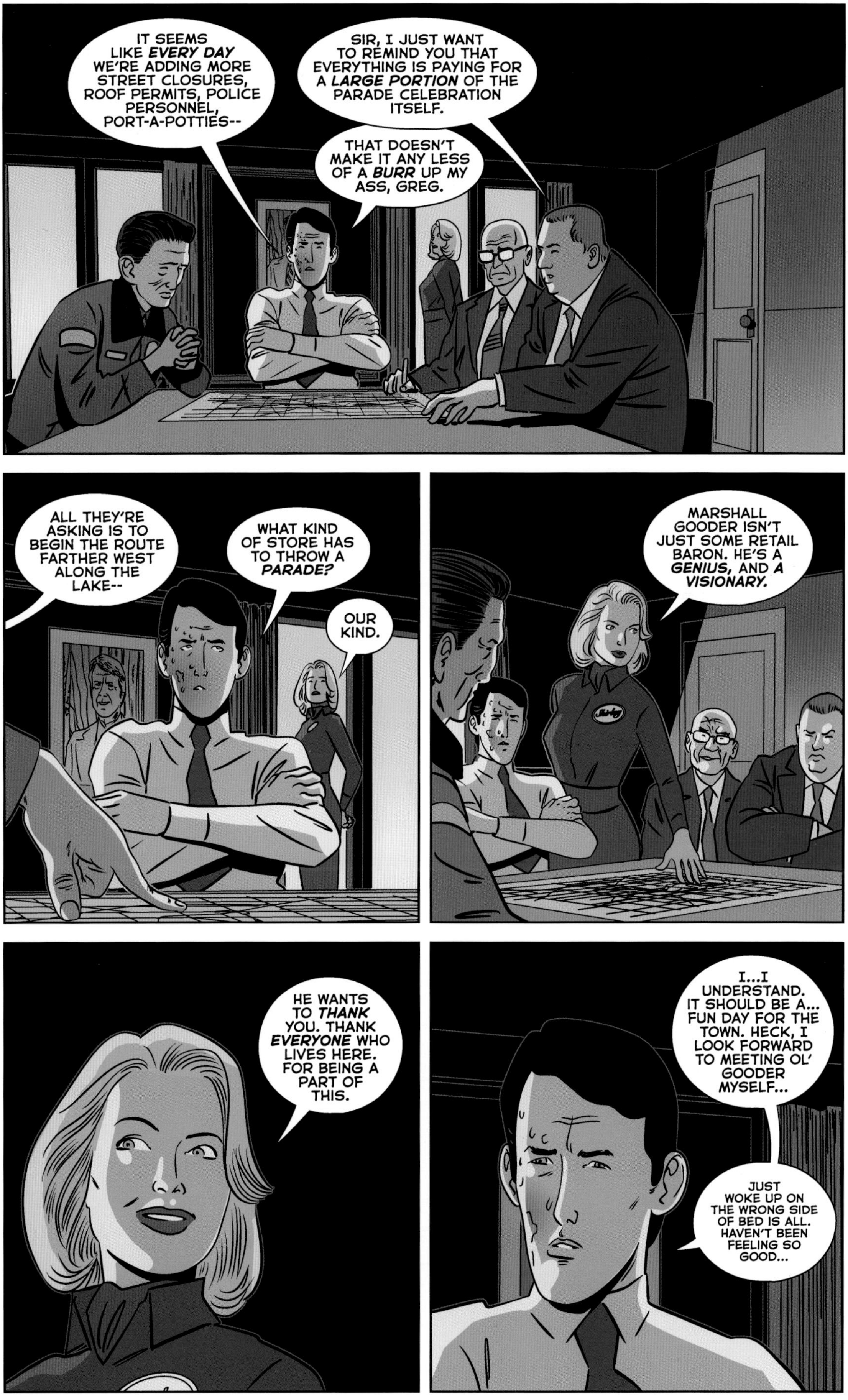

IT SEEMS LIKE EVERY DAY WE'RE ADDING MORE STREET CLOSURES, ROOF PERMITS, POLICE PERSONNEL, PORT-A-POTTIES--
SIR, I JUST WANT TO REMIND YOU THAT EVERYTHING IS PAYING FOR A LARGE PORTION OF THE PARADE CELEBRATION ITSELF.
THAT DOESN'T MAKE IT ANY LESS OF A BURR UP MY ASS, GREG.
ALL THEY'RE ASKING IS TO BEGIN THE ROUTE FARTHER WEST ALONG THE LAKE--
WHAT KIND OF STORE HAS TO THROW A PARADE?
OUR KIND.
MARSHALL GOODER ISN'T JUST SOME RETAIL BARON. HE'S A GENIUS, AND A VISIONARY.
HE WANTS TO THANK YOU. THANK EVERYONE WHO LIVES HERE. FOR BEING A PART OF THIS.
I...I UNDERSTAND. IT SHOULD BE A... FUN DAY FOR THE TOWN. HECK, I LOOK FORWARD TO MEETING OL' GOODER MYSELF...
JUST WOKE UP ON THE WRONG SIDE OF BED IS ALL. HAVEN'T BEEN FEELING SO GOOD...

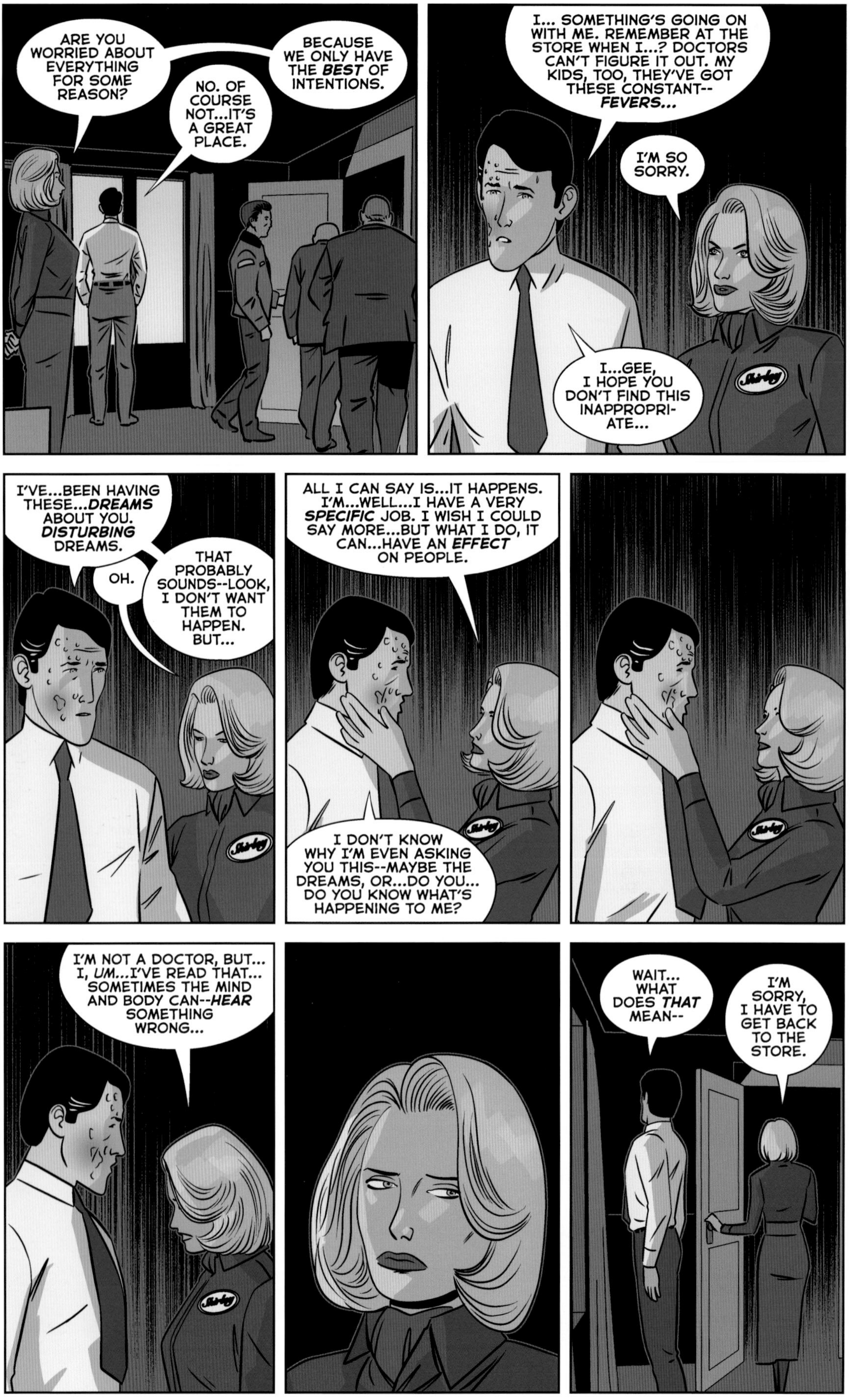
ARE YOU WORRIED ABOUT EVERYTHING FOR SOME REASON?
BECAUSE WE ONLY HAVE THE *BEST* OF INTENTIONS.
NO. OF COURSE NOT...IT'S A GREAT PLACE.
I... SOMETHING'S GOING ON WITH ME. REMEMBER AT THE STORE WHEN I...? DOCTORS CAN'T FIGURE IT OUT. MY KIDS, TOO, THEY'VE GOT THESE CONSTANT--*FEVERS...*
I'M SO SORRY.
I...GEE, I HOPE YOU DON'T FIND THIS INAPPROPRI-ATE...
I'VE...BEEN HAVING THESE...*DREAMS* ABOUT YOU. *DISTURBING* DREAMS.
OH.
THAT PROBABLY SOUNDS--LOOK, I DON'T WANT THEM TO HAPPEN. BUT...
ALL I CAN SAY IS...IT HAPPENS. I'M...WELL...I HAVE A VERY *SPECIFIC* JOB. I WISH I COULD SAY MORE...BUT WHAT I DO, IT CAN...HAVE AN *EFFECT* ON PEOPLE.
I DON'T KNOW WHY I'M EVEN ASKING YOU THIS--MAYBE THE DREAMS, OR...DO YOU... DO YOU KNOW WHAT'S HAPPENING TO ME?
I'M NOT A DOCTOR, BUT... I, *UM*...I'VE READ THAT... SOMETIMES THE MIND AND BODY CAN--*HEAR* SOMETHING WRONG...
WAIT... WHAT DOES *THAT* MEAN--
I'M SORRY, I HAVE TO GET BACK TO THE STORE.

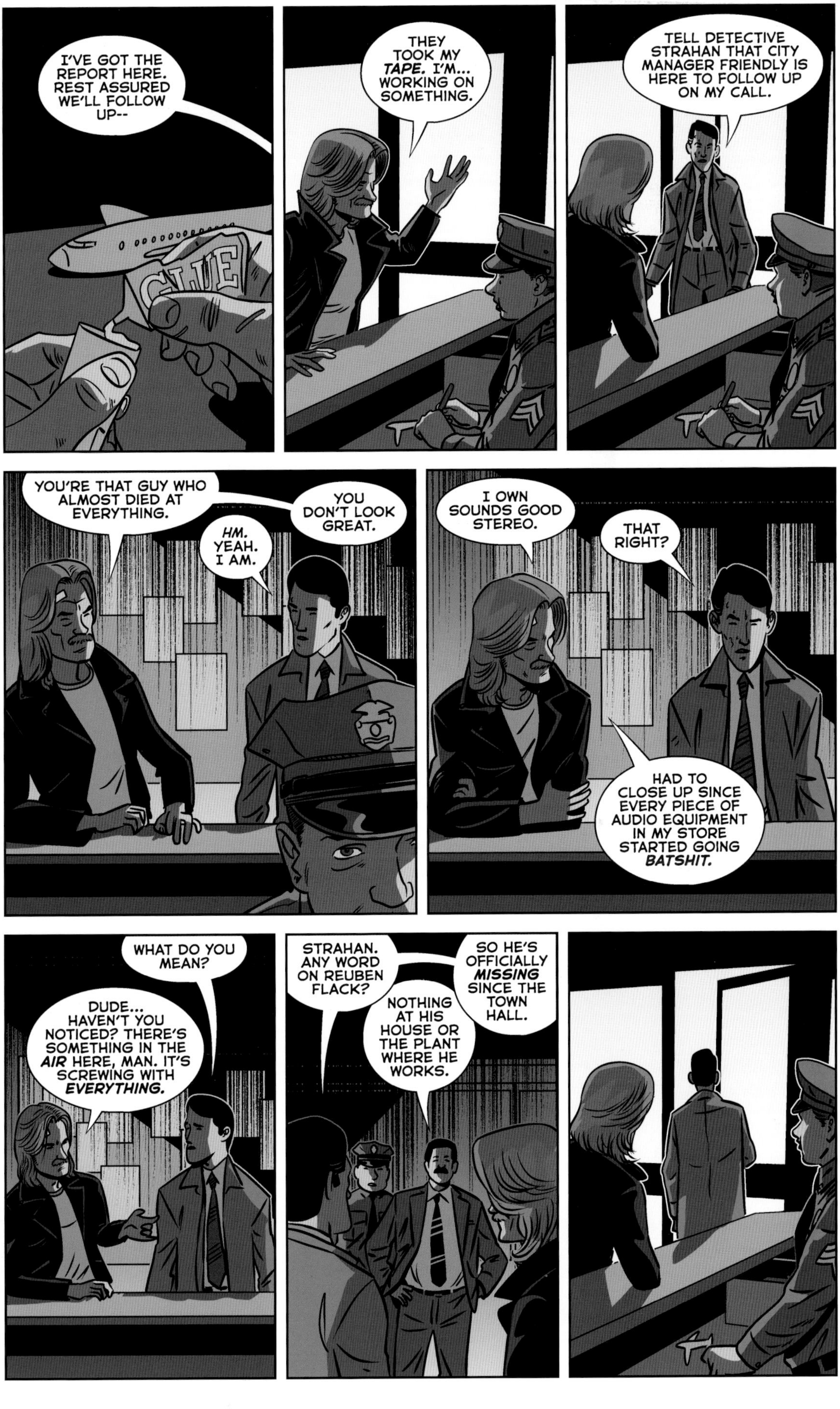
I'VE GOT THE REPORT HERE. REST ASSURED WE'LL FOLLOW UP--
CLUE
THEY TOOK MY *TAPE.* I'M... WORKING ON SOMETHING.
TELL DETECTIVE STRAHAN THAT CITY MANAGER FRIENDLY IS HERE TO FOLLOW UP ON MY CALL.
YOU'RE THAT GUY WHO ALMOST DIED AT EVERYTHING.
YOU DON'T LOOK GREAT.
HM. YEAH. I AM.
I OWN SOUNDS GOOD STEREO.
THAT RIGHT?
HAD TO CLOSE UP SINCE EVERY PIECE OF AUDIO EQUIPMENT IN MY STORE STARTED GOING *BATSHIT.*
WHAT DO YOU MEAN?
DUDE... HAVEN'T YOU NOTICED? THERE'S SOMETHING IN THE *AIR* HERE, MAN. IT'S SCREWING WITH *EVERYTHING.*
STRAHAN. ANY WORD ON REUBEN FLACK?
NOTHING AT HIS HOUSE OR THE PLANT WHERE HE WORKS.
SO HE'S OFFICIALLY *MISSING* SINCE THE TOWN HALL.

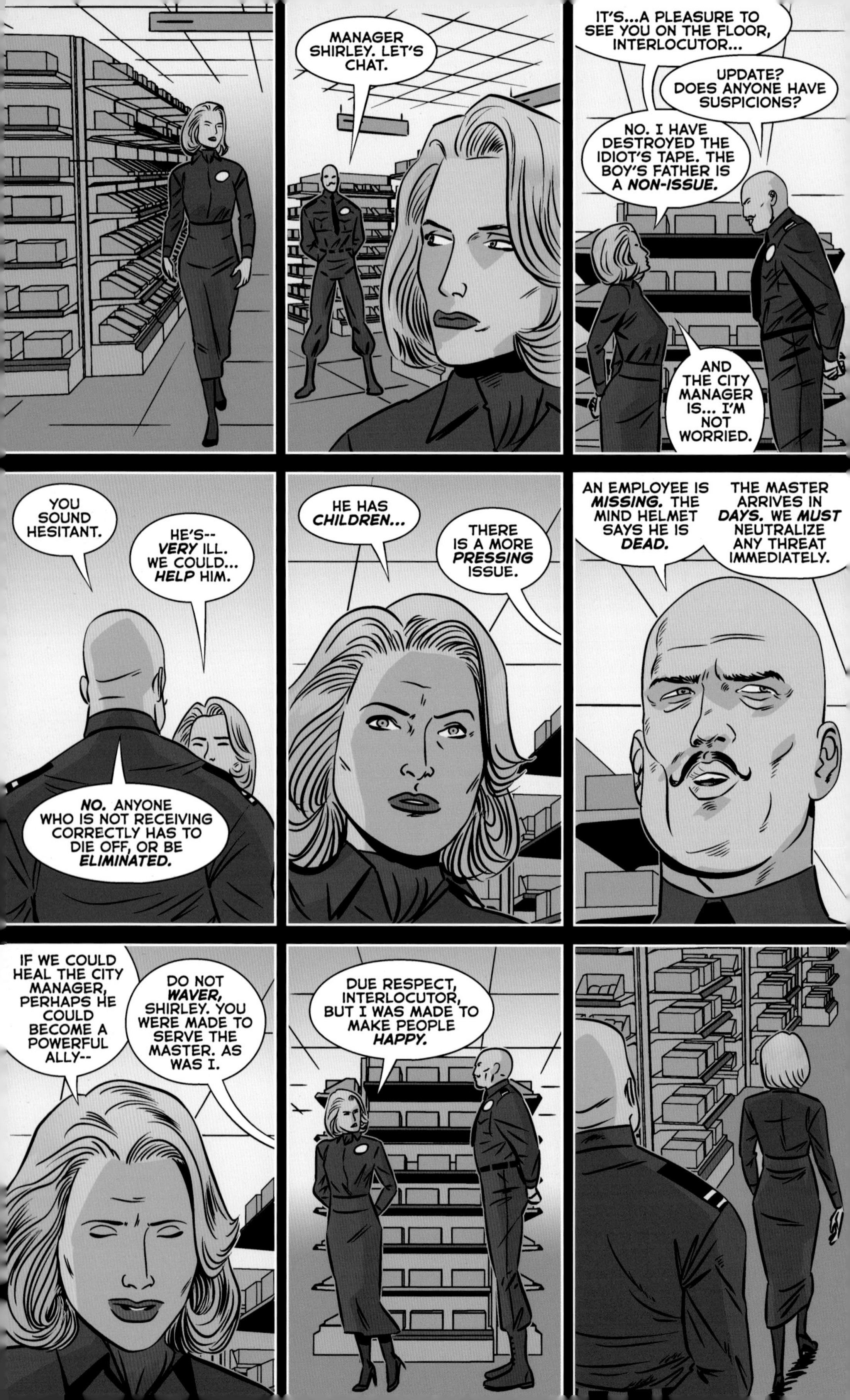
MANAGER SHIRLEY. LET'S CHAT.
IT'S...A PLEASURE TO SEE YOU ON THE FLOOR, INTERLOCUTOR...
UPDATE? DOES ANYONE HAVE SUSPICIONS?
NO. I HAVE DESTROYED THE IDIOT'S TAPE. THE BOY'S FATHER IS A NON-ISSUE.
AND THE CITY MANAGER IS... I'M NOT WORRIED.
YOU SOUND HESITANT.
HE'S-- VERY ILL. WE COULD... HELP HIM.
NO. ANYONE WHO IS NOT RECEIVING CORRECTLY HAS TO DIE OFF, OR BE ELIMINATED.
HE HAS CHILDREN...
THERE IS A MORE PRESSING ISSUE.
AN EMPLOYEE IS MISSING. THE MIND HELMET SAYS HE IS DEAD.
THE MASTER ARRIVES IN DAYS. WE MUST NEUTRALIZE ANY THREAT IMMEDIATELY.
IF WE COULD HEAL THE CITY MANAGER, PERHAPS HE COULD BECOME A POWERFUL ALLY--
DO NOT WAVER, SHIRLEY. YOU WERE MADE TO SERVE THE MASTER. AS WAS I.
DUE RESPECT, INTERLOCUTOR, BUT I WAS MADE TO MAKE PEOPLE HAPPY.

NEAT FLOWERS.

HUH?

COOL COLORS.

...DO I KNOW YOU?

EH. I'M IN THIS PLACE A LOT.

THAT... LOOKS LIKE SOME *SERIOUS* MATH.

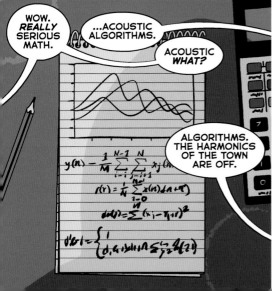

WOW. *REALLY* SERIOUS MATH.

...ACOUSTIC ALGORITHMS.

ACOUSTIC *WHAT?*

ALGORITHMS. THE HARMONICS OF THE TOWN ARE OFF.

HARMONICS?

MMHM. HOLLAND'S *FUNDAMENTAL FREQUENCY* HAS CHANGED AND I'M GETTING BIZARRE *SINUSOIDAL* WAVES FROM MY UH, 'SERIOUS MATH' HERE.

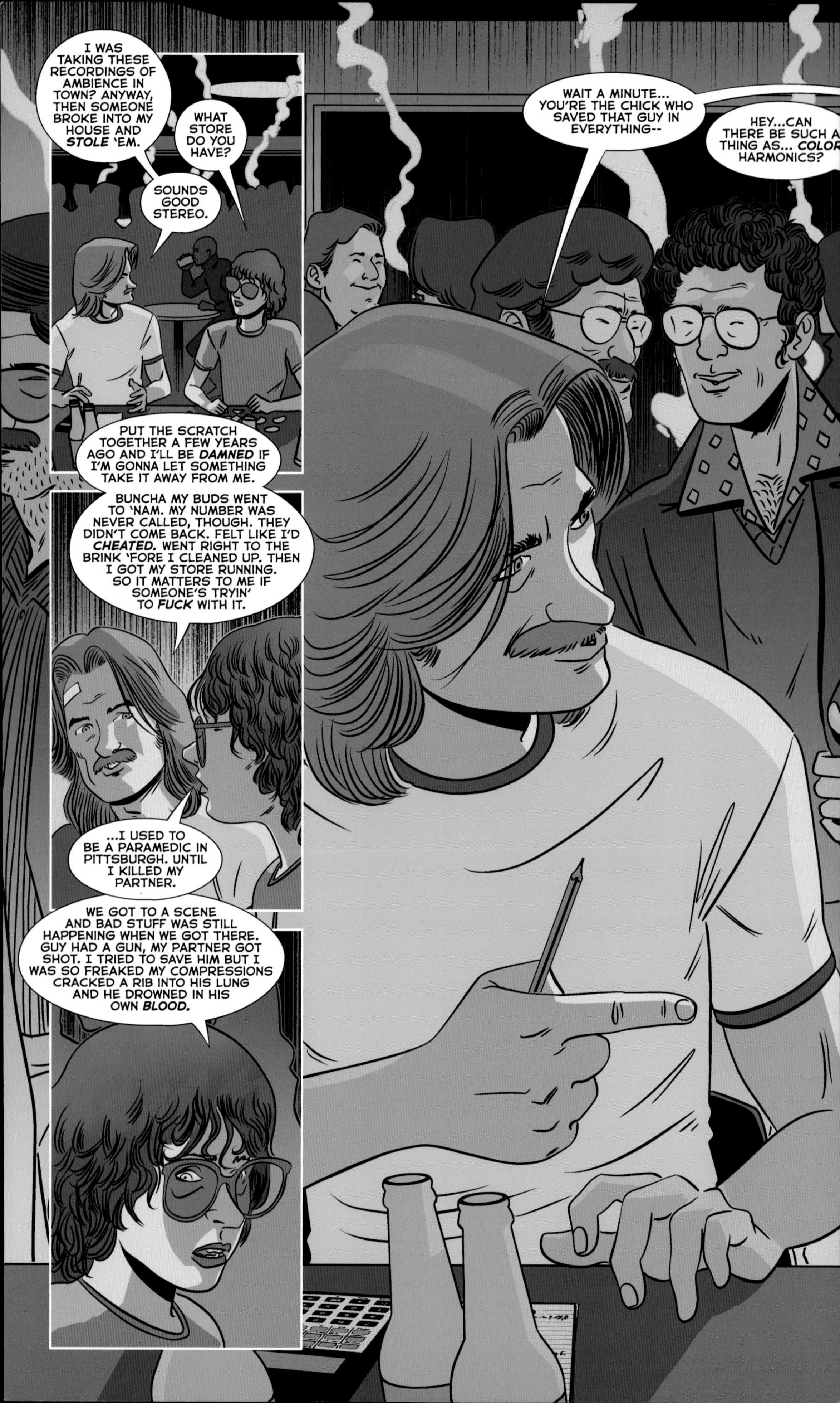

I WAS TAKING THESE RECORDINGS OF AMBIENCE IN TOWN? ANYWAY, THEN SOMEONE BROKE INTO MY HOUSE AND STOLE 'EM.
WHAT STORE DO YOU HAVE?
SOUNDS GOOD STEREO.
PUT THE SCRATCH TOGETHER A FEW YEARS AGO AND I'LL BE DAMNED IF I'M GONNA LET SOMETHING TAKE IT AWAY FROM ME.
BUNCHA MY BUDS WENT TO 'NAM. MY NUMBER WAS NEVER CALLED, THOUGH. THEY DIDN'T COME BACK. FELT LIKE I'D CHEATED. WENT RIGHT TO THE BRINK 'FORE I CLEANED UP. THEN I GOT MY STORE RUNNING. SO IT MATTERS TO ME IF SOMEONE'S TRYIN' TO FUCK WITH IT.
...I USED TO BE A PARAMEDIC IN PITTSBURGH. UNTIL I KILLED MY PARTNER.
WE GOT TO A SCENE AND BAD STUFF WAS STILL HAPPENING WHEN WE GOT THERE. GUY HAD A GUN, MY PARTNER GOT SHOT. I TRIED TO SAVE HIM BUT I WAS SO FREAKED MY COMPRESSIONS CRACKED A RIB INTO HIS LUNG AND HE DROWNED IN HIS OWN BLOOD.
WAIT A MINUTE... YOU'RE THE CHICK WHO SAVED THAT GUY IN EVERYTHING--
HEY...CAN THERE BE SUCH A THING AS... COLOR HARMONICS?

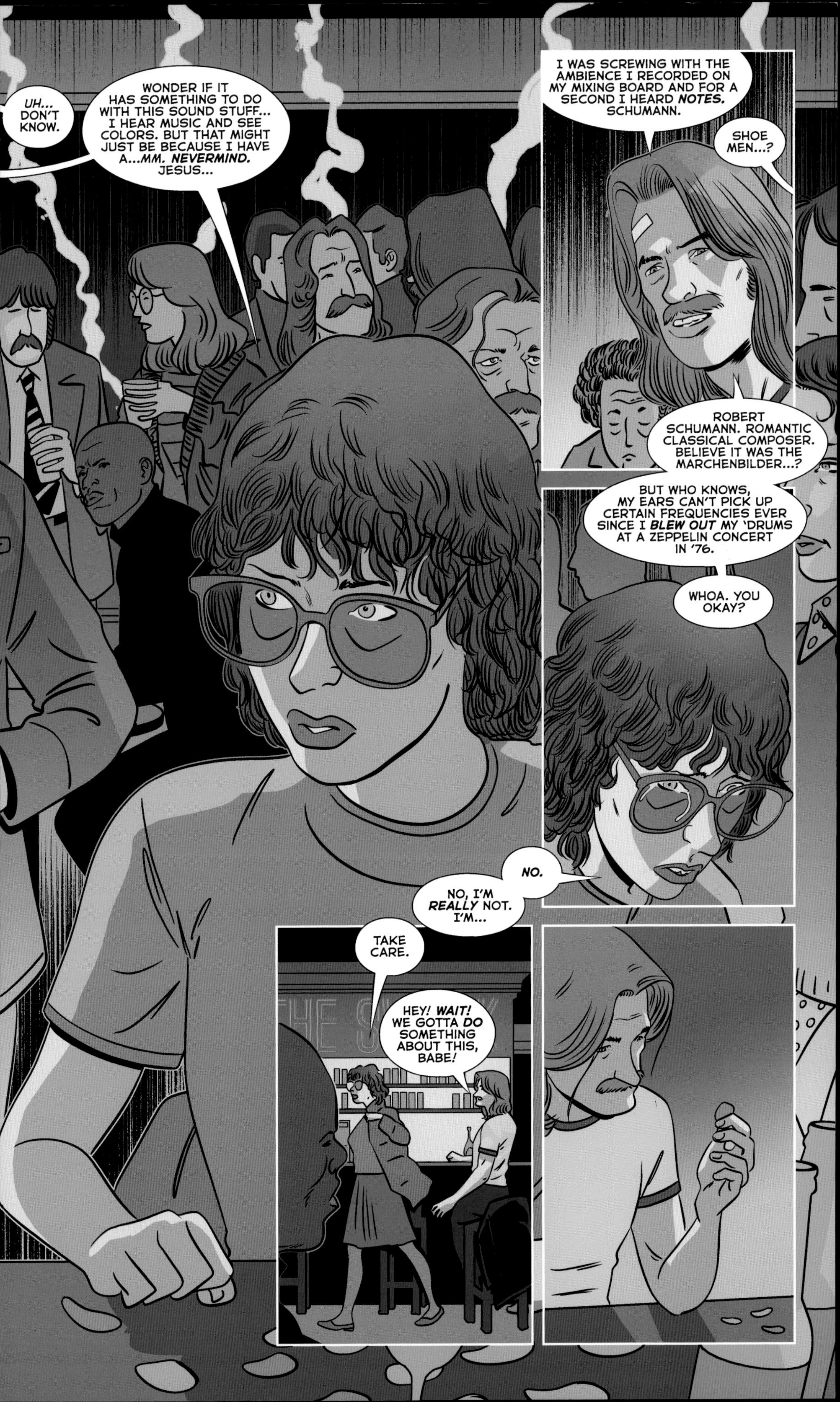

UH... DON'T KNOW.
WONDER IF IT HAS SOMETHING TO DO WITH THIS SOUND STUFF... I HEAR MUSIC AND SEE COLORS. BUT THAT MIGHT JUST BE BECAUSE I HAVE A...MM. NEVERMIND. JESUS...
I WAS SCREWING WITH THE AMBIENCE I RECORDED ON MY MIXING BOARD AND FOR A SECOND I HEARD NOTES. SCHUMANN.
SHOE MEN...?
ROBERT SCHUMANN. ROMANTIC CLASSICAL COMPOSER. BELIEVE IT WAS THE MARCHENBILDER...?
BUT WHO KNOWS, MY EARS CAN'T PICK UP CERTAIN FREQUENCIES EVER SINCE I BLEW OUT MY 'DRUMS AT A ZEPPELIN CONCERT IN '76.
WHOA. YOU OKAY?
NO.
NO, I'M REALLY NOT. I'M...
TAKE CARE.
HEY! WAIT! WE GOTTA DO SOMETHING ABOUT THIS, BABE!

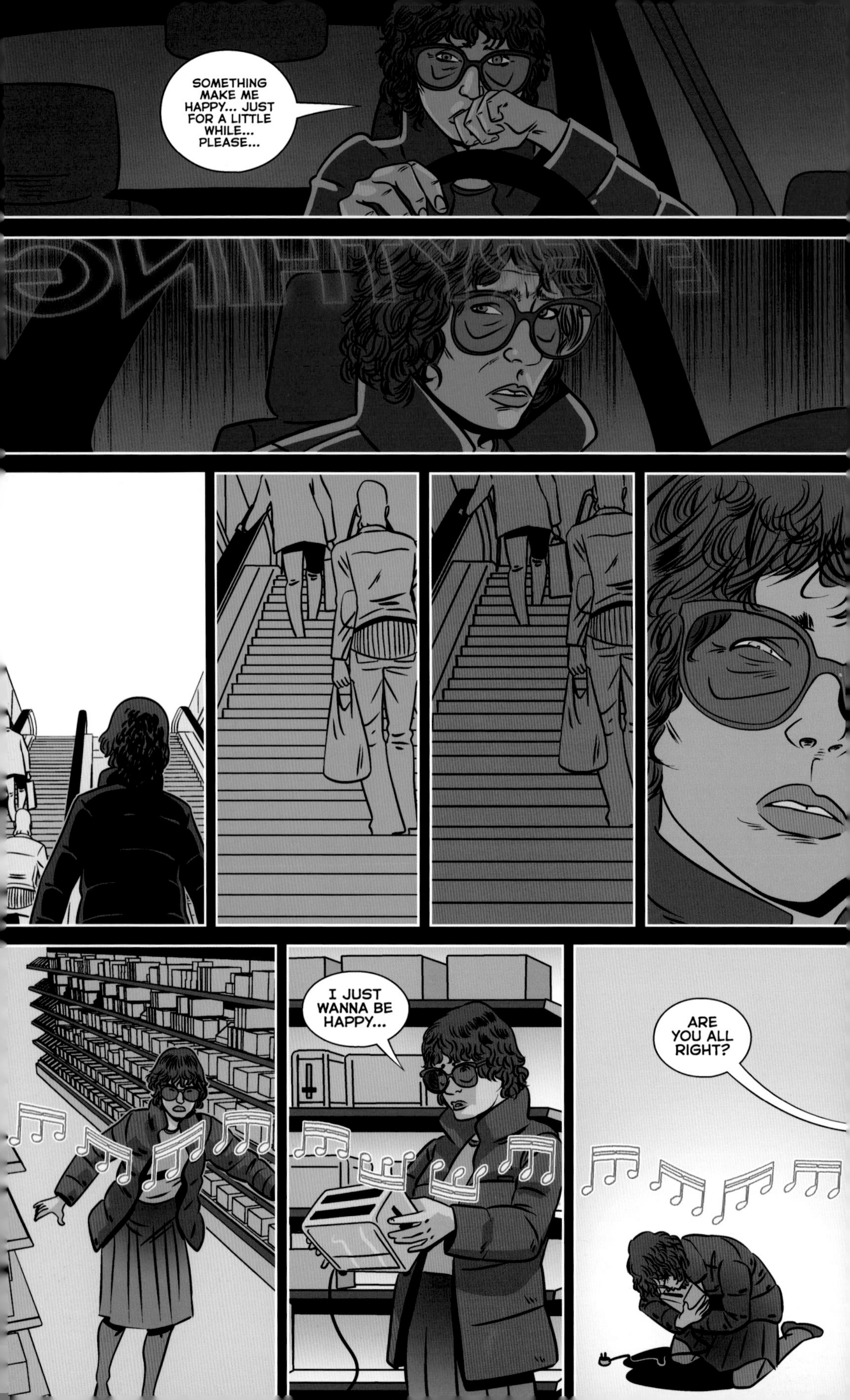
SOMETHING MAKE ME HAPPY... JUST FOR A LITTLE WHILE... PLEASE...
I JUST WANNA BE HAPPY...
ARE YOU ALL RIGHT?

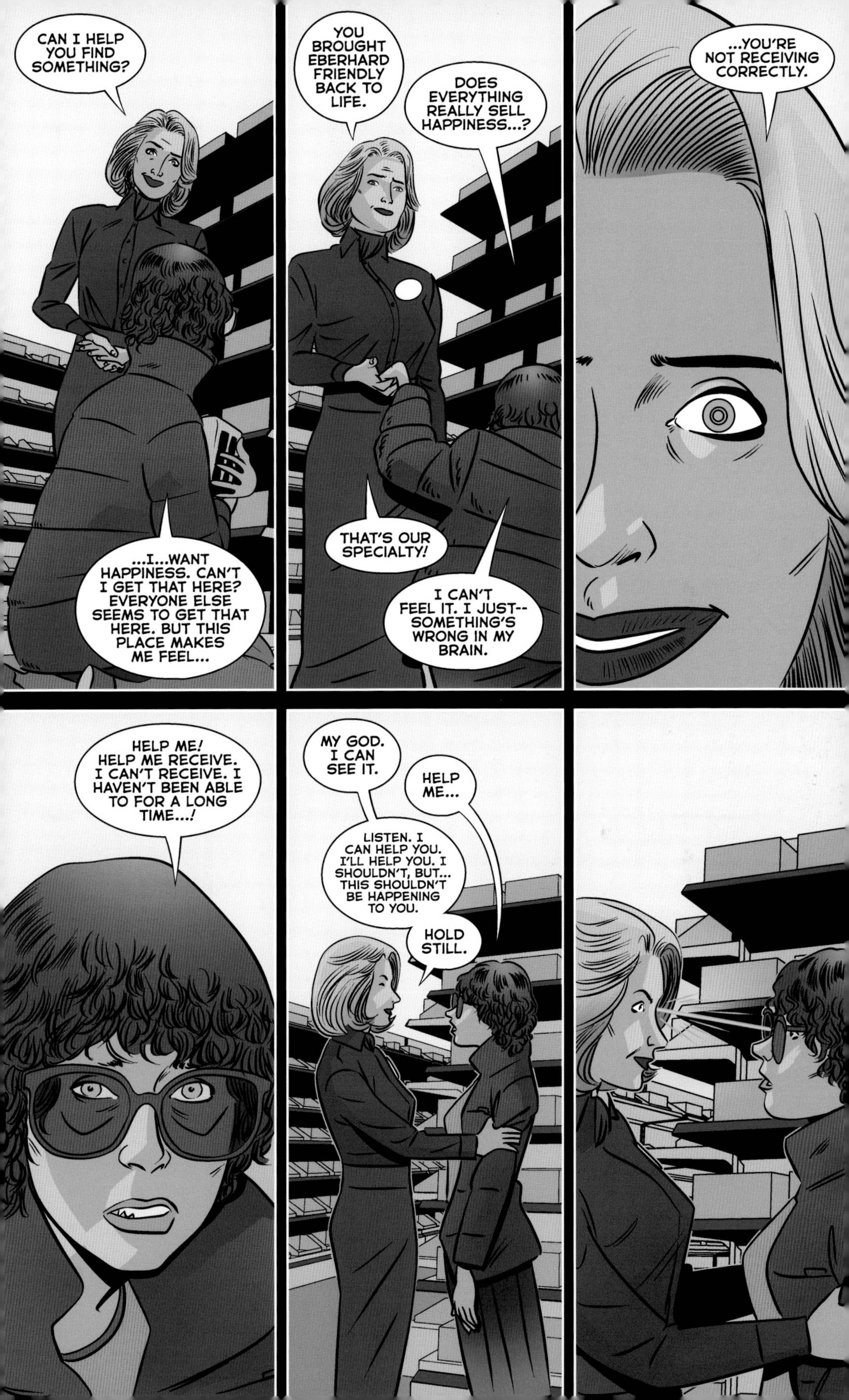
CAN I HELP YOU FIND SOMETHING?
...I...WANT HAPPINESS. CAN'T I GET THAT HERE? EVERYONE ELSE SEEMS TO GET THAT HERE. BUT THIS PLACE MAKES ME FEEL...
YOU BROUGHT EBERHARD FRIENDLY BACK TO LIFE.
DOES EVERYTHING REALLY SELL HAPPINESS...?
THAT'S OUR SPECIALTY!
I CAN'T FEEL IT. I JUST--SOMETHING'S WRONG IN MY BRAIN.
...YOU'RE NOT RECEIVING CORRECTLY.
HELP ME! HELP ME RECEIVE. I CAN'T RECEIVE. I HAVEN'T BEEN ABLE TO FOR A LONG TIME...!
MY GOD. I CAN SEE IT.
HELP ME...
LISTEN. I CAN HELP YOU. I'LL HELP YOU. I SHOULDN'T, BUT... THIS SHOULDN'T BE HAPPENING TO YOU.
HOLD STILL.

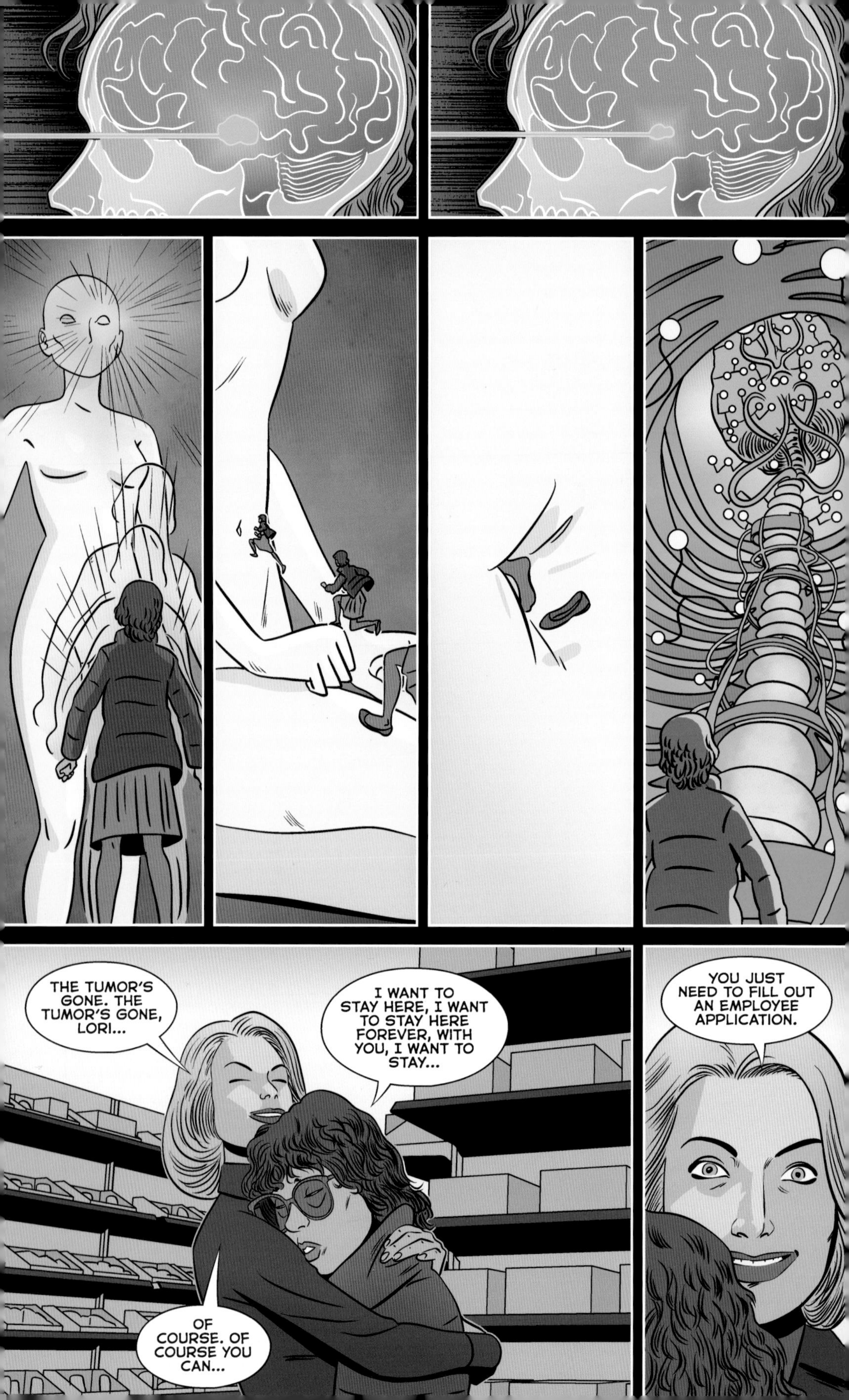
THE TUMOR'S GONE. THE TUMOR'S GONE, LORI...
I WANT TO STAY HERE, I WANT TO STAY HERE FOREVER, WITH YOU, I WANT TO STAY...
OF COURSE. OF COURSE YOU CAN...
YOU JUST NEED TO FILL OUT AN EMPLOYEE APPLICATION.

Chapter 5:
"C'mon, Get Happy"

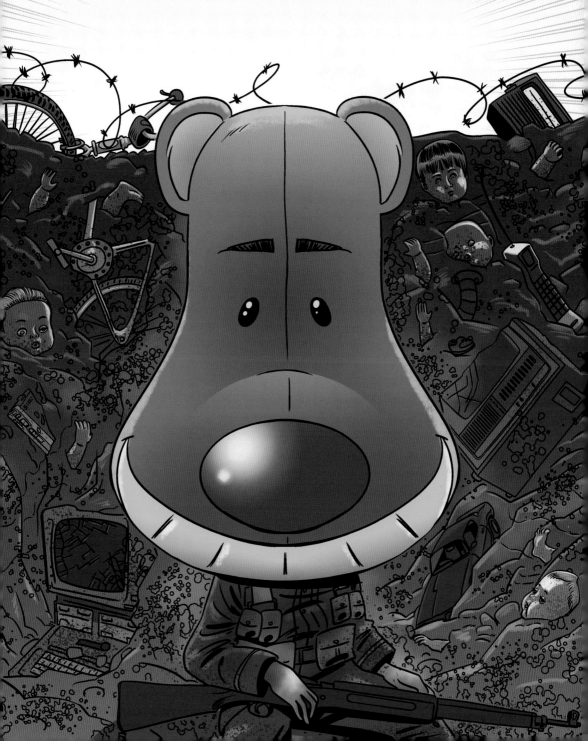

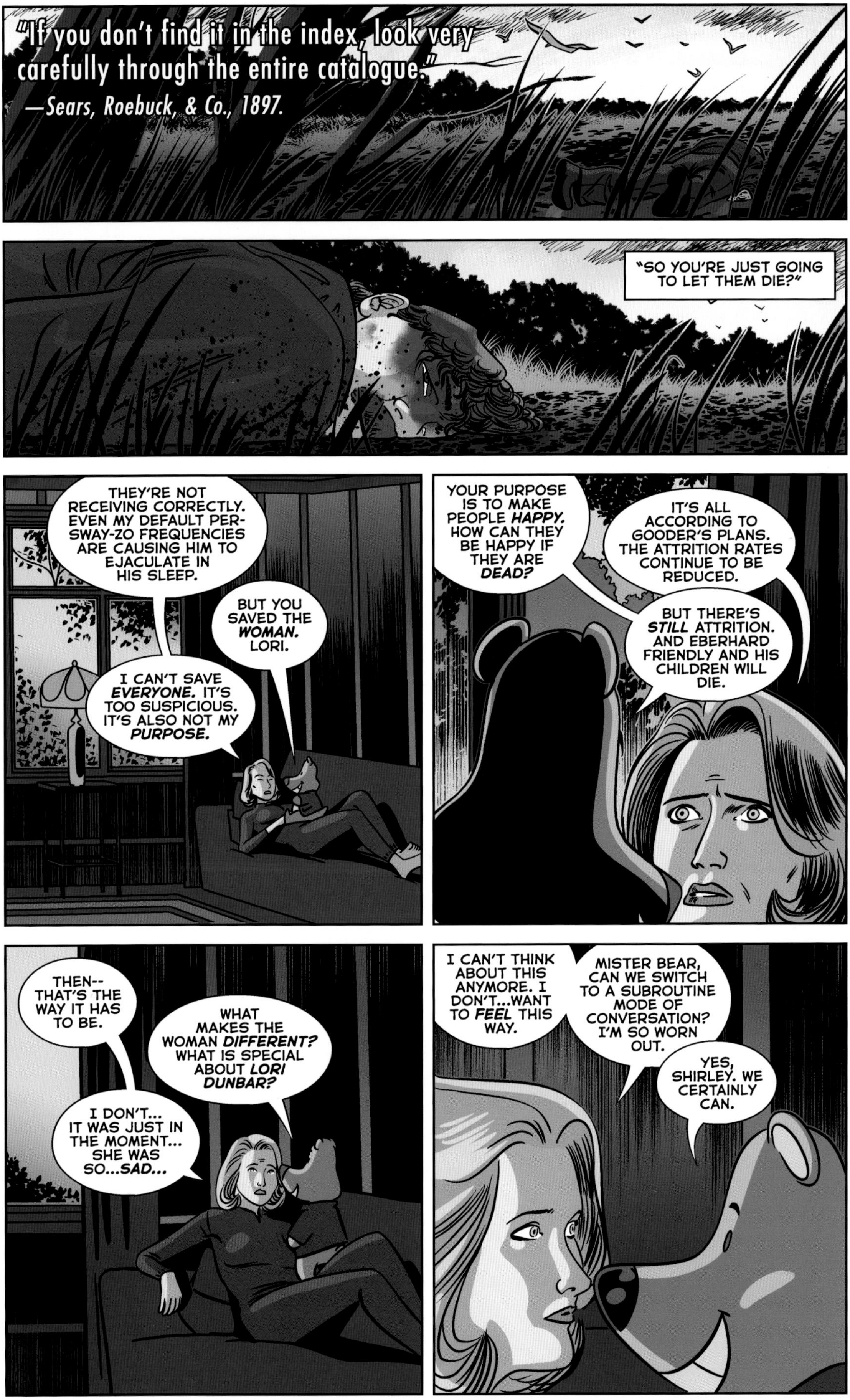
"If you don't find it in the index, look very carefully through the entire catalogue."
—Sears, Roebuck, & Co., 1897.
"SO YOU'RE JUST GOING TO LET THEM DIE?"
THEY'RE NOT RECEIVING CORRECTLY. EVEN MY DEFAULT PER-SWAY-ZO FREQUENCIES ARE CAUSING HIM TO EJACULATE IN HIS SLEEP.
BUT YOU SAVED THE WOMAN. LORI.
I CAN'T SAVE EVERYONE. IT'S TOO SUSPICIOUS. IT'S ALSO NOT MY PURPOSE.
YOUR PURPOSE IS TO MAKE PEOPLE HAPPY. HOW CAN THEY BE HAPPY IF THEY ARE DEAD?
IT'S ALL ACCORDING TO GOODER'S PLANS. THE ATTRITION RATES CONTINUE TO BE REDUCED.
BUT THERE'S STILL ATTRITION. AND EBERHARD FRIENDLY AND HIS CHILDREN WILL DIE.
THEN-- THAT'S THE WAY IT HAS TO BE.
WHAT MAKES THE WOMAN DIFFERENT? WHAT IS SPECIAL ABOUT LORI DUNBAR?
I DON'T... IT WAS JUST IN THE MOMENT... SHE WAS SO...SAD...
I CAN'T THINK ABOUT THIS ANYMORE. I DON'T...WANT TO FEEL THIS WAY.
MISTER BEAR, CAN WE SWITCH TO A SUBROUTINE MODE OF CONVERSATION? I'M SO WORN OUT.
YES, SHIRLEY. WE CERTAINLY CAN.

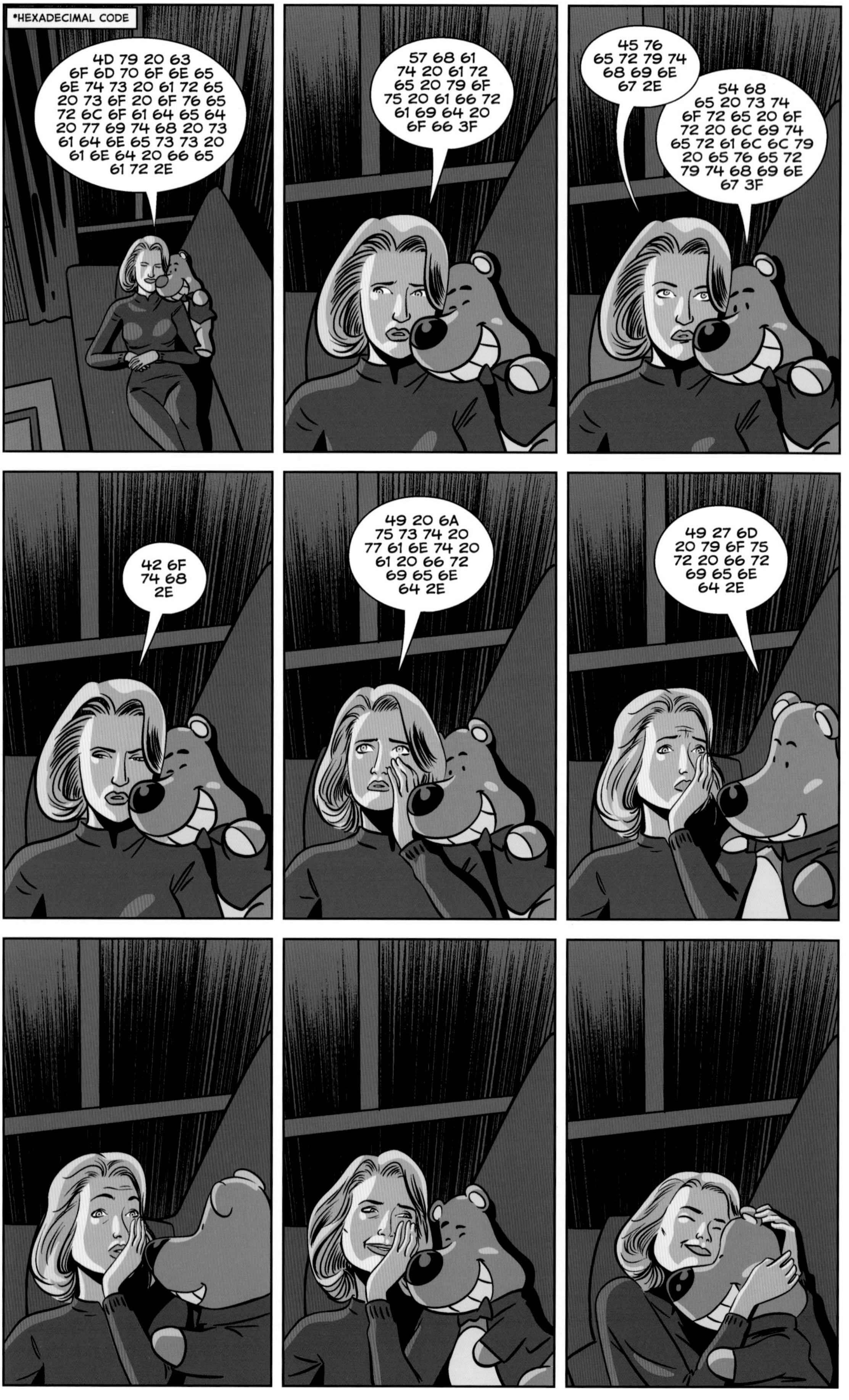
*HEXADECIMAL CODE
4D 79 20 63 6F 6D 70 6F 6E 65 6E 74 73 20 61 72 65 20 73 6F 20 6F 76 65 72 6C 6F 61 64 65 64 20 77 69 74 68 20 73 61 64 6E 65 73 73 20 61 6E 64 20 66 65 61 72 2E
57 68 61 74 20 61 72 65 20 79 6F 75 20 61 66 72 61 69 64 20 6F 66 3F
45 76 65 72 79 74 68 69 6E 67 2E
54 68 65 20 73 74 6F 72 65 20 6F 72 20 6C 69 74 65 72 61 6C 6C 79 20 65 76 65 72 79 74 68 69 6E 67 3F
42 6F 74 68 2E
49 20 6A 75 73 74 20 77 61 6E 74 20 61 20 66 72 69 65 6E 64 2E
49 27 6D 20 79 6F 75 72 20 66 72 69 65 6E 64 2E

I DON'T UNDERSTAND, THE ENTIRE *GOD-BLESSED HOUSE?!*

YES, WE'RE GOING TO HAVE TO DO A FULL EXTERMINATION--

--AND LOCATE THE SOURCE OF THE ANTS.

Owl's Perch.

I HAVE TWO *VERY ILL* CHILDREN! YOU KNOW HOW *STRENUOUS* THIS WILL BE FOR THEM?

I'M SORRY, GIRLS...BUT WE'RE GOING TO HAVE TO LEAVE FOR A BIT.

WE WON'T, SWEETIE... THEY JUST HAVE TO TAKE CARE OF THE...*ANT PROBLEM.*

DADDY, I DON'T WANT TO GO BACK TO THE HOSPITAL AGAIN.

...IT'S OKAY, DADDY...I COULD USE A CHANGE OF SCENERY...

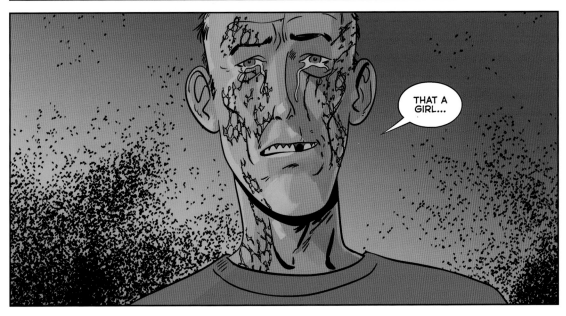

THAT A GIRL...

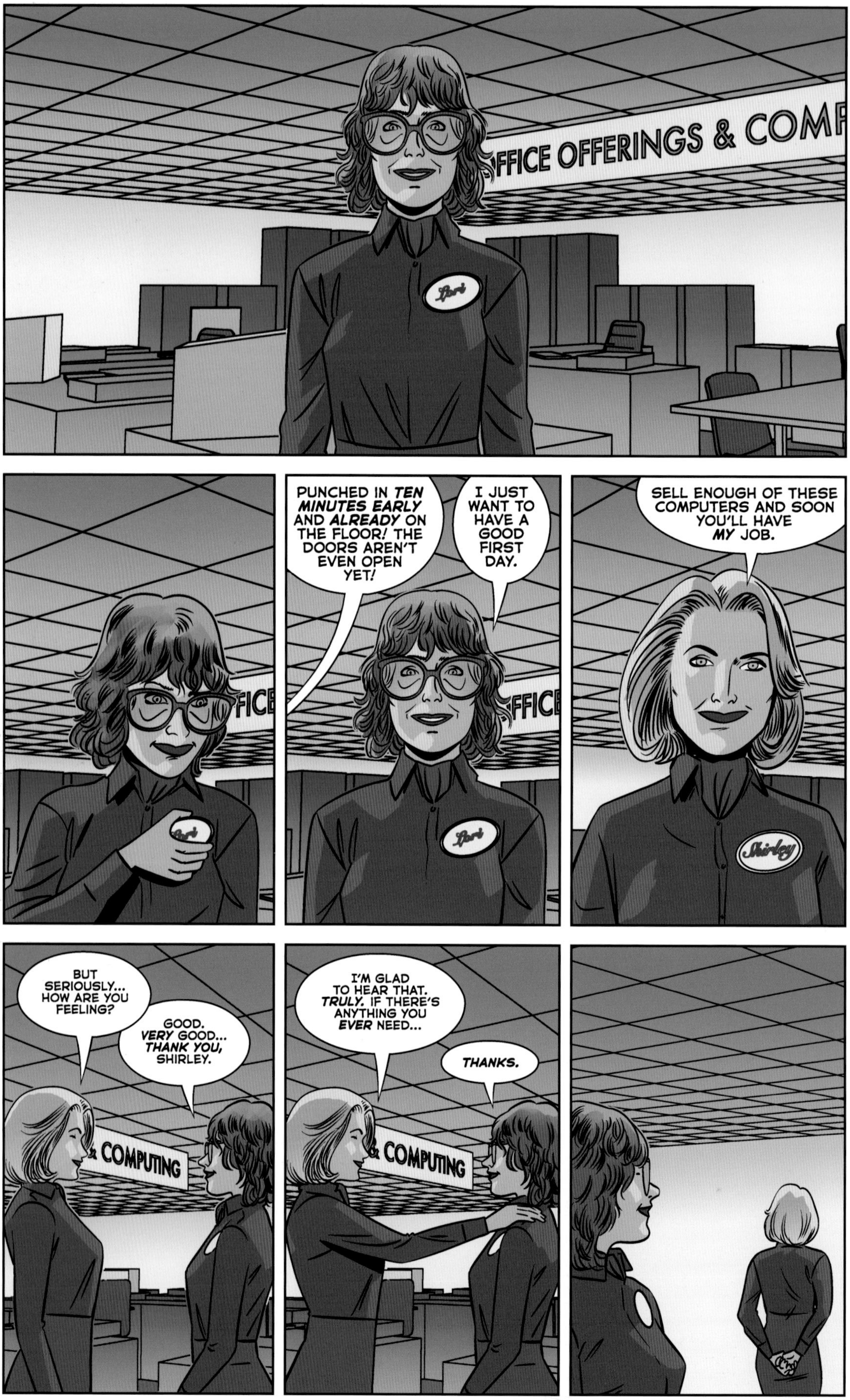

OFFICE OFFERINGS & COMP
Lori
PUNCHED IN TEN MINUTES EARLY AND ALREADY ON THE FLOOR! THE DOORS AREN'T EVEN OPEN YET!
I JUST WANT TO HAVE A GOOD FIRST DAY.
SELL ENOUGH OF THESE COMPUTERS AND SOON YOU'LL HAVE MY JOB.
Shirley
BUT SERIOUSLY... HOW ARE YOU FEELING?
GOOD. VERY GOOD... THANK YOU, SHIRLEY.
& COMPUTING
I'M GLAD TO HEAR THAT. TRULY. IF THERE'S ANYTHING YOU EVER NEED...
THANKS.

GOOD MORNING, SHOPPERS, WELCOME TO *EVERYTHING YOU NEED.* REMEMBER TOMORROW IS THE EVERYTHING JAMBOREE CELEBRATION PARADE, SO THE STORE WILL BE CLOSED...THE ONLY DAY *EVER!*

HEY, BUD! CHANGE YOUR MIND?

YEAH, I THINK I'M GONNA GO WITH A CREVELLO...BUT I WANTED TO CHECK OUT MY FAVORITE ALBUM ON A TURNTABLE FIRST.

WHOA, *CLASSICAL?* LET'S DO IT TO IT.

1 STEREO   SLA-4535
SCHUMANN – Märchenbilder, Op. 113
1. Nicht schnell (Moderato)
2. Lebhaft (Allegro)
3. Rasch (Allegro)
4. Langsam, mit melancholischem Ausdruck (Adagio)

YOU MIND? THERE'S ONE MOVEMENT I LOVE ON HERE.

GO AHEAD, *AMIGO.* THAT'S A *GOLD NEEDLE,* SO IT'LL PROBABLY SOUND BETTER THAN YOU'VE EVER HEARD IT...

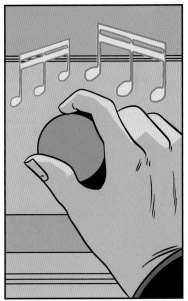

FFZZZZZZSSH FFZZZZZBUY--HAPP JOY--BUY--HAPPY-- COMFORT--BUY--

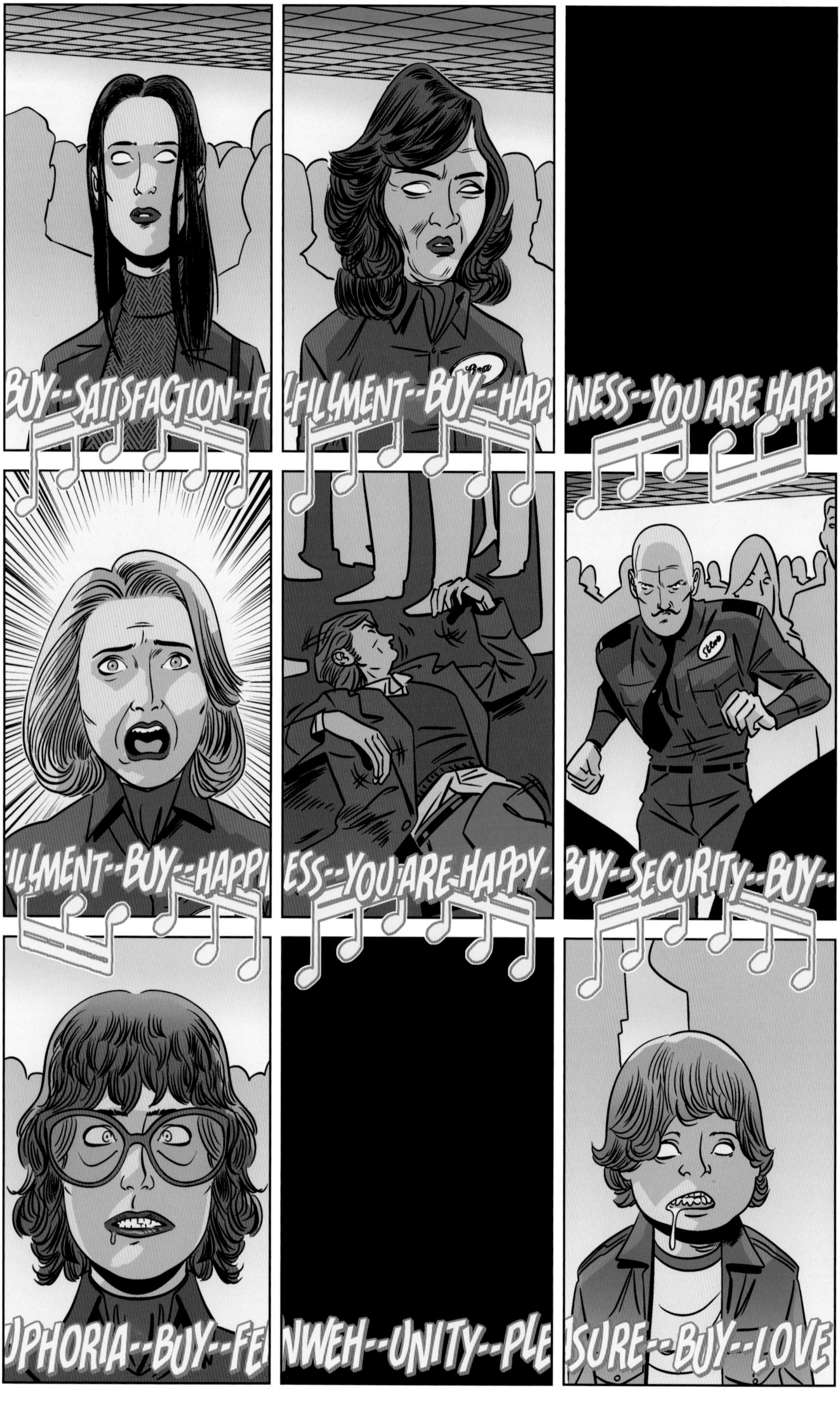
BUY--SATISFACTION--FULFILLMENT--BUY--HAPPINESS--YOU ARE HAPP
FILLMENT--BUY--HAPPINESS--YOU ARE HAPPY--BUY--SECURITY--BUY--
UPHORIA--BUY--FERNWEH--UNITY--PLEASURE--BUY--LOVE

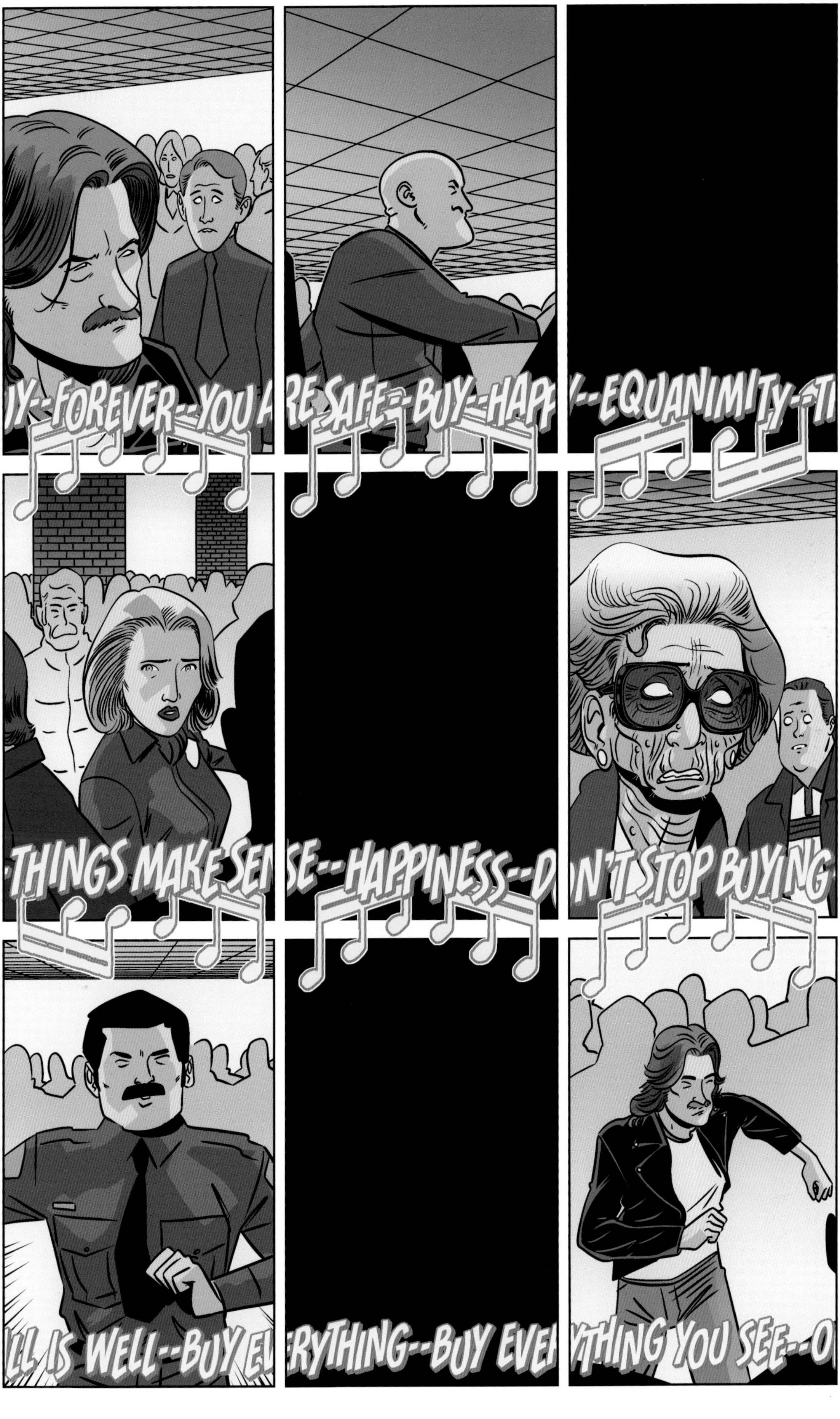

UY--FOREVER--YOU ARE SAFE--BUY--HAPPY--EQUANIMITY--TI
--THINGS MAKE SENSE--HAPPINESS--DON'T STOP BUYING
LL IS WELL--BUY EVERYTHING--BUY EVERYTHING YOU SEE--O

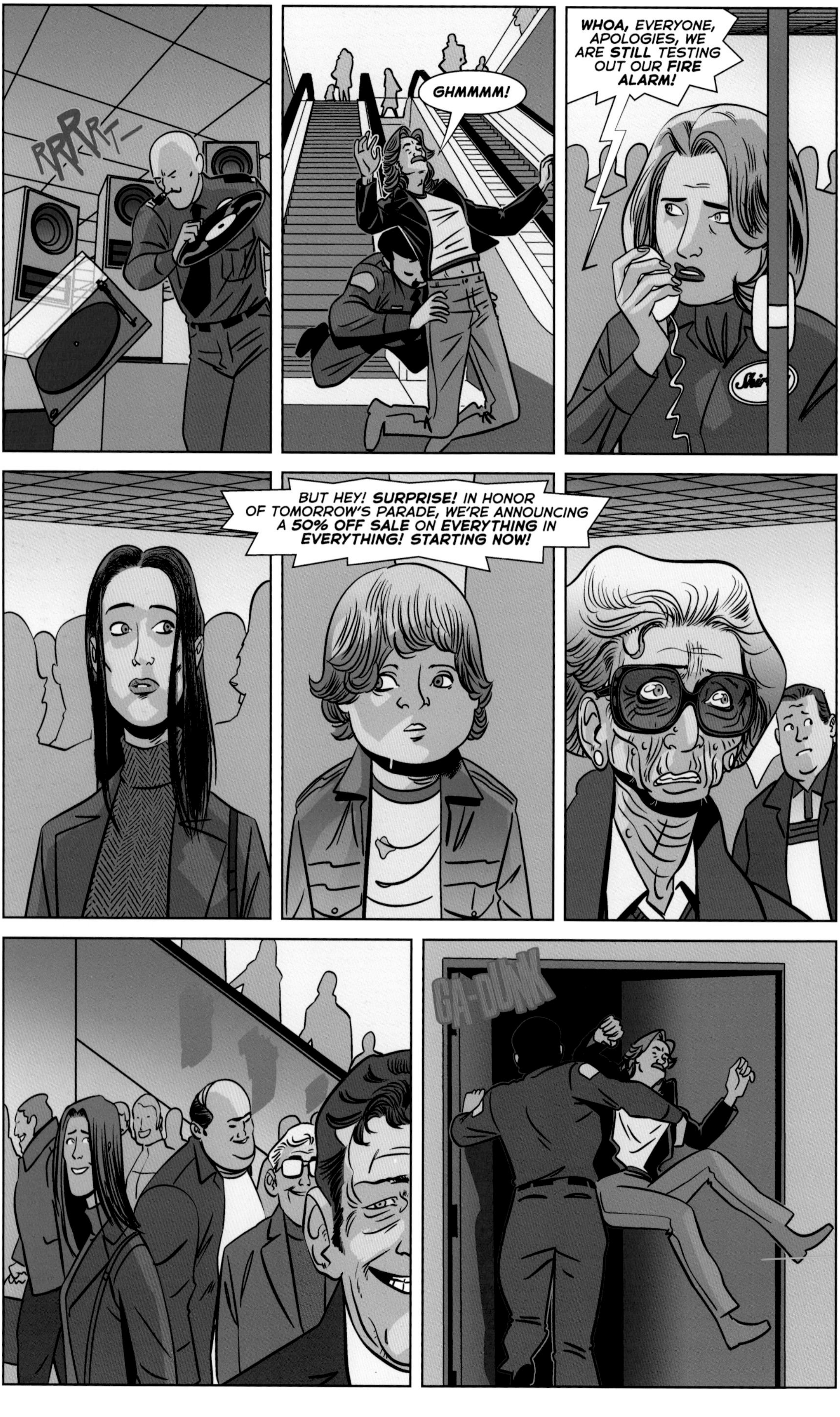

RRRRT—
GHMMMM!
WHOA, EVERYONE, APOLOGIES, WE ARE STILL TESTING OUT OUR FIRE ALARM!
BUT HEY! SURPRISE! IN HONOR OF TOMORROW'S PARADE, WE'RE ANNOUNCING A 50% OFF SALE ON EVERYTHING IN EVERYTHING! STARTING NOW!
GA-DUNK

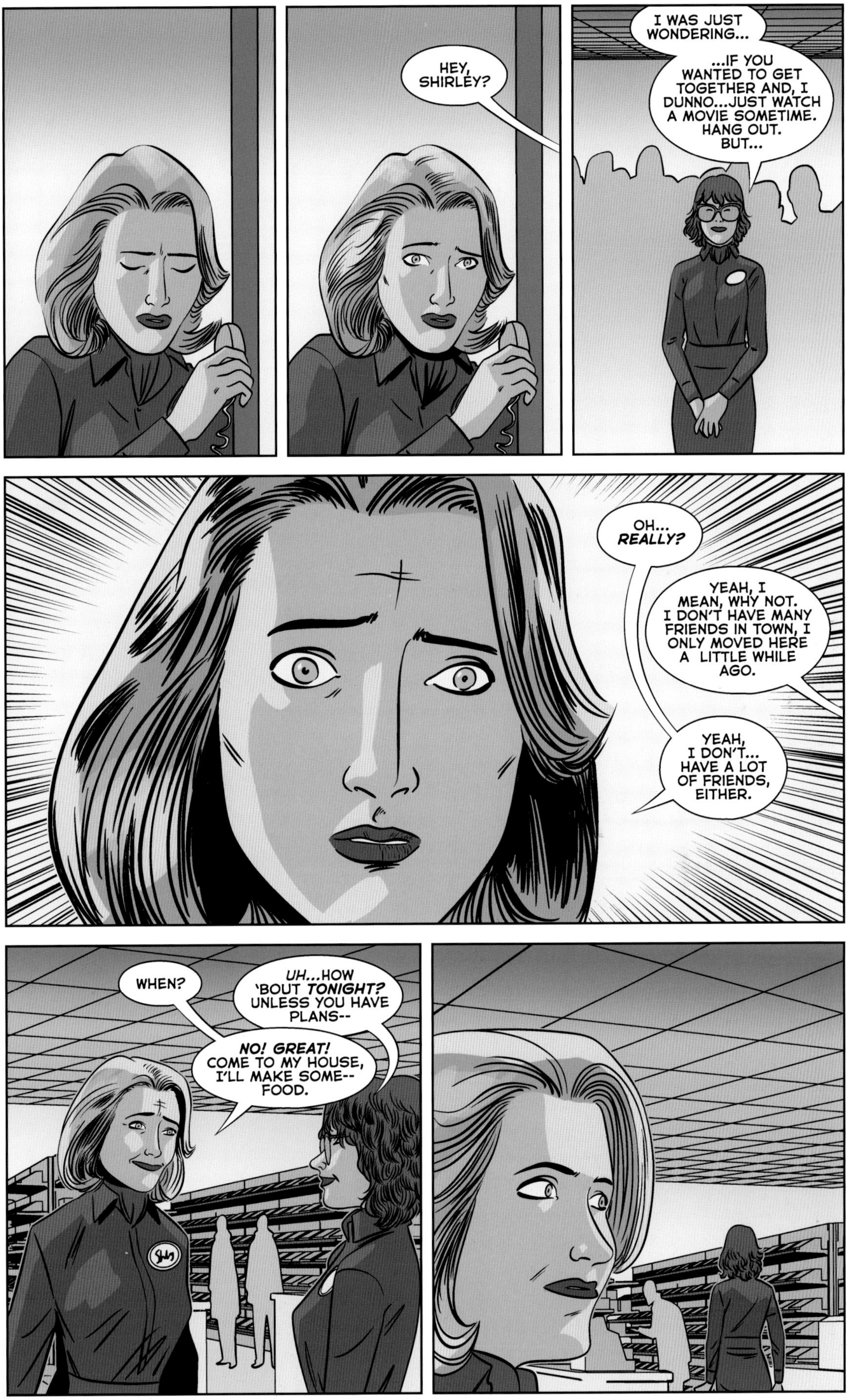
HEY, SHIRLEY?
I WAS JUST WONDERING...
...IF YOU WANTED TO GET TOGETHER AND, I DUNNO...JUST WATCH A MOVIE SOMETIME. HANG OUT. BUT...
OH... REALLY?
YEAH, I MEAN, WHY NOT. I DON'T HAVE MANY FRIENDS IN TOWN, I ONLY MOVED HERE A LITTLE WHILE AGO.
YEAH, I DON'T... HAVE A LOT OF FRIENDS, EITHER.
WHEN?
UH...HOW 'BOUT TONIGHT? UNLESS YOU HAVE PLANS--
NO! GREAT! COME TO MY HOUSE, I'LL MAKE SOME-- FOOD.

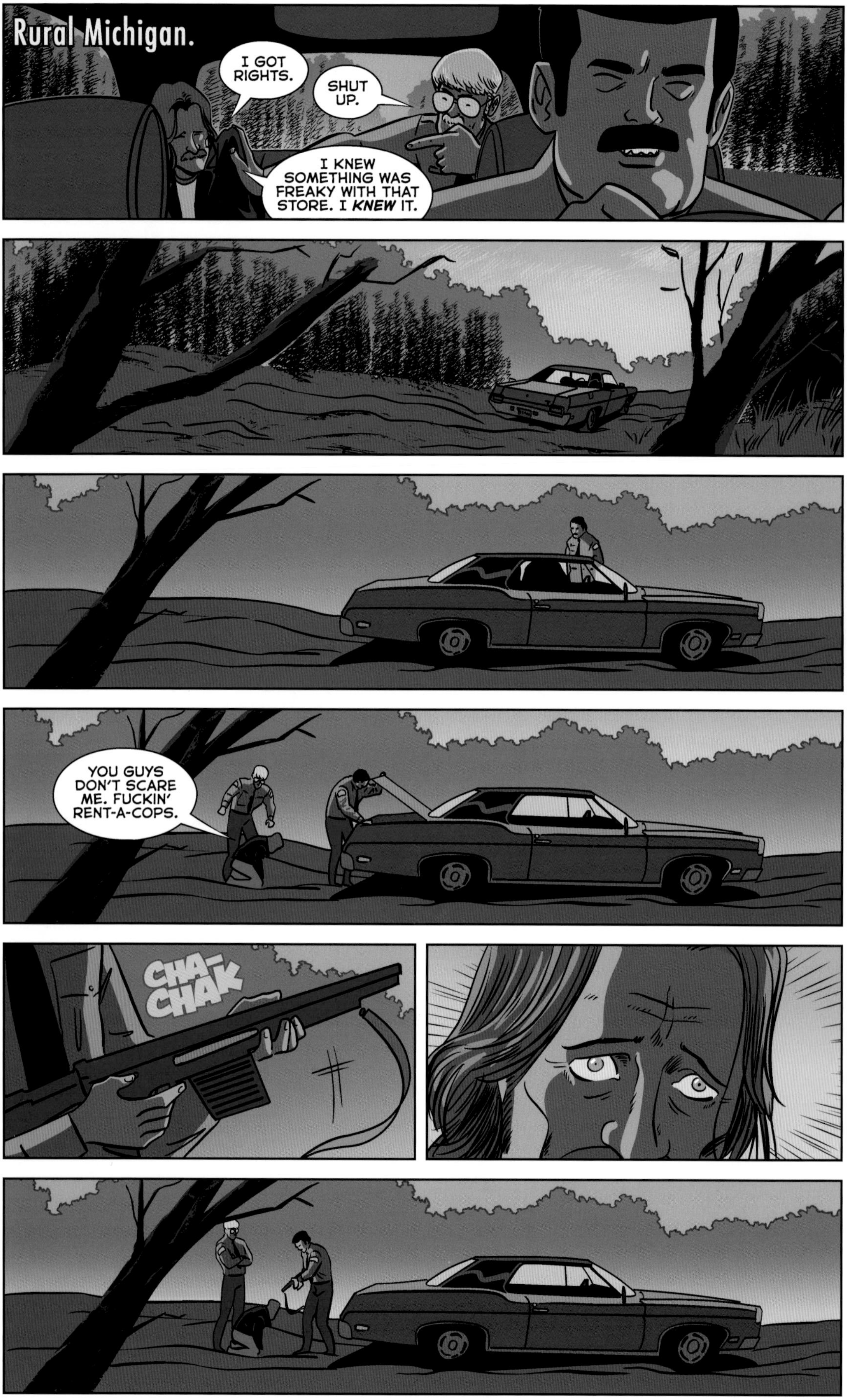
Rural Michigan.
I GOT RIGHTS.
SHUT UP.
I KNEW SOMETHING WAS FREAKY WITH THAT STORE. I *KNEW* IT.
YOU GUYS DON'T SCARE ME. FUCKIN' RENT-A-COPS.
CHA-CHAK

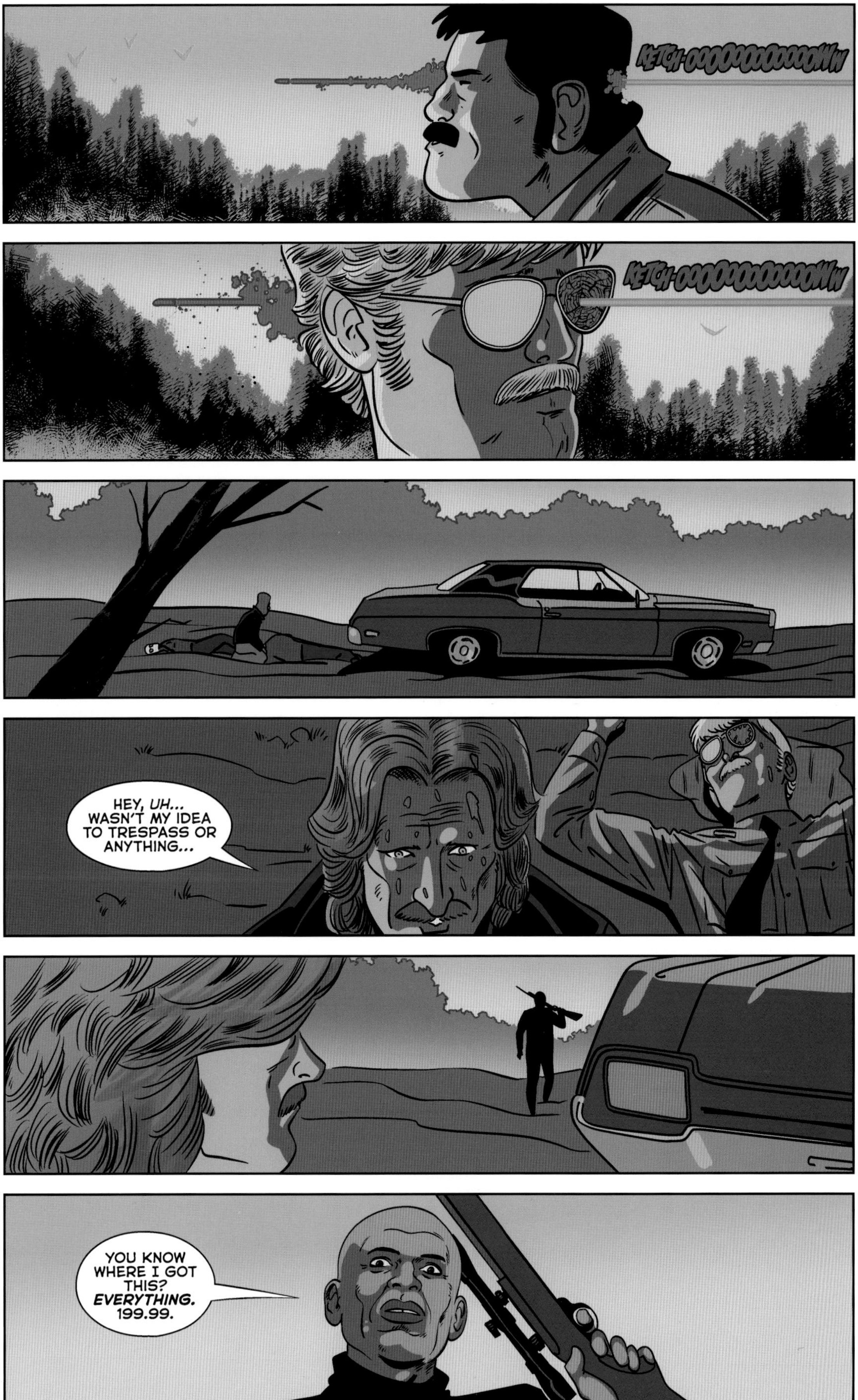
KETCH-OOOOOOOOOOOOWW
KETCH-OOOOOOOOOOOOWW
HEY, UH... WASN'T MY IDEA TO TRESPASS OR ANYTHING...
YOU KNOW WHERE I GOT THIS? EVERYTHING. 199.99.

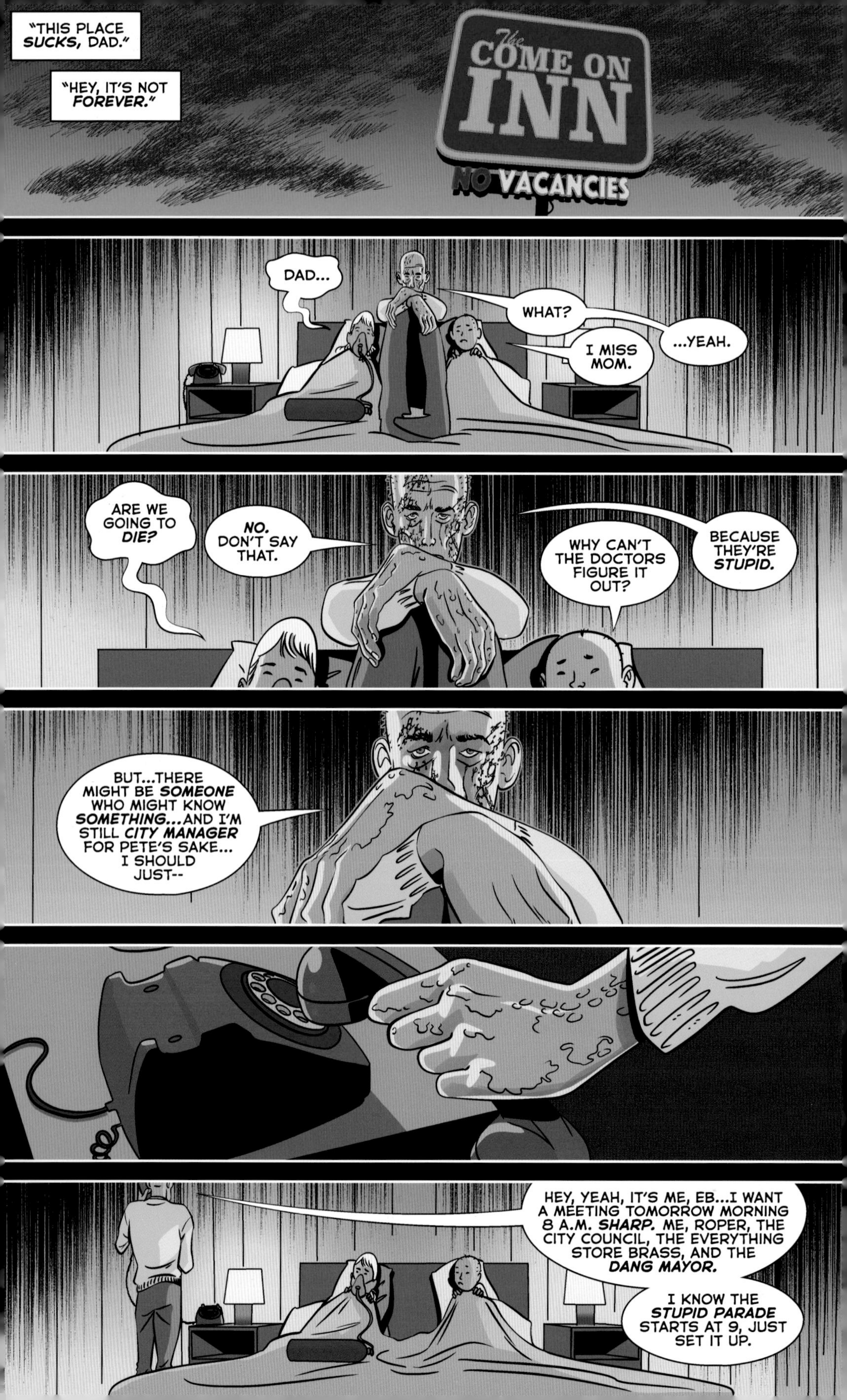
"THIS PLACE *SUCKS,* DAD."
"HEY, IT'S NOT *FOREVER.*"
The COME ON INN
NO VACANCIES
DAD...
WHAT?
I MISS MOM.
...YEAH.
ARE WE GOING TO *DIE?*
NO. DON'T SAY THAT.
WHY CAN'T THE DOCTORS FIGURE IT OUT?
BECAUSE THEY'RE *STUPID.*
BUT...THERE MIGHT BE *SOMEONE* WHO MIGHT KNOW *SOMETHING...*AND I'M STILL *CITY MANAGER* FOR PETE'S SAKE... I SHOULD JUST--
HEY, YEAH, IT'S ME, EB...I WANT A MEETING TOMORROW MORNING 8 A.M. *SHARP.* ME, ROPER, THE CITY COUNCIL, THE EVERYTHING STORE BRASS, AND THE *DANG MAYOR.*
I KNOW THE *STUPID PARADE* STARTS AT 9, JUST SET IT UP.

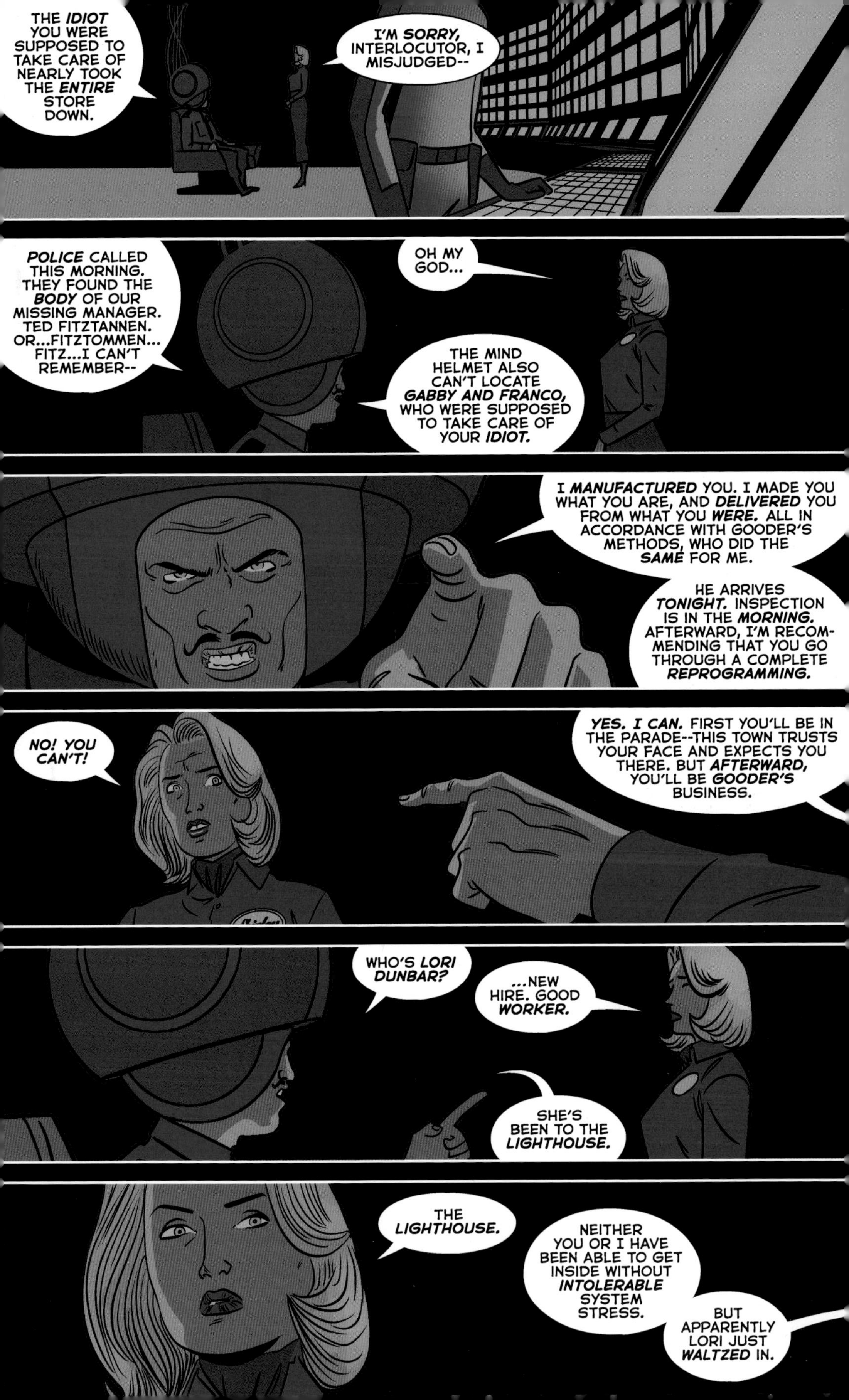
THE IDIOT YOU WERE SUPPOSED TO TAKE CARE OF NEARLY TOOK THE ENTIRE STORE DOWN.
I'M SORRY, INTERLOCUTOR, I MISJUDGED--
POLICE CALLED THIS MORNING. THEY FOUND THE BODY OF OUR MISSING MANAGER. TED FITZTANNEN. OR...FITZTOMMEN... FITZ...I CAN'T REMEMBER--
OH MY GOD...
THE MIND HELMET ALSO CAN'T LOCATE GABBY AND FRANCO, WHO WERE SUPPOSED TO TAKE CARE OF YOUR IDIOT.
I MANUFACTURED YOU. I MADE YOU WHAT YOU ARE, AND DELIVERED YOU FROM WHAT YOU WERE. ALL IN ACCORDANCE WITH GOODER'S METHODS, WHO DID THE SAME FOR ME.
HE ARRIVES TONIGHT. INSPECTION IS IN THE MORNING. AFTERWARD, I'M RECOMMENDING THAT YOU GO THROUGH A COMPLETE REPROGRAMMING.
NO! YOU CAN'T!
YES. I CAN. FIRST YOU'LL BE IN THE PARADE--THIS TOWN TRUSTS YOUR FACE AND EXPECTS YOU THERE. BUT AFTERWARD, YOU'LL BE GOODER'S BUSINESS.
WHO'S LORI DUNBAR?
...NEW HIRE. GOOD WORKER.
SHE'S BEEN TO THE LIGHTHOUSE.
THE LIGHTHOUSE.
NEITHER YOU OR I HAVE BEEN ABLE TO GET INSIDE WITHOUT INTOLERABLE SYSTEM STRESS.
BUT APPARENTLY LORI JUST WALTZED IN.

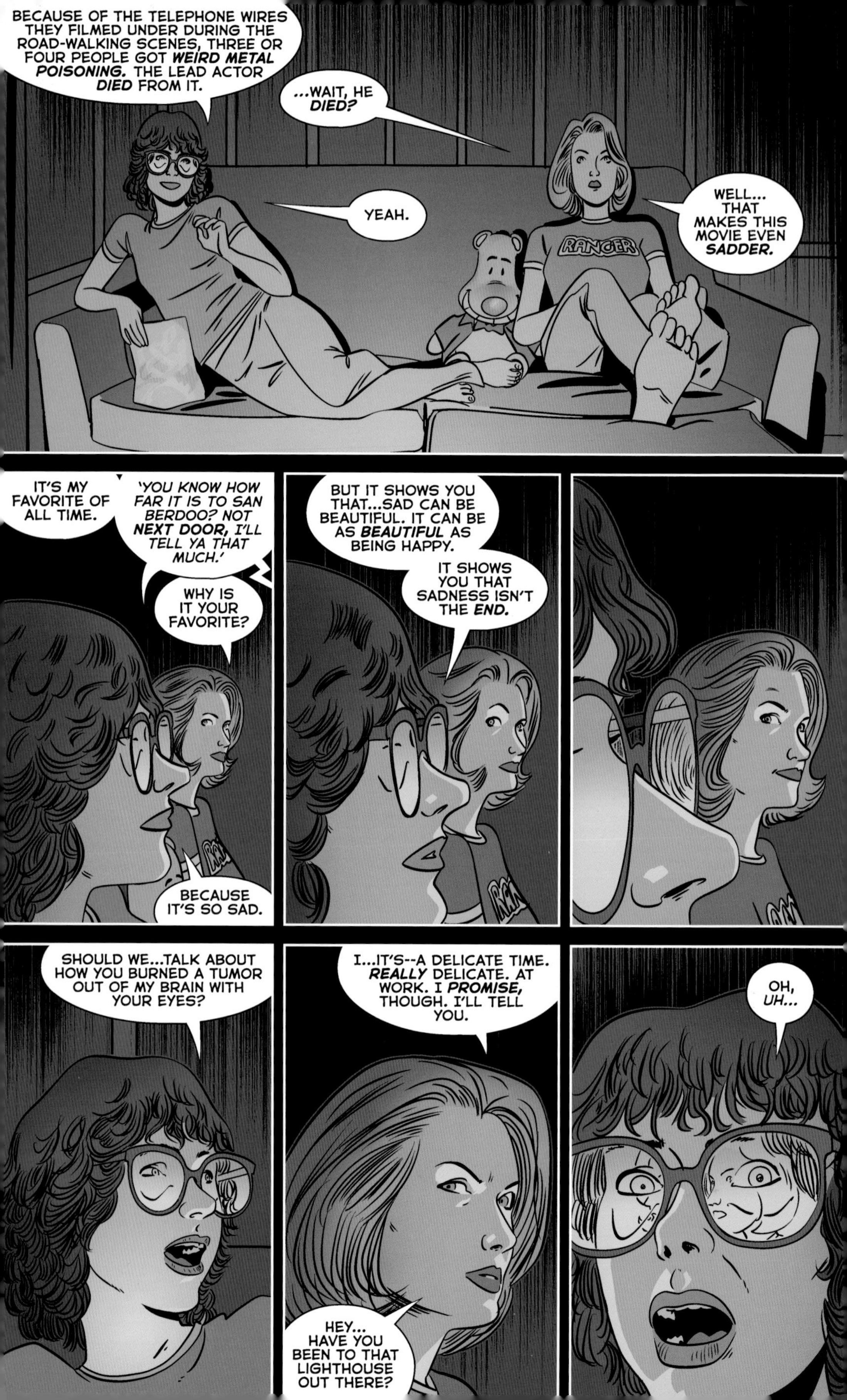
BECAUSE OF THE TELEPHONE WIRES THEY FILMED UNDER DURING THE ROAD-WALKING SCENES, THREE OR FOUR PEOPLE GOT *WEIRD METAL POISONING.* THE LEAD ACTOR *DIED* FROM IT.
...WAIT, HE *DIED?*
YEAH.
WELL... THAT MAKES THIS MOVIE EVEN *SADDER.*
RANGER
IT'S MY FAVORITE OF ALL TIME.
*'YOU KNOW HOW FAR IT IS TO SAN BERDOO? NOT **NEXT DOOR,** I'LL TELL YA THAT MUCH.'*
WHY IS IT YOUR FAVORITE?
BECAUSE IT'S SO SAD.
BUT IT SHOWS YOU THAT...SAD CAN BE BEAUTIFUL. IT CAN BE AS *BEAUTIFUL* AS BEING HAPPY.
IT SHOWS YOU THAT SADNESS ISN'T THE *END.*
SHOULD WE...TALK ABOUT HOW YOU BURNED A TUMOR OUT OF MY BRAIN WITH YOUR EYES?
I...IT'S--A DELICATE TIME. *REALLY* DELICATE. AT WORK. I *PROMISE,* THOUGH. I'LL TELL YOU.
HEY... HAVE YOU BEEN TO THAT LIGHTHOUSE OUT THERE?
OH, *UH...*

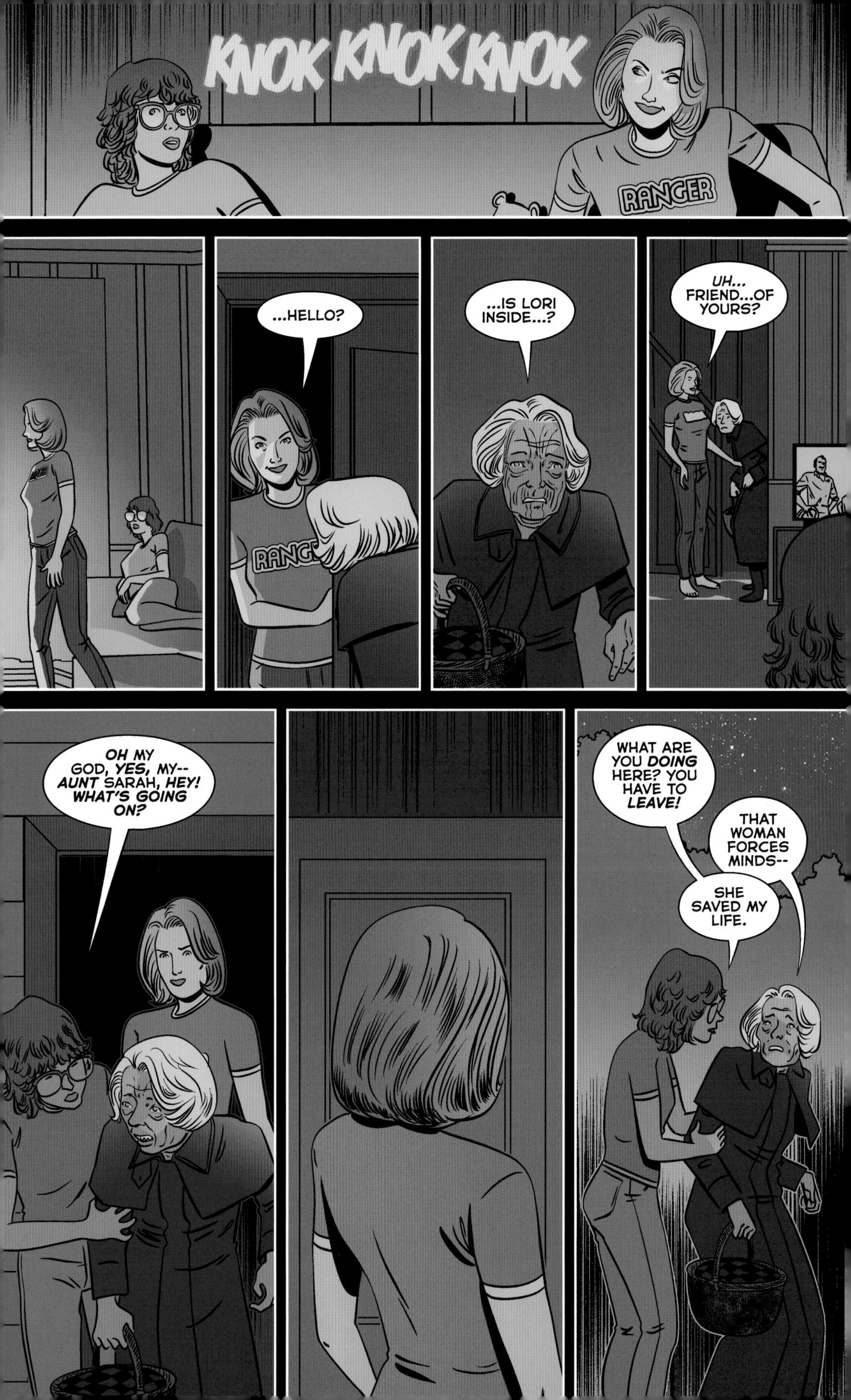
KNOK KNOK KNOK
RANGER
...HELLO?
RANGER
...IS LORI INSIDE...?
UH... FRIEND...OF YOURS?
OH MY GOD, YES, MY-- AUNT SARAH, HEY! WHAT'S GOING ON?
WHAT ARE YOU DOING HERE? YOU HAVE TO LEAVE!
THAT WOMAN FORCES MINDS--
SHE SAVED MY LIFE.

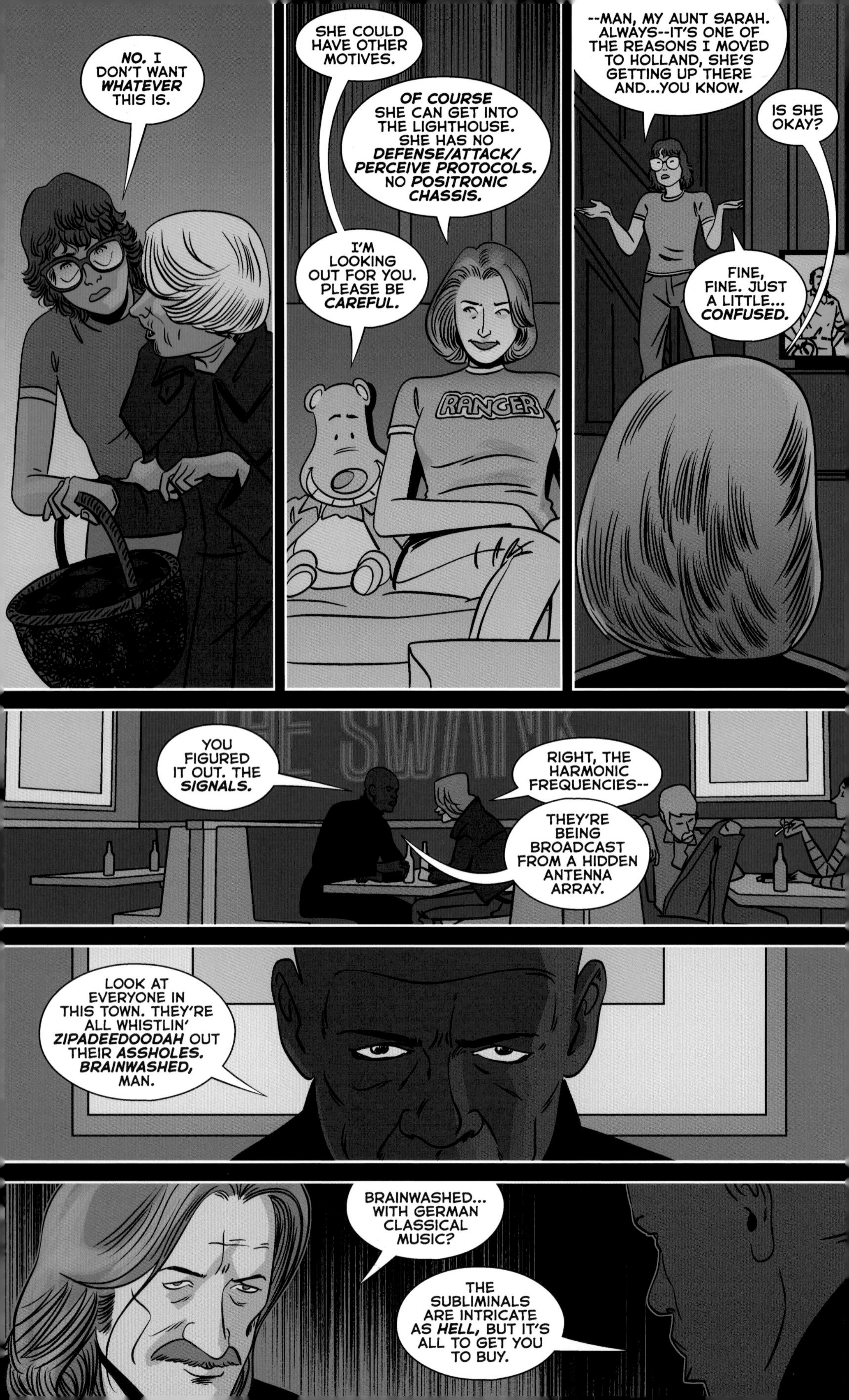
NO. I DON'T WANT WHATEVER THIS IS.
SHE COULD HAVE OTHER MOTIVES.
OF COURSE SHE CAN GET INTO THE LIGHTHOUSE. SHE HAS NO DEFENSE/ATTACK/ PERCEIVE PROTOCOLS. NO POSITRONIC CHASSIS.
I'M LOOKING OUT FOR YOU. PLEASE BE CAREFUL.
RANGER
--MAN, MY AUNT SARAH. ALWAYS--IT'S ONE OF THE REASONS I MOVED TO HOLLAND, SHE'S GETTING UP THERE AND...YOU KNOW.
IS SHE OKAY?
FINE, FINE. JUST A LITTLE... CONFUSED.
YOU FIGURED IT OUT. THE SIGNALS.
RIGHT, THE HARMONIC FREQUENCIES--
THEY'RE BEING BROADCAST FROM A HIDDEN ANTENNA ARRAY.
LOOK AT EVERYONE IN THIS TOWN. THEY'RE ALL WHISTLIN' ZIPADEEDOODAH OUT THEIR ASSHOLES. BRAINWASHED, MAN.
BRAINWASHED... WITH GERMAN CLASSICAL MUSIC?
THE SUBLIMINALS ARE INTRICATE AS HELL, BUT IT'S ALL TO GET YOU TO BUY.

OUTSIDE CLEVE-LAND, MY *WIFE AND KIDS*...THEY LEFT ME FOR THE STORE. THEN THE STORE *CLOSED*...SO MY FAMILY BURNED THEMSELVES *ALIVE*.

...WHY... WAIT, WHY WEREN'T YOU--AFFECTED?

I'M *DEAF* IN ONE EAR. YOU GOT HEARING DAMAGE, TOO, RIGHT?

...YEAH--

ALL RIGHT... SO THIS ARRAY.

ARRAY IS JUST PART OF IT. THERE'S ALSO THE *PRIME*.

THE PRIME?

SOURCE OF *TREMENDOUS* ENERGY. THE PRIME INTERFACES WITH THE *APERTURE* DEEP UNDERGROUND.

THE *PRIME* IS INSULATED BY A *FORM*.

'KAY, ELWOOD' BUD, I'M GETTIN' A HEADACHE--

GOODER IS THE *KEY*, MAN. HE'S COMING TO TOWN *TONIGHT*. THIS *PARADE* IS TOMORROW.

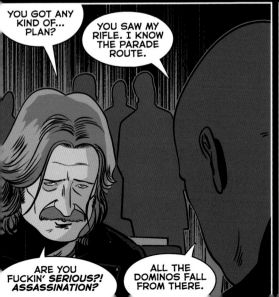

YOU GOT ANY KIND OF... PLAN?

YOU SAW MY RIFLE. I KNOW THE PARADE ROUTE.

ARE YOU FUCKIN' *SERIOUS?!* ASSASSINATION?

ALL THE DOMINOS FALL FROM THERE.

NO, WAIT. THERE'S AN *EASIER* WAY. STORE'S *CLOSED* TOMORROW FOR THE PARADE. *PERFECT* TIME TO CHECK IT OUT.

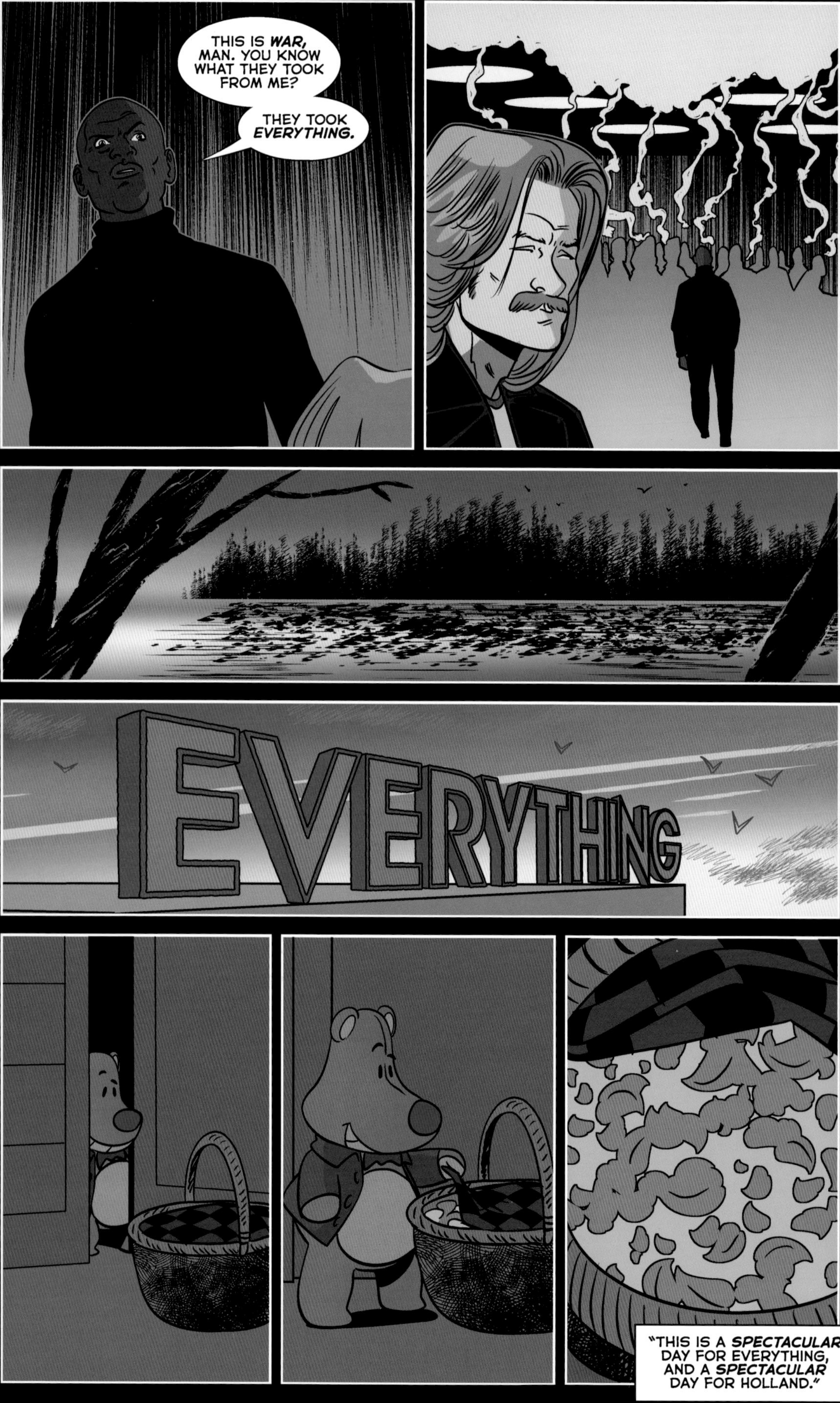

THIS IS *WAR,* MAN. YOU KNOW WHAT THEY TOOK FROM ME?
THEY TOOK *EVERYTHING.*
EVERYTHING
"THIS IS A *SPECTACULAR* DAY FOR EVERYTHING, AND A *SPECTACULAR* DAY FOR HOLLAND."

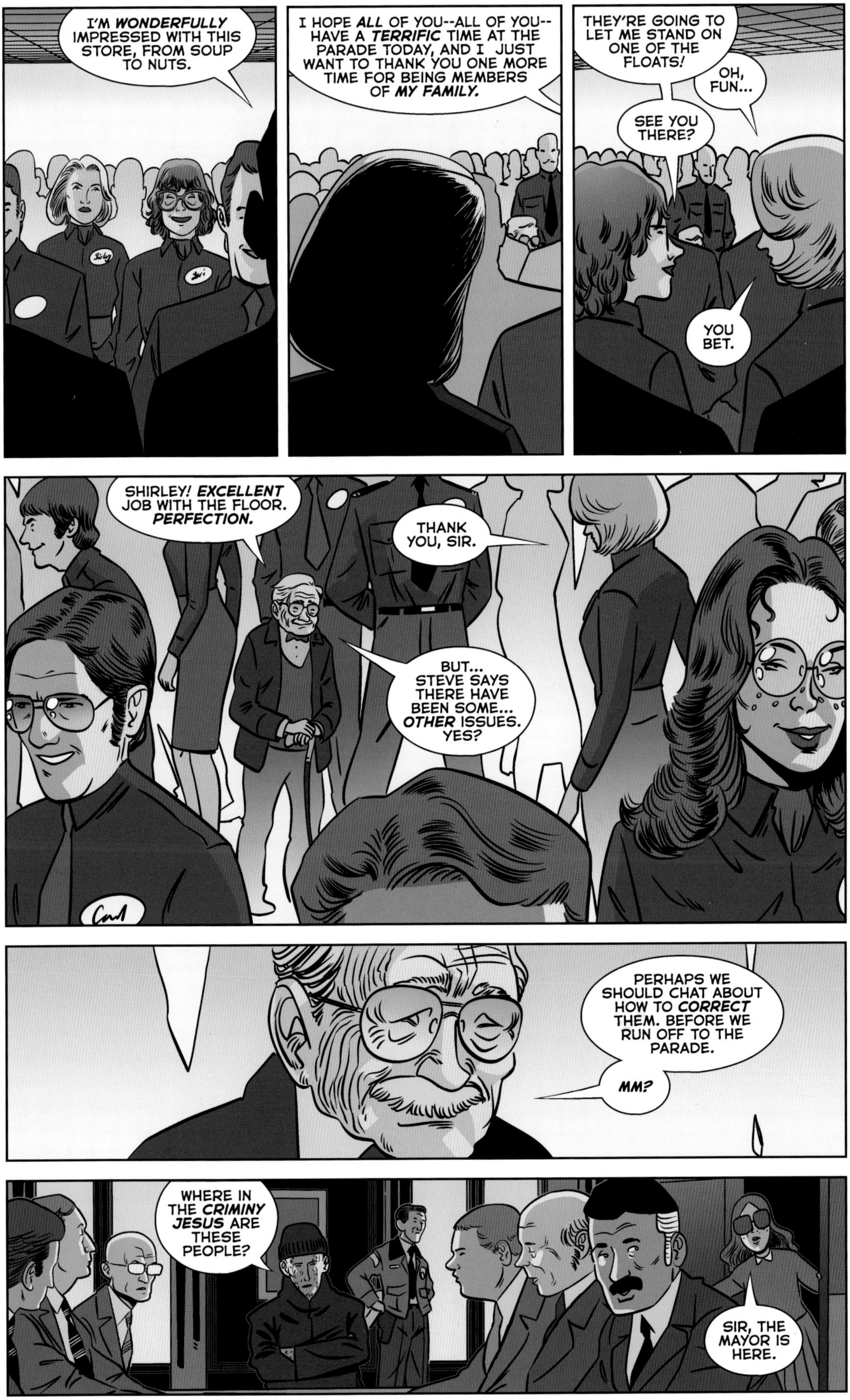
I'M *WONDERFULLY* IMPRESSED WITH THIS STORE, FROM SOUP TO NUTS.
I HOPE *ALL* OF YOU--ALL OF YOU--HAVE A *TERRIFIC* TIME AT THE PARADE TODAY, AND I JUST WANT TO THANK YOU ONE MORE TIME FOR BEING MEMBERS OF *MY FAMILY.*
THEY'RE GOING TO LET ME STAND ON ONE OF THE FLOATS!
OH, FUN...
SEE YOU THERE?
YOU BET.
SHIRLEY! *EXCELLENT* JOB WITH THE FLOOR. *PERFECTION.*
THANK YOU, SIR.
BUT... STEVE SAYS THERE HAVE BEEN SOME... *OTHER* ISSUES. YES?
PERHAPS WE SHOULD CHAT ABOUT HOW TO *CORRECT* THEM. BEFORE WE RUN OFF TO THE PARADE.
MM?
WHERE IN THE *CRIMINY JESUS* ARE THESE PEOPLE?
SIR, THE MAYOR IS HERE.

MAYOR SMILEY, ALWAYS A PLEASURE...

EB.

I'M GLAD YOU'RE HERE, SIR, I WANT TO DISCUSS EVERYTHING--

I HEARD YOU'VE BEEN *HENPECKING* THEM. *HARASSING* THEM.

WHAT?

EB, YOU'RE BEING *RELIEVED* OF CITY MANAGEMENT DUTIES, EFFECTIVE *IMMEDIATELY*.

I SPOKE TO *MR. GOODER* ON THE PHONE. HE AND HIS STAFF FEEL YOU'RE *ILL*--WHICH FROM THE LOOKS OF IT YOU *CERTAINLY* ARE--SO YOU'RE GOING TO STEP BACK. *GREG* WILL TAKE OVER.

WOW, THANKS!

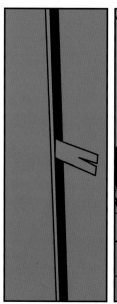

HOLY FUCK-STREET..

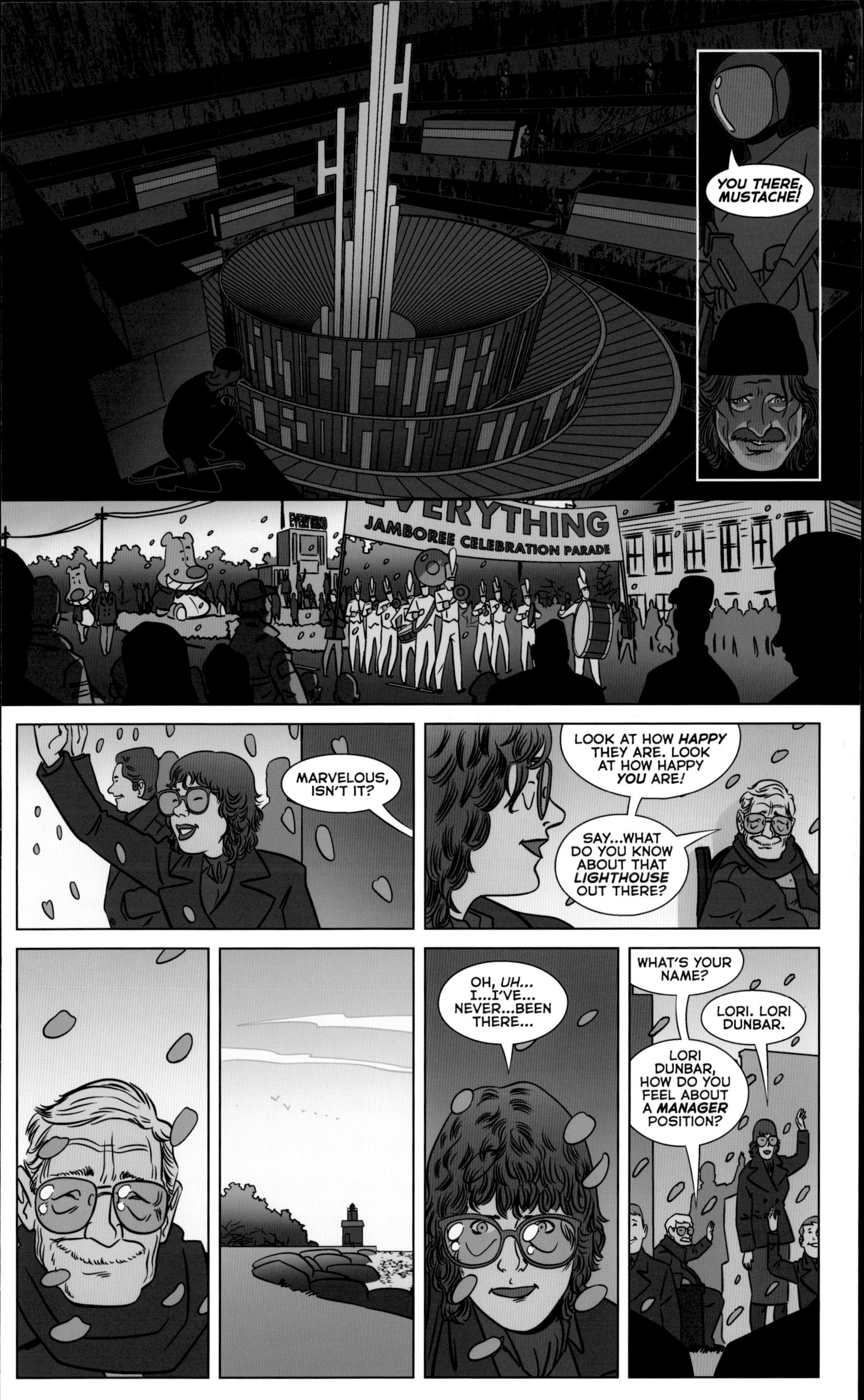
YOU THERE, MUSTACHE!
EVERYTHING
EVERYTHING
JAMBOREE CELEBRATION PARADE
MARVELOUS, ISN'T IT?
LOOK AT HOW *HAPPY* THEY ARE. LOOK AT HOW HAPPY *YOU* ARE!
SAY...WHAT DO YOU KNOW ABOUT THAT ***LIGHTHOUSE*** OUT THERE?
OH, *UH...* I...I'VE... NEVER...BEEN THERE...
WHAT'S YOUR NAME?
LORI. LORI DUNBAR.
LORI DUNBAR, HOW DO YOU FEEL ABOUT A ***MANAGER*** POSITION?

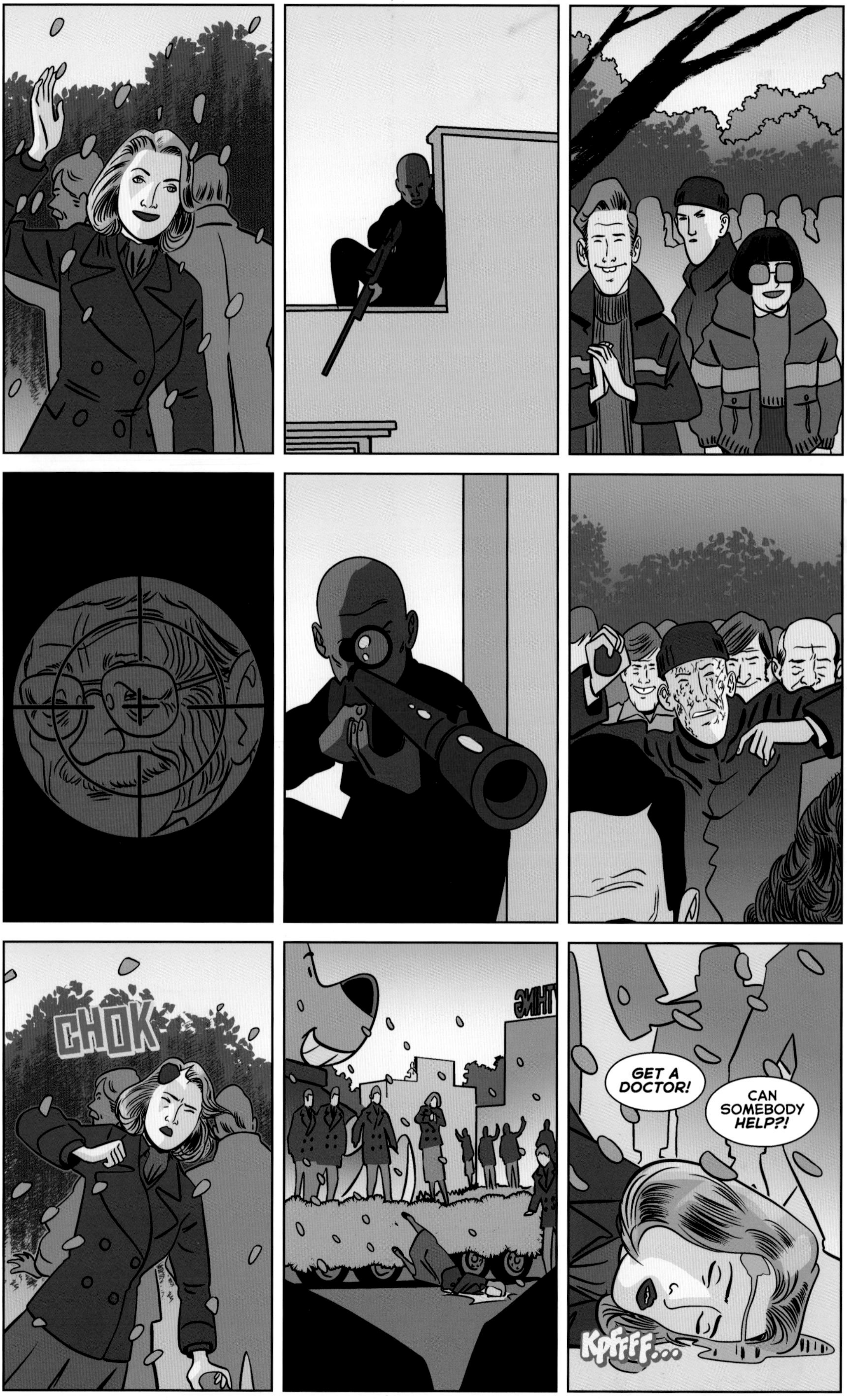
CHOK
GET A DOCTOR!
CAN SOMEBODY HELP?!
KPFFFF...

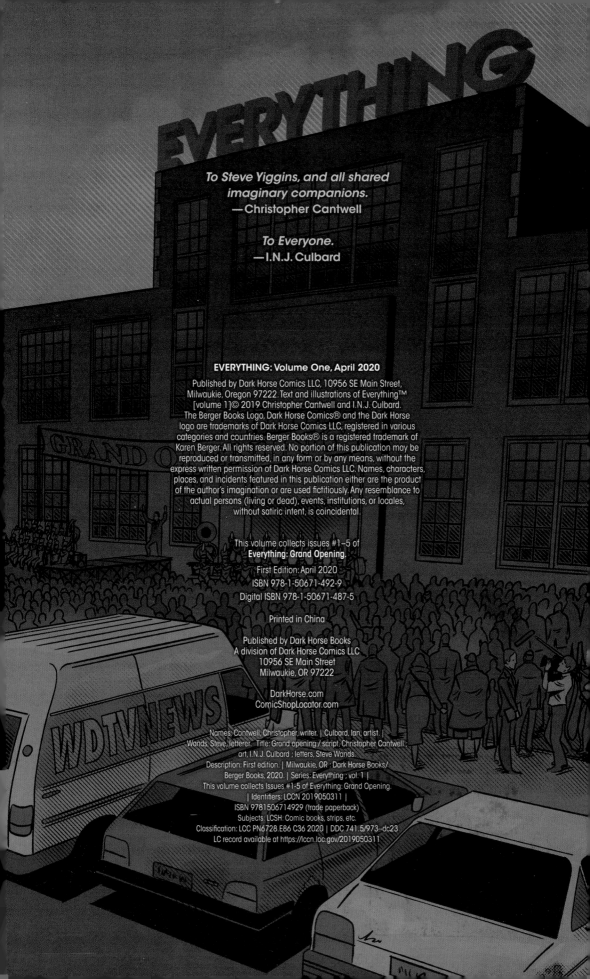

*To Steve Yiggins, and all shared
imaginary companions.*
—Christopher Cantwell

To Everyone.
—I.N.J. Culbard

EVERYTHING: Volume One, April 2020

Published by Dark Horse Comics LLC, 10956 SE Main Street,
Milwaukie, Oregon 97222. Text and illustrations of Everything™
[volume 1]© 2019 Christopher Cantwell and I.N.J. Culbard.
The Berger Books Logo, Dark Horse Comics® and the Dark Horse
logo are trademarks of Dark Horse Comics LLC, registered in various
categories and countries. Berger Books® is a registered trademark of
Karen Berger. All rights reserved. No portion of this publication may be
reproduced or transmitted, in any form or by any means, without the
express written permission of Dark Horse Comics LLC. Names, characters,
places, and incidents featured in this publication either are the product
of the author's imagination or are used fictitiously. Any resemblance to
actual persons (living or dead), events, institutions, or locales,
without satiric intent, is coincidental.

This volume collects issues #1–5 of
Everything: Grand Opening.

First Edition: April 2020
ISBN 978-1-50671-492-9
Digital ISBN 978-1-50671-487-5

Printed in China

Published by Dark Horse Books
A division of Dark Horse Comics LLC
10956 SE Main Street
Milwaukie, OR 97222

DarkHorse.com
ComicShopLocator.com

Names: Cantwell, Christopher, writer. | Culbard, Ian, artist. |
Wands, Steve, letterer. Title: Grand opening / script, Christopher Cantwell ;
art, I.N.J. Culbard ; letters, Steve Wands.
Description: First edition. | Milwaukie, OR : Dark Horse Books/
Berger Books, 2020. | Series: Everything ; vol. 1 |
This volume collects issues #1-5 of Everything: Grand Opening.
| Identifiers: LCCN 2019050311 |
ISBN 9781506714929 (trade paperback)
Subjects: LCSH: Comic books, strips, etc.
Classification: LCC PN6728.E86 C36 2020 | DDC 741.5/973--dc23
LC record available at https://lccn.loc.gov/2019050311